The Native American Mascot Controversy

A Handbook

Edited by
C. Richard King

THE SCARECROW PRESS, INC.
Lanham • Toronto • Plymouth, UK
2010

Published by Scarecrow Press, Inc.
A wholly owned subsidiary of The Rowman & Littlefield Publishing Group, Inc.
4501 Forbes Boulevard, Suite 200, Lanham, Maryland 20706
http://www.scarecrowpress.com

Estover Road, Plymouth PL6 7PY, United Kingdom

British Library Cataloguing in Publication Information Available

Library of Congress Cataloging-in-Publication Data

The Native American mascot controversy : a handbook / edited by C. Richard King.
    p. cm.
  Includes bibliographical references and index.
  ISBN 978-0-8108-6731-4 (cloth : alk. paper) — ISBN 978-0-8108-6732-1 (ebook)
  1. Indians as mascots. 2. Sports team mascots—Social aspects—United States. 3.
Indians of North America—Social conditions—20th century. I. King, C. Richard, 1968-
  GV714.5.N38 2010
  306.483—dc22
                                    2010017012

Printed in the United States of America

Dedicated to the next generation in hopes that one day
empathy and justice will prevail

Contents

Preface

This volume offers an overview of the controversies surrounding Native American mascots over the past 40 years. It trains its attention on education to reveal the significance of the continued use of such symbols, artifacts, and identities and the efforts to combat them. Informed by numerous studies that have stressed the centrality of educational institutions to the perpetuation of racial imagery, identities, and inequalities through Native American mascots, it endeavors to elucidate the dangers and damages associated with them. I begin with the premise that such use contributes to the stereotyping of American Indians and consequently to the miseducation of our students (Davis, 2002; Pewewardy, 1991, 1998, 2001; Staurowsky, 1999), transforming schools and stadiums into hostile environments for indigenous peoples (Baca, 2004). Importantly, as "invented traditions," Native American mascots foster the creation of if "imagined communities" that quite passionately defend the use of such imagery in the face of opposition (King, 2002).

Gathering together primary source materials, legal documents and resolutions, scholarly studies, and position papers, this volume seeks to make plain the history and significance of Native American mascots as well as the social struggles that they have increasingly incited over the past quarter century. Thus, this sourcebook is as much a window on changing perceptions of American Indians, race, and history as it is a catalog of efforts to secure justice, advance understanding, and promote change.

I will not reiterate each contribution here but merely offer an outline of the contents. The volume opens with a series of essays that highlight core concerns with Native American mascots, including racism, gender, stereotyping, and whiteness. They provide readers with a strong introduction to why such imagery matters and why so many people have worked against its use over the past 40 years. On this foundation, the contributions in the second section unpack the educational issues raised by Native American mascots, particularly their propensity to miseducate, contribute to a hostile environment, and reinforce other forms of ethnic fraud. Moreover, selections in this section offer insight into how schools have gone about changing mascots and the negligible impact it has had on alumni giving. In the third section, the discussion shifts directly to struggle over mascots and their meaning. Individual essays consider arguments offered in support of them, legal and extralegal effort to retain them, and grassroots opposition to them. Next, Part IV reprints a range of primary sources, including policies and resolution endorsed by governmental bodies, tribal councils, advocacy groups, professional organizations, and educational institutions as well as proposed legislation. The volume closes with a set of additional resources: a list of organizations advocating change, a chronology of American Indian mascot and nickname changes, and an exhaustive bibliography.

REFERENCES

Baca, L. (2004). Native images in schools and the racially hostile environment. *Journal of Sport and Social Issues, 28*, 71–78.

Davis, L. R. (2002). The problems with Native American mascots. *Multicultural Education, 9*, 11–14.

King, C. R. (2002). Defensive dialogues: Native American mascots, anti-Indianism, and educational institutions. *Studies in Media & Information Literacy Education, 2*(1). Retrieved from http://www.utpress.utoronto.ca/journal/ejournals/simile

Pewewardy, C. D. (1991). Native American mascots and imagery: The struggle of unlearning Indian stereotypes. *Journal of Navaho Education, 9*, 19–23.

Pewewardy, C. D. (1998). Fluff and feathers: Treatment of American Indians in the literature and the classroom. *Equity and Excellence in Education, 31*, 69–76.

Pewewardy, C. D. (2001). Educators and mascots: Challenging contradictions. In C. R. King & C. F. Springwood (Eds.), *Team spirits: Essays on the history and significance of Native American mascots* (pp. 257–279). Lincoln: University of Nebraska Press.

Staurowsky, E. J. (1999). American Indian imagery and the miseducation of America. *Quest, 51*, 382–392.

Acknowledgments

As with all creative and critical endeavors, this volume reflects the hard work, dedication, and struggle of many people. First and foremost, it derives from the blood, sweat, and tears of advocates and educators within and beyond Indian Country who have invested in the pursuit of justice, civil rights, and dignity. To them, I owe my deepest debt of gratitude both for what they have taught me and for how they endeavored to make the world a better place. I have benefited over the years leading up to this book from the guidance, counsel, and inspiration of many leaders and scholars in the movement against the use of Indianness in sport, including Lawrence Baca, Laurel Davis, Norman Denzin, Stephanie Fryberg, Harvey and Carol Gunderson, Suzan Shown Harjo, Stephen Kaufman, Cornell Pewewardy, David Prochaska, Carol Spindel, Ellen Staurowsky, Charlene Teeters, and especially Chuck Springwood.

This book was made possible by the initial interest, deep commitment, and inexhaustible patience of Stephen Ryan. I am grateful to him for his support throughout the journey to publication.

I benefited, moreover, from the hard work of Debbie Brudie and Rose Smetana, who played a crucial role in securing permissions, a time-consuming and frustrating burden. A completion grant from the College of Liberal Arts at Washington State University went a long way toward offsetting the costs associated with obtaining these permissions.

My colleagues in Comparative Ethnic Studies at Washington State University deserve much credit for creating an intellectual community that nurtures good work. I appreciate especially the contributions of David J.

Leonard, Carmen Lugo-Lugo, Mary Bloodsworth-Lugo, Lisa Guerrero, and Kim Christen. My work is better thanks to them.

Finally, I must acknowledge the love and support of my family. Abbey and Ellory continue to amaze me and provide important opportunities to forget about work and instead play Wii, bake cookies, or go for an adventure. And not enough can be said for what Marcie has given me and made me capable of over the years. Shine on, my rare jewel!

Part I

BACKGROUND

Too often, discussions of Native American mascots in the media suggest the key issue is offensiveness. Such a framing prevents a full understanding of why such names, images, and logos matter: They exclude history, take mascots out of context, discourage an appreciation of how race and gender matter, and reduce the question to one of feelings and opinion. The contributions to this section seek to reframe the issue and to provide readers with a knowledge base to understand where Native American mascots came from, how they are significant, and why they should be eliminated.

1

Chiefs, Braves, and Tomahawks: The Use of American Indians as University Mascots

Robert Longwell-Grice and Hope Longwell-Grice

Many colleges continue to use Native American images as their mascots despite mounting calls to cease this practice. Attempts to change these mascots have not always been successful because of the deep support these mascots and images engender. Using a postcolonial critical framework, we discuss here the various justifications given for using Native American images as mascots, describe the effect their continued use has, and urge action to effect change that is educationally, politically, and culturally sound.

Resolutions to ban Indian mascots and logos have come from (among other organizations) the American Indian Education Association, the National Education Association, the United Indians Nation of Oklahoma, the National Congress of American Indians, the American Indian Movement, the National Rainbow Coalition, the National Association for the Advancement of Colored People, and the Center for Study of Sports in Society (Pewewardy, 2000). In an editorial, the National Collegiate Athletic Association (NCAA) Minority Opportunities and Interests Committee came out in support of the elimination of Indian names and mascots as symbols for sports teams (Whitcomb, 1998). Additionally, in April of 2001, the U.S. Commission on Civil Rights also called for an end to the use of Indian names. Missing from this list, however, are any college student personnel organizations. Perhaps it is because we, too, accept the argument that these mascots honor Native Americans. Perhaps we do not see the potential damage our lack of action has on our campuses. Or are we hesitant to openly critique our colleagues and our employers? Student affairs offices need to take a more active role in educating people about why use of these mascots and images is inappropriate. First, however, we need to educate ourselves about why this is so. This paper

(1) discusses the various justifications given for the use of Native American images as mascots; (2) describes the effect their continued use has on Indians, non-Indians, and universities; and (3) suggests the necessity for support of and action to effect change that is educationally, politically, and culturally sound.

We have entered into this project through a postcolonial theoretical framework to describe how the political, social, cultural, and psychological operations of colonialist ideologies work to maintain hierarchies in society (Tyson, 1999). This lens can help explain the power of mascots as symbols and rituals and, more specifically, the implications of using Native Americans as mascots. McLaren (1999) explains the inherent risks of symbols and rituals: "The most enduring of rituals are able to draw essential symbols into an inclusive totality and self-subsistent whole that can sustain itself while enabling those symbols to maintain their difference from others, yet at the same time harmonizing with them and complementing them" (p. xiv).

In this instance, although mascots can facilitate our "rallying behind" the image, we hope to show that given the disembodiment of Indianness from the image of an Indian mascot runs the risk of continuing to "other" a nondominant culture in society and maintains the group's status in society.

THE ARGUMENTS FOR INDIAN MASCOTS

> The argument supporting the use of Native Americans as mascots falls into three broad categories—tradition, money, and broader societal support. Those who favor using Native Americans as mascots argue the mascots honor and celebrate Indians.
>
> —Dawn Marie Neeson, Students for Chief Illiniwek, April 4, 2000
> (quoted in Vanderford, 1996)

Supporters (in this case, Students for Chief Illiniwek) feel that their mascot is part of the school's tradition, and changing the mascot is simply giving in to politically correct pressure groups. However, others argue, and we concur, that mascot support, like other examples of stereotyping, is also linked to emotional and economic arguments and a long history of society-sponsored racism (Pewewardy, 2000; Whitt, 1995; Rouse & Hanson, 1991).

Emotionally, mascots appeal to a sense of "tradition" and the pride in and affiliation with an institution that administrators and faculty work hard to cultivate. A common assumption is that to take a mascot away is to undermine the traditions that have been developed over the years. However, the following cases demonstrate that the origins of these mascots were harmless or unintentional.

In 1926, assistant band director Ray Dvarak of the University of Illinois conceived of the idea of performing an American Indian dance during half-time of the Illinois–Pennsylvania football game in Philadelphia (Students for Chief Illiniwek, 2000). The University of Illinois football coach at the time suggested calling the Indian symbol Chief Illiniwek. Chief Illiniwek ran onto the field "doing a lively Indian dance," saluted the Pennsylvania rooters, and then smoked a peace pipe with William Penn (impersonated by another University of Illinois student). The crowd loved it and a tradition was born. The Chief has appeared at halftime of every home University of Illinois football game ever since.

A second example, at Central Michigan University, the school's mascot appeared in 1925 as a dragon. Then, in 1927 "a drive began to adopt a new and more official name for the athletic teams that could be used in write-ups and cheers" (Central Michigan University, Official Athletic Site, 2000). As a result, the mascot was changed to the Bearcat. However, in 1941, Central's football coach went to the student council with an idea he had of changing the mascot to the "Chippewas," for the Indian tribes that were once scattered about the region. He argued that:

> The name "Chippewa" opens up unlimited opportunities for pageantry and showmanship for the band as well as athletic teams. The Indian Chief would be an outstanding marker for athletic uniforms, the Indian pow-wow could replace the pep meeting and Indian ceremonies could be conducted on many occasions. School flags could be made much more attractive and finally all types of Indian lore have a strong appeal and could be used to great advantage. (p. 2)

Media depictions and educational misrepresentations are likely to contribute to widespread stereotyping about Native American peoples. The appeal to stereotypical notions in using Indians, chiefs, braves, and so forth is evident in these examples. For coaches and players, the idea that they could be "braves" or "chiefs" is prominent.

Appeals to stereotypes can be seen in the dance, the music, and the symbols used by these mascots. As we have noted, this did not go unnoticed by the individuals in charge. Economically, these mascots make it easy to sell goods because their stereotypical symbols appeal to alumni, students, and community supporters. The logos and related goods make use of the mascot, and spinoffs on the Native American motif are easily manipulated to continually develop new products to sell. The tie-in for other university departments, such as development offices, is clear as well. At Arkansas State University, for example, the booster club is called the "Indians Club" and there is a separate club for kids called the "Lil' Indians Club." According to the Indians Club scholarship fund, for $100 one can become a "Brave" and for $250 one can become a "Chief" (ASUIndians.com, 2001).

Changing the mascot, according to supporters, has the potential to negatively affect giving. There is no question that any change that can be perceived as having the potential for harming alumni giving must be cautiously approached. Colleges and universities are dependent on alumni giving, so curtailment of giving would harm students, staff, and faculty alike.

Universities are not alone in their racialized representations of indigenous people for profit, and they may be seen as reflecting societal norms. The dominant culture in the United States has long sanctioned racially harmful behaviors toward Native Americans (Pewewardy, 2000; Deloria & Lytle, 1998). Deloria's work provides many more specific examples throughout the history of America, including the savage Indian image to facilitate the removal of Indians from the east coast in early American times. The Puritan view of Indians as a morally and spiritually inferior people helped justify U.S. expansion and the expropriation of Indian land (Segal & Stineback, 1977). Ethnic identity was (and is) political and economic, and defined (defines) boundaries that set groups apart. In times of strife, stereotypical images can arise to help one group gain an advantage over another. By portraying Native Americans as savages or heathens, white Americans established a feeling that Indians were "less worthy" and gained the backing of the majority of Americans. In areas where competition over economic resources is present or in times of conflict or competition, the intentional negative and self-serving stereotyping of Native Americans continues (Boxberger, 1989) and can become exaggerated (Rouse & Hanson, 1991).

If the stereotyping is intentional, as Rouse and Hanson (1991), Boxberger (1989), and Segal and Stineback (1977) feel it is, could it be that supporters of these "traditions" feel it is important that the dominant culture think of Native Americans as an extinguished culture/civilization so that they can profit from the marketing of Native America? With this in mind, it is important to consider what purposes, intended or otherwise, the continued use of Native American mascots serves.

DECONSTRUCTING PLEAS TO POSTERITY

As stated earlier, there seem to be three major points to the supporters' arguments for maintaining images of Native Americans for mascots. The preponderance of the evidence in this area seems to negate these assumptions. We take time here to rebut the supporters' claims.

Given the recent history of some of these mascots, it could be argued that the "tradition" argument is not as solid as supporters would have us believe. At the University of Miami–Ohio (RedHawks Online, 2000), the name "Redskins" first appeared in the school paper in 1928 with little notice. It wasn't until 1931, when the university's lone publicity man announced the new nickname, that it became permanent.

Since many colleges and universities have changed mascots over the years, the precedent for changing mascots has been established. Besides the University of Miami–Ohio, other universities that have changed their Indian mascots include St. John's University (Redstorm), Shippensburg University (Ship), and Stanford University (Cardinals), to name just a few. One can also legitimately question if sports teams (including players and coaches) really need the imagery of a savage Indian to produce a winning team. There are certainly a large number of winning teams who do not use such imagery, and coaches should be sufficiently versed in the psychology of motivation that such appeals to players do not need to be made.

Beyond the appeal to tradition associated with a mascot, there are moral traditions that institutions like to foster and maintain. Among these are the beliefs embraced by the organizations and associations with whom universities affiliate. For example, the NCAA has a commitment to ethnic student welfare. In a guest editorial for the *NCAA News*, Charles Whitcomb (1998), chair of the NCAA Minority Opportunities and Interests Committee, wrote:

> Member institutions with Indian mascots that present Indian caricatures and mimic ceremonial rites do not comply with the NCAA's commitment to ethnic student welfare. . . . These mascots are perpetuating negative stereotypes of an ethnic group and diminishing the right and opportunity of Native Americans to appropriately identify their culture. It is simply another form of institutional racism. (p. 2)

One explanation for the continued use of Native American mascots relates to the marketing of Native America—particularly the images, symbols, and spirituality of the culture. This is an example of what Whitt (1995) calls cultural imperialism. When the spiritual knowledge, rituals, and objects of historically subordinated cultures are transformed into commodities, economic and political powers merge to produce cultural imperialism. As a form of oppression exerted by a dominant society upon other cultures, and typically a source of economic profit, cultural imperialism secures and deepens the subordinated status of those cultures (p. 3).

Whitt argues that it is inconsequential if the behavior is unconscious or intentional since the results are the same: extending the political power, securing the social control, and furthering the economic profit of the dominant culture. The reasons for the initial selection of Native Americans as mascots appear to be as much an economic and marketing gimmick as anything else. There is no doubt that now, under a G. W. Bush administration, more than ever, higher education institutions will be facing budget constraints. Every dollar is important to colleges and universities. We do not want to underrepresent the importance of fiscal concerns or the high-stakes nature of these concerns. In this regard, two recent incidents involving Indian mascots stand out.

At the University of North Dakota, an alumnus threatened to withhold a $100 million contribution he had pledged for the purpose of building the school a new hockey arena if the school changed its "Fighting Sioux" mascot (Brownstein, 2001). The president of the University of North Dakota, responding to concerns about the mascot, had formed a committee, which met for five months, to look into the controversy. It appeared that the president was open to phasing out the name but, when the supporter threatened to withhold his pledge, the school's board of trustees unanimously voted to keep the mascot. Here, the lack of action appears to have yielded at least a short-term economic benefit for the institution.

On the other side, the University of Miami–Ohio did take action to change its mascot and does not appear to have suffered from a decline in alumni support and giving—which some schools explain is a reason not to drop their Indian mascots. According to senior communications director Richard Little, the University of Miami–Ohio trustees decided to change the mascot so that their incoming president would not have to contend with what had become a contentious issue (personal communication, March 3, 2000). In the fall of 1996, the University of Miami–Ohio changed its Redskin mascot to the Red-Hawk. One trustee resigned over the issue, but Mr. Little contended that there is no data to support the contention that the change has hurt the institution financially.

Given the problems of using Indian mascots as outlined in this article, why would anyone select them as mascots and why do we as spectators and fans support them? One explanation may be that those who created the mascot symbol did not see it as stereotypical or racist in nature. It is only now, with the advantage of years of knowledge and experience, that people are beginning to see these symbols as wrong (Delgado & Stefancic, 1992). Dennis (1981) contends that people engage in racist behavior because they are reasonably sure that there is support for it; and since many of these mascots were created when overt racist acts were common in this country, it should not be altogether surprising that no one spoke up against the use of Indian mascots at the time. In many ways, this reinforces Davis (1989), who says that humans categorize other humans to make sense of their world.

Those who initially chose the American Indian mascots were responding to the category they had placed Native Americans into as a result of their own experiences vis-à-vis popular culture and traditional education. Their experiences were rarely firsthand interactions with Native Americans. Little concern was given to whether the mascots selected were portraying a stereotype that could fan the flames of racism or discrimination. Although some people who support Indian mascots claim that the mascots honor Indians, with little appreciation given for tribal customs or reality, schools have created their own image of the "Indian."

That it is a false image never penetrates the mind of the halftime spectators, since it simply reinforces the mascot they learned in the classrooms and textbooks (Trimble, 1988). Spectators who witness the mascot accept the mascot unconditionally since it reinforces their categorization. Further, since this categorization is subconscious, attempts to unlearn it and confront it are met with defensiveness, hostility, and an unwillingness to consider the possibility that the categorization may result in racist or biased behavior.

RISKS IN DOING AND NOT DOING

According to the documentary *In Whose Honor* (Rosenstein, 1997), the national protest movement against the use of Native American mascots began at the University of Illinois, Urbana-Champaign, in 1987 by Charlene Teeters. Teeters, a Spokane Indian, was a graduate student at the University of Illinois and attended a football game where the university's mascot, Chief Illiniwek, was present. Teeters was so appalled by the depiction of Native Americans by this mascot—and by the other fans acting as Indians—that she decided to return the following Saturday to protest Chief Illiniwek.

The bastardization of traditional and sacred practices is not limited to Chief Illiniwek. Flutes, whistles, and drums are important in Native American ceremonies and are even considered to be spiritual in nature. The use of these instruments and the music that accompanies a mascot performing at a halftime show trivializes their importance and is out of place on the playing field. The wearing of feathers, buckskin, and war paint all lend themselves to an imagery that degrades Native Americans and their culture and distorts people's perceptions.

The symbols mascots use—tomahawks, spears, war whoops, and headdresses—also are a stereotyped vision of Native Americans as savages—and certainly not as a people who are among us today (Pewewardy, 1992). All of these images prevent the dominant culture from understanding the historical and current culture of indigenous people. Since the mascot image simply reinforces or affirms our stereotype, the image must have been implanted earlier in our lives.

The films we watch and the books we read have grouped Indians into four groups: the noble savage, the generic Indian, the living fossil, and the savage. Although serious efforts have been made to raise our collective consciousness, many of these efforts have been undermined by the superficial treatment they receive in school (Charles, 1993). In their study among college students at the University of Texas, University of Wisconsin–LaCrosse, and University of North Dakota, Rouse and Hanson (1991) sought to determine if students at the University of North Dakota and University of Wisconsin had more factual knowledge about Native Americans due to their relative close proximity to Indian reservations than students at the University of Texas, which is not near a reservation. Their study showed no statistical differences among the students' factual knowledge of Native Americans or in the cultural stereotypes they held about Native Americans. These stereotypes were not always negative, but they were inaccurate. Further, the University of Wisconsin and University of North Dakota students held greater negative personal stereotypes (Indians are lazy, weak, undependable, unpatriotic), felt that Indians were to blame for their own problems, and were less likely to favor self-determination for Indians. This study also showed that all three samples received most of their information about Native Americans from TV and movies, and that their high school curriculums had, on average, 1.46 books on Native Americans. What this study shows is that while a lack of visibility may contribute to ignorance about a minority group, higher visibility may not dispel these biases. Native American mascots contribute to the problem by playing to the stereotypes that people hold about Native Americans. It is our belief that given the educational mission of colleges and universities, people who work at them cannot ignore this use of oppressive images. The costs are too high.

CONCLUSION

There are several ways that student affairs professionals can protest the use of Indian mascots. First and foremost, we as student affairs professionals can educate ourselves and then act as educators of students, faculty, and staff about the developmental, community, institutional, and antipluralistic effects of using Native Americans as mascots. As individuals, we need to stop lending our support to their continued use. We should not wear clothing with Indian images as logos, display these mascots in our offices, or use them for publicity. Rather than referring to teams as "Redskins" or "Warriors," we can refer to them as "the Florida State team" or the "University of Illinois team." We should not participate in culturally demeaning actions such as the tomahawk chop or "war chants." At a recent conference of the Southern Association of College Student Affairs (SACSA), a major speaker from Florida State University led the crowd in the tomahawk chop—and many participated enthusiastically. We can each show our disapproval through letters to the president, the board of trustees, the director of athletics, and alumni, informing them that we do not support the use of Indian mascots. Those of us who are responsible for educational programming on campus can make use of resources like *In Whose Honor?* (Rosenstein, 1997) or invite guest speakers to teach students about this issue. These are steps all of us can take whether or not we work at a school with an Indian mascot. Those of us at school without these mascots have a responsibility to a broader community, which includes lending our support to organizations addressing the mascot issue. It is not inappropriate for universities to take a leadership role in this oppressive practice. NASPA and other student affairs organizations should weigh in on the issue as well by passing a resolution urging all colleges and universities to discontinue the use of Indian mascots. The use of school mascots is an issue that needs to be addressed by student affairs; and with a new millennium upon us, now is the time.

NOTE

This essay was originally published in 2002 in the *Journal of Student Affairs, 40* (2–3).

REFERENCES

ASUIndians.com: The official website of Arkansas State Athletics. (2001). Retrieved from http://asuindians.fansonly.com/

Boxberger, D. L. (1989). *To fish in common: The ethno history of Lummi Indian salmon fishing.* Lincoln: University of Nebraska Press.

Brownstein, A. (2001, February 23). A battle over a name in the land of the Sioux. *Chronicle of Higher Education, 47,* 24A–25A.

Central Michigan University, Official Athletic Site—Traditions. Retrieved from http://cmuchippewas.fansonly.com/

Charles, J. (1993). *Of mascots and tomahawk chops: Stereotypes of American Indians and the English teacher's response.* Paper presented at the annual meeting of the national teachers of English. Retrieved from ERIC database. (ED355535)

Davis, P. C. (1989). Law as micro aggression. In R. Delgado and J. Stefancic (Eds.), *Critical race theory: The cutting edge.* Philadelphia: Temple Press.

Delgado, R., & Stefancic, J. (1992). Images of the outsider in American law and culture: Can free expression remedy systemic social ills? In R. Delgado and J. Stefancic (Eds.), *Critical race theory: The cutting edge*. Philadelphia: Temple Press.

Deloria, V., Jr., & Lytle, C. M. (1998). *The nations within: The past and future of American Indian sovereignty*. Austin: University of Texas Press.

Dennis, R. (1981). Socialization and racism: The white experience. In B. P. Bowser & R. G. Hunt (Eds.), *Impacts of racism on white Americans* (pp. 71–85). Beverly Hills, CA: Sage.

Department of the Interior, Bureau of Indian Affairs (2000). *Federal Registry, 65*(49).

McLaren, P. (1999). *Schooling as a ritual performance: Toward a political economy of educational symbols and gestures*. Lanham, MD: Rowman & Littlefield.

Pewewardy, C. D. (1992). The "tomahawk chop": The continuous struggle of unlearning "Indian" stereotypes. Retrieved from ERIC database. (ED355066)

Pewewardy, C. D. (2000). Why educators should not ignore Indian mascots. *Multicultural Perspectives, 2*(1).

RedHawks Online. (2000). The Official Website of the Miami RedHawks Athletic Department—Traditions. Retrieved from http://www.muredhawks.com/

Rosenstein, J. (Producer). (1997). *In whose honor?* (Videorecording).

Rouse, L., & Hanson, J. (1991). American Indian stereotyping, resource competition, and status-based prejudice. *American Indian Culture and Research Journal, 15*(3), 1–17.

Segal, C. M., & Stineback, D. C. (1977). *Puritans, Indians and manifest destiny*. New York: G. P. Putnam's Sons.

Students for Chief Illiniwek. (2000). Retrieved from http://www.savethechief.com

Trimble, J. E. (1988). Stereotypical images, American Indians, and prejudice. In P. A. Katz & D. A. Taylor (Eds.), *Eliminating racism: Profiles in controversy*. New York: Plenum Press.

Tyson, L. (1999). *Critical theory today: A user-friendly guide*. New York: Garland.

Vanderford, H. A. (1996). What's in a name? Heritage of hatred: The school mascot controversy. *Journal of Law and Education, 25*(2), 381–383.

Whitcomb, C. (1998). Indian mascot shows lack of respect. *NCAA News* [Editorial]. Retrieved from http://www.ncaa.org/news/archive

Whitt, L. A. (1995). Cultural imperialism and the marketing of Native America. *American Indian Culture and Research Journal, 19*(3), 1–31.

2

Teach Them Respect Not Racism: Common Themes and Questions About the Use of "Indian" Logos

Barbara E. Munson

"Indian" logos and nicknames create, support, and maintain stereotypes of a race of people. When such cultural abuse is supported by one or many of society's institutions, it constitutes institutional racism. It is not conscionable that our public schools (and those of Wisconsin, in particular) be the vehicle of institutional racism. The logos, along with other societal abuses and stereotypes, separate, marginalize, confuse, intimidate, and harm Native American children and create barriers to their learning throughout their school experience. Additionally, the logos teach non-Indian children that it is all right to participate in culturally abusive behavior. Children spend a great deal of their time in school, and schools have a very significant impact on their emotional, spiritual, physical, and intellectual development. As long as such logos remain, both Native American and non-Indian children are learning to tolerate racism in our schools. The following illustrate the common questions and statements that I have encountered in trying to provide education about the "Indian" logo issue.

"We have always been proud of our 'Indians.'" People are proud of their high school athletic teams, even in communities where the team name and symbolism does not stereotype a race of people. In developing high school athletic traditions, schools have borrowed from Native American cultures the sacred objects, ceremonial traditions, and components of traditional dress that were most obvious, without understanding their deep meaning or appropriate use. High school traditions were created without in-depth knowledge of Native traditions; they are replete with inaccurate depictions of Indian people, and promote and maintain misguided stereotypes of rich and varied cultures. High school athletic traditions have taken the trappings of Native cultures

onto the playing field where young people have played at being "Indian."
Over time, and with practice, generations of children in these schools have
come to believe that the pretended "Indian" identity is more than what it is.

"We are honoring Indians; you should feel honored." Native people are
saying that they don't feel honored by this symbolism. We experience it as no
less than a mockery of our cultures. We see objects sacred to us—such as the
drum, eagle feathers, face painting, and traditional dress—being used, not in
sacred ceremony or in any cultural setting, but in another culture's *game*. We
are asking that the public schools stop demeaning, insulting, harassing, and
misrepresenting Native peoples, their cultures, and their religions for the sake
of school athletics. Why must some schools insist on using symbols of a *race*
of people? Other schools are happy with their logos that offend no human
being. Why do some schools insist on categorizing Indian people along with
animals and objects? If your team name were the Pollacks, Niggers, Gooks,
Spics, Honkies, or Krauts and someone from the community found the name
and symbols associated with it offensive and asked that it be changed, would
you not change the name? If not, why not? I apologize for using this example
but have found no way to get this point across without using similar derogatory names for other racial and ethnic groups.

"Why is the term 'Indian' offensive?" The term "Indian" was given to
indigenous people on this continent by an explorer who was looking for
India, a man who was lost and who subsequently exploited the indigenous
people. "Indian" is a designation we have learned to tolerate; it is not the
name we call ourselves. We are known by the names of our Nations—Oneida
(Onyota'a:ka), Hochunk, Stockbridge-Munsee, Menominee (Omaeqnome-
new), Chippewa (Anishanabe), Potawatomi, and so forth. There are many
different nations with different languages and different cultural practices
among the Native American peoples—as in Europe there are French, Swiss,
Italian, German, Polish, English, Irish, Yugoslavs, Swedes, Portuguese, Lat-
vians, and so on.

*"Why is an attractive depiction of an Indian warrior just as offensive
as an ugly caricature?"* Both depictions present and maintain stereotypes.
Both firmly place Indian people in the past, separate from our contemporary
cultural experience. It is difficult, at best, to be heard in the present when
someone is always suggesting that your real culture only exists in museums.
The logos keep us marginalized and are a barrier to our contributing here
and now. Depictions of mighty warriors of the past emphasize a tragic part
of our history; focusing on wartime survival; they ignore the strength and
beauty of our cultures during times of peace. Many Indian cultures view life
as a spiritual journey filled with lessons to be learned from every experience
and from every living being. Many cultures put high value on peace, right

action, and sharing. Indian men are not limited to the role of warrior; in many of our cultures, a good man is learned, gentle, patient, wise, and deeply spiritual. In present time as in the past, our men are also sons and brothers, husbands, uncles, fathers, and grandfathers. Contemporary Indian men work in a broad spectrum of occupations, wear contemporary clothes, and live and love just as men do from other cultural backgrounds. The depictions of Indian "braves," "warriors," and "chiefs" also ignore the roles of women and children. Although there are patrilineal Native cultures, many Indian Nations are both matrilineal and child centered. Indian cultures identify women with the Creator because of their ability to bear children, and with the Earth, which is Mother to us all. In most Indian cultures, the highest value is given to children; they are closest to the Creator and they embody the future. In many Native traditions, each generation is responsible for the children of the seventh generation in the future.

"We never intended the logo to cause harm." That no harm was intended when the logos were adopted may be true. It is also true that we Indian people are saying that the logos are harmful to our cultures, and especially to our children, in the present. When someone says you are hurting him or her by your action and if you persist, then the harm becomes intentional.

"We are paying tribute to Indians." Indian people do not pay tribute to one another by the use of logos, portraits, or statues. The following are some ways that we exhibit honor:

In most cultures, to receive an eagle feather is a great honor; often, such a feather also carries great responsibility.

An honor song at a powwow or other ceremony is a way of honoring a person or a group.

- We honor our elders and leaders by asking them to share knowledge and experience with us or to lead us in prayer. We defer to elders. They go first in many ways in our cultures.
- We honor our young by not doing things to them that would keep them from becoming who and what they are intended to be.
- We honor one another by listening and not interrupting.
- We honor those we love by giving them our time and attention.
- Sometimes we honor people through gentle joking.
- We honor others by giving to them freely what they need or what belongs to them already because they love it more or could use it better than we do.

"Aren't you proud of your warriors?" Yes, we are proud of the warriors who fought to protect our cultures and preserve our lands. We are proud and we don't want them demeaned by being "honored" in a sports activity on a

playing field. Our people died tragically in wars motivated by greed for our lands. Our peoples have experienced forced removal and systematic genocide. Our warriors gave their sacred lives in often vain attempts to protect the land and preserve the culture for future generations. Football is a game.

"This is not an important issue." If it is not important, then why are school boards willing to tie up their time and risk potential lawsuits rather than simply change the logos? I, as an Indian person, have never said it is unimportant. Most Indian adults have lived through the pain of prejudice and harassment in schools when they were growing up, and they don't want their children to experience more of the same. The National Congress of American Indians, the Great Lakes Inter-Tribal Council, the Oneida Tribe, and the Wisconsin Indian Education Association have all adopted formal position statements because this is a very important issue to Indian people. This issue speaks to our children being able to form a positive Indian identity and to develop appropriate levels of self-esteem. In addition, it has legal ramifications in regard to pupil harassment and equal access to education. If it is not important to people of differing ethnic and racial backgrounds within the community, then change the logos because they are hurting the community's Native American population.

"What if we drop derogatory comments and clip art and adopt pieces of real *Indian culturally significant ceremony, like powwows and sacred songs?"* Though well-intended, these solutions are culturally naive and would exchange one pseudo culture for another. Powwows are gatherings of Native people that give us the opportunity to express our various cultures and strengthen our sense of Native American community. Powwows have religious, as well as social, significance. To parody such ceremonial gatherings for the purpose of cheering on the team at homecoming would multiply exponentially the current pseudo-cultural offensiveness. Bringing Native religions onto the playing field through songs of tribute to the "Great Spirit" or Mother Earth would increase the mockery of Native religions even more than the current use of drums and feathers. High school football games are secular; the Creator and Mother Earth are sacred.

"We are helping you preserve your culture." The responsibility for the continuance of our cultures falls to Native people. We accomplish this by surviving, living, and thriving; in so doing, we pass on to our children our stories, traditions, religions, values, arts, and languages. We sometimes do this important work with people from other cultural backgrounds, but they do not and cannot continue our cultures for us. Our ancestors did this work for us, and we continue to carry the culture for the generations to come. Our cultures are living cultures—they are passed on, not "preserved."

"This logo issue is just about political correctness." Using the term "political correctness" to describe the attempts of concerned Native American

parents, educators, and leaders to remove stereotypes from the public schools trivializes a survival issue. A history of systematic genocide has decimated over 95% of the indigenous population of the Americas. Today, the average life expectancy of Native American males is age 45. The teen suicide rate among Native people is several times higher than the national average. Stereotypes, ignorance, silent inaction, and even naive innocence damage and destroy individual lives and whole cultures. Racism kills.

"What do you mean, there is hypocrisy involved in retaining an 'Indian' logo?" Imagine that you are a child in a society where your people are variously depicted as stoic, brave, honest, a mighty warrior, fierce, savage, stupid, dirty, drunken, and only good when dead. Imagine going to a school where many of your classmates refer to your people as "dirty squaws" and "timber niggers." Imagine hearing your peers freely, loudly, and frequently say such things as "Spear an Indian, save a walleye" or more picturesquely proclaim, "Spear a pregnant squaw, save a walleye." Imagine that the teachers and administration do not forbid this kind of behavior. Imagine that this same school holds aloft an attractive depiction of a Plains Indian chieftain and cheers on its "Indian" team. Imagine that in homecoming displays, cheers, and artwork you see your people depicted inaccurately in ways that demean your cultural and religious practices. Imagine that when you bring your experiences to the attention of your school board and request change, they simply ignore you and decide to continue business as usual. Imagine that the same school board states publicly that it opposes discriminatory practices, provides equal educational opportunity, and supports respect for cultural differences.

"Why don't community members understand the need to change? Isn't it a simple matter of respect?" On one level, yes. But in some communities, people have bought into local myths and folklore presented as accurate historical facts. Sometimes these myths are created or preserved by local industry. Also, over the years, athletic and school traditions grow up around the logos. These athletic traditions can be hard to change when much of a community's ceremonial and ritual life, as well as its pride, becomes tied to high school athletic activities. Finally, many people find it difficult to grasp a different cultural perspective. Not being from an Indian culture, they find it hard to understand that things that are not offensive to themselves might be offensive or even harmful to someone who is from a Native culture. Respecting a culture different from the one you were raised in requires some effort. Even if a person lives in a different culture, insight and understanding of that culture will require interaction, listening, observing, and a willingness to learn. The Native American population, in most school districts displaying "Indian" logos, is proportionally very small. When one of us confronts the logo issue, that person, his or her children and other family members, and anyone else in the

district who is Native American become targets of insults and threats; we are shunned and further marginalized—our voices become even harder to hear from behind barriers of fear and anger. We appreciate the courage, support, and sometimes the sacrifice of all who stand with us by speaking out against the continued use of "Indian" logos. When you advocate for the removal of these logos, you are strengthening the spirit of tolerance and justice in your community; you are modeling for all our children thoughtfulness, courage, and respect for self and others.

"Is there any common ground on this issue?" All of Wisconsin's public schools are required to have a nondiscrimination statement and a policy to provide enforcement. Through Act 31, all schools are required to provide education (in the classroom, not on the basketball court) about Wisconsin's Woodland Indians. Many schools have adopted strategic plans emphasizing cultural sensitivity and awareness. These measures should establish considerable common ground between Indian people requesting the removal of the logos and the public schools. Until the logos are removed, however, they are no more than broken promises and hollow, hypocritical rhetoric.

3

Native Americans as Sports Mascots

Sharon Pray Muir

Using "Indians" as mascots for sports teams is opposed by most Native Americans, yet the tradition is often enthusiastically supported by European Americans. Supporters of the practice maintain that they are honoring the Native heritage, that some American Indians are overly sensitive, or that the controversy illustrates extreme political correctness. Opponents regard it as a classic example of institutional racism. They contend that the tradition is offensive, that it interferes with the respectful understanding of Native cultures, or that it scars some Native Americans emotionally and psychologically.[1] They also note that Native mascots are culturally inaccurate or demeaning and that they perpetuate negative, historically inaccurate portrayals of American Indians as savages, Why, opponents ask, would anyone choose a human group as a mascot if the group in question objected to it, especially when there are so many acceptable alternatives? What seems to be creative, cute, or comical to some people may be seen as mocking, trivializing, and dehumanizing by others.

A droll editorial in *Time* magazine suggested that sports nicknames originally were named for "animals that specialize in messy predation (lions, sharks, falcons, and so forth) or human groups famous for rapine and pillage (pirates, buccaneers, Vikings, conquistadors, bandits, and raiders)." It noted that more recent nicknames included some associated with the "nostalgic violence of cowboys and Indians (Braves, Redskins, Chiefs, Indians, Outlaws, Cowboys, Wranglers and Rangers)."[2]

Professional, university, and school teams have responded to the controversy in various ways. Some teams have changed their names, such as a team at Eastern Michigan University that discarded its Huron mascot to become

the Eagles. Others have retained Native names but eliminated offensive caricatures, such as Central Michigan University's Chippewas. Still others have
studied the issue and kept both their Native mascots and the objectionable
trappings, notably the Atlanta Braves with their chant and tomahawk chop.

A few states have asked schools to voluntarily change Native team names.
In one, Wisconsin, only a few schools have done so, while most "continue to
cling to what they see as a harmless tradition."[3] The Unity '94 Conference
asked newspapers to stop printing Native team names. At least two publish-
ers changed their policies, though in different ways. The Minneapolis *Star
Tribune* began identifying such teams only by their city (e.g., Kansas City
and Washington in place of Chiefs and Redskins). The Portland *Oregonian*
followed suit, except that it continued to print tribal names (e.g., Chicago's
Blackhawks).[4]

Criteria have been suggested for assessing the use of Native Americans as
mascots. One principal of a Native American school proposed 13 questions
to consider, including whether the mascots are respectful of Indian cultures
or rooted in Hollywood fiction.[5] Television personality Larry King asked
some teams with Native mascots if they would "name it that if [you] were
just starting out."[6]

Another test of this practice involves role reversal, in which people consider the issue as if it were their own culture were being singled out: How
might you feel if a sports mascot portrayed a group to which you belong?
In response, proponents of Native mascots argue that they are not offended
when Buffalo Bill or pioneers are mascots. But that comparison may miss
the point, because neither one denigrates a culture. Giago suggests that
a more apt comparison would be one in which cheerleaders painted their
faces black, wore Afro wigs, or acted out crude stereotypes of African
Americans.[7]

NOTES

This essay was originally published in January–February 1999 in *Social Education,*
63(1), 56–57.

1. Cornel Pewewardy, *The tomahawk chop: The continuous struggle of unlearning
"Indian" stereotypes*. Paper presented at the annual conference of the National Indian
Education Association, Albuquerque, NM, November 1992. Retrieved from ERIC
database. (ED355066)
2. John Lee, "What's in a nickname," *Time* (January 19, 1987): 82.
3. Herbert Buchanan, "Sports mascots," *Scholastic Update* [Teachers edition]
(February 10, 1995): 13.

4. Mark Fitzgerald, "Drop Indian sports terms, minorities say," *Editor & Publisher* (August 13, 1994): 19.

5. Pewewardy, *The tomahawk chop*, 2.

6. Cited by Tim Giago, "Drop the chop! Indian nicknames just aren't right," *New York Times* (March 13, 1994): 19.

7. Tim Giago, "I hope the Redskins lose," *Newsweek* (January 27, 1992).

4

The Problems with Native American Mascots

Laurel R. Davis

Sport has not been widely discussed in the field of multicultural education, yet sport is central to the lives of many students. It is critical that multicultural educators attend to the field of sport, because it plays a significant role in the socialization of youth. There are many sport-related topics that multicultural educators could address. This article focuses on the existence of Native American mascots in school-sponsored sport.

Because of the prevalence of stereotypes of Native Americans in United States popular culture, many have difficulty understanding the problems with Native American mascots. Even those who oppose these mascots often have trouble clearly articulating the reasons for their opposition. The purpose of this article is to lay out the main arguments against the use of Native American mascots. All of the arguments mentioned in this article are used by activists who are working to eliminate these mascots.

THE MASCOTS ARE RACIST STEREOTYPES

The most common argument against Native American mascots (and by "Native American mascots" I also refer to the many other items that are popular in U.S. culture) is that they represent racist stereotypes of Native Americans. Stereotypes of Native Americans appear in movies; government seals; advertisements and symbols for products like butter, beer, and paper; and statues and paintings that non-Natives have in their homes. Scholars have observed two main stereotypes: the "bloodthirsty savage," which conveys the notions that Native Americans are wild, aggressive, violent, and brave; and the "noble savage," which conveys the notions that Native Americans are primitive, childlike, silent, and part of the natural world (Bataille & Silet, 1980; Hilger, 1986; Lyman, 1982; Williams, 1980).

It is the stereotype of Native Americans as bloodthirsty savage that led non-Natives to choose Native American mascots for sport. Traits associated with this stereotype—such as having a fighting spirit and being aggressive, brave, stoic, dedicated, and proud—are associated with sport; thus, selecting a Native American mascot links sport teams with such traits. The appeal of this stereotype to many in sport is illustrated by the following quotations from supporters of Native American mascots: "I can think of no greater tribute to the American Indian than to name a team's warriors after courageous, cunning—and feared—warriors of the Indian nations, the braves" (Shepard, 1991, p. 14A); and "I look at that mascot, that Indian head, and it stirs me up. I think of getting real aggressive, and it brings out the aggressiveness in me. And it makes me go out there and really wrestle hard and fight hard, you know, because that's what those Indians were" (cited in Davis, 1993, p. 15).

When all the mascots representing Native Americans are considered (e.g., Indians, Redskins, Braves, Chiefs), it turns out that Native Americans are the most common mascot in U.S. sport. The other mascots that are most common are animals, most of which are also associated with aggression and fighting (e.g., tigers). Many consider it offensive that Native Americans are perceived and used as symbols in the same way as animals.

Stereotypes are misleading generalizations about a category of people. When people believe stereotypes, they tend to think that all, or almost all, people who belong to a particular category behave in the same way, and they tend to ignore the wide diversity of behavior exhibited by people within the category. Regarding the stereotype associated with the mascots, not all Native Americans in the past were aggressive, brave, dedicated fighters. And today, most Native Americans do not occupy their time fighting. Many non-Natives are aggressive, brave, dedicated fighters. Of course, many Native Americans take pride in their ethnic/racial background and are dedicated people. But do they have more pride and dedication than other groups? And, since Native Americans have extremely high rates of suicide, health problems, and poverty, asserting that this racial group has more pride than other groups is shallow.

The stereotype of Native Americans as aggressive is particularly offensive because it distorts the historical reality of European and European American aggression (i.e., the white invasion of Native American lands and subsequent conquering of people on these lands). Belief in this stereotype works to obscure the oppression, violence, and genocide initiated by European Americans against Native Americans, and serves as justification for these acts. This stereotype is part of a mythological history of the western United States, according to which cowboys and so-called pioneers led a glorious and adventurous life fighting Native Americans. One reason the resistance to elimination of Native American mascots is so vigorous and emotionally charged is because when the activists critique the mascots they are also criticizing a form of American identity that is linked to myths about the western United States (Davis, 1993).

Native American mascots, and most other images of Native Americans in popular culture, are stereotypes that focus on the past, and thus these stereotypes reinforce the problematic view that associates Native Americans only with the past. This stereotyping works to obscure the lives of contemporary Native Americans. As one interview subject said, "Respect the living Indian, you know. Don't memorialize us. . . . [The mascots are] almost like a monument to the vanished American Indian" (Davis, 1993, p. 13). Recognizing and understanding the lives of contemporary Native Americans challenges this stereotype.

Native American mascots misrepresent, distort, and trivialize many aspects of Native American cultures, such as drumming, dancing, singing, and some aspects of religion. As an interview subject stated, "I compose memorial songs, I compose burial songs for my grandmothers and my grandfathers, my family. And when people [imitate] that at an athletic event, like at a baseball game, it hurts me, to see that people are making a mockery of me. We don't do that, what they're doing, this chanting" (Davis, 1993, p. 13). Most of those who support the mascots do not understand the meanings or realities of Native American lives and cultures. Thus, it is particularly ironic that many who want to retain Native American mascots think they are honoring Native Americans. As another interview subject asserted, "How can you honor me, when you don't know the first damn thing about me?" (Davis, 1993, p. 14).

Another irony related to the belief that Native Americans are being honored by the mascots is that "positive" views of Native Americans, and the practice of using symbols of Native Americans to represent sport teams and the like, began soon after the last of the Native American nations were conquered or subdued (Davis, 1993). Thus, one has to ask, who is being "honored" by Native American mascots, Native Americans or those who subdued Native Americans?

The mascots and most other images of Native Americans in popular culture lump all nations (i.e., "tribes") of Native Americans together, incorrectly conveying that there is a single Native American culture and rendering the diversity of Native American cultures invisible. For example, only some Native American nations have political structures that are dominated by a male chief, and headdresses are worn by members of only some nations.

Ethnic and racial groups other than Native Americans have occasionally been used as mascots. There are several reasons why these mascots are not as problematic as Native American mascots. First, these other mascots tend to either represent a people that lived in the past and are not alive today (e.g., Spartans) or were selected by people from the named ethnic group (e.g., Scots). Second, most of the mascots that represent other ethnic groups do not have the same association with aggression (e.g., Irish). And third, Native Americans should not have to condition their responses to be the same as other ethnic/racial groups.

One of the reasons many do not see Native American mascots as stereotypes and as racist is that the majority of these images seem to be positive. Most stereotypes of racial and ethnic groups are obviously negative, such as African Americans as criminals and Mexican Americans as lazy. It is easier to understand that overtly negative stereotypes are stereotypes and are racist. On the other hand, some stereotypes appear to be positive, such as Asians as intelligent, Jews as good at business, and Native Americans as brave. Yet despite their positive tone, these are problematic stereotypes in that many people from these groups do not fit the stereotype, and underneath the positive facade lie some problematic beliefs and consequences. For example, the stereotype that all Asians are intelligent contributes to the extra pressure and discrimination many Asian Americans face, and this stereotype is often used to disparage other groups. The stereotype that all Jews are good in business serves as a foundation for another stereotype—that Jews are taking over the world economy, a stereotype that has been used to legitimate anti-Semitic actions such as the Holocaust. There are problematic beliefs and consequences that stem from the so-called positive stereotypes of Native Americans as well.

Some people argue that they should be able to retain their Native American mascots if they portray the mascots in a culturally authentic and nonstereotypical manner. There are three problems with this idea. One is that a school or team cannot control how others, such as the media and other schools or teams, use their mascot. For example, the media might print a headline announcing an "attack" by a team with the Native American mascot. The second problem with this idea is that the schools or teams with the Native American mascots will not be able to avoid stereotypes. Native Americans are a category of people who live in many different societies, each with a different culture, and within each Native American society there is much diversity. Thus, how does one portray what Native Americans are "really like?" Imagine creating a mascot that represented African Americans, Jewish Americans, Puerto Ricans, or European Americans. Because of the wide diversity of people within these categories, any mascot one could imagine would be a stereotype. Third, it is inappropriate for non-Natives to imitate Native Americans, even if they do so in a culturally accurate way. We would find it offensive to see a Christian portray herself as Jewish or an European American portray himself as African American, even if the portrayal is culturally accurate (e.g., using an authentic dialect and clothing). Imitating another's culture, even if we do it accurately, seems like we are mimicking and mocking the other, especially if the imitation is done for entertainment, like it is at a sporting event.

The mascot stereotypes influence the way non-Natives both perceive and treat Native Americans. The mascot stereotypes limit the abilities of the public to understand Native American realities. As the late Michael Dorris (1992) put it, "War-bonnetted apparitions pasted to football helmets or baseball caps act as opaque, impermeable curtains, solid walls of white noise that for many citizens block or distort all vision of the nearly 2 million native Americans today" (p. 19A).

THE MASCOTS HAVE A NEGATIVE IMPACT ON NATIVE AMERICAN LIVES

A second argument against the mascots is that they have a negative impact on Native American lives. Many people argue that symbols, such as images and language, are trivial issues that do not matter, yet reams of scholarship demonstrate that symbols exert a significant influence on both our perceptions and behaviors.

Native American mascots create a hostile climate for many Native Americans and sensitive non-Natives in the schools and communities with these mascots. It is hard to feel comfortable in and committed to a school or community and perform to the best of one's ability in school or work when constantly surrounded by offensive stereotypes.

The mascots negatively influence the self-image and self-esteem of Native Americans, especially children. One activist tells the story of how she instilled pride in her children regarding their Native American heritage and she thought her children were secure—yet when she took them to a game with a Native American mascot, she witnessed a major "blow to their self-esteem" as they "sank in their seats," not wanting to be identified as Native American (Davis, 1993). Another activist called the mascot issue a "mental health" issue (Ode, 1992, p. 2E).

Mascot stereotypes affect more than mental health and comfort within a school/community. Other problems Native Americans commonly face, such as poverty, cultural destruction, poor health, and inadequate education, are intertwined with public images of Native Americans. These images played a role in creating such problems, and now these images constrain Native American efforts to effectively address such problems.

Because of the current power structure in the United States, the quality of lives Native Americans will lead in the future depends on whether the general public has an accurate understanding of past and present Native American lives. If members of the public cannot understand the problem with Native American mascots, they certainly will not understand sovereignty or other issues that affect the quality of Native American lives.

NATIVE AMERICANS SHOULD CONTROL IMAGES OF THEMSELVES

A third argument against the mascots is that Native Americans should have control over societal definitions of who they are. Currently, Native Americans have little power to shape public images of themselves, and the voices of Native Americans are rarely heard. Non-Natives continually assert that the mascots are honoring Native Americans, despite the fact that most pan-ethnic Native American organizations (i.e., organizations consisting of Native American nations from throughout the United States) have stated otherwise (Rosenstein, 1996). One Native American writer said, "I'll decide what honors me and what doesn't. . . . Minority groups have had enough of whites telling them what to think" (MacPhie, 1991, p. 19A). It is plain arrogance and a lack of respect when non-Natives think that they know more about Native Americans and what honors them than do the Native Americans themselves.

Of course, one can find some people from every racial or ethnic group to agree with any opinion, as the various people from one racial or ethnic group never all have the same opinion, so supporters of Native American mascots have been able to find Native Americans (and other people of color) to defend their use of these mascots. Many Native Americans have learned stereotypes of Native Americans from the same sources that non-Natives have. Some Native Americans have even profited from selling images of these stereotypes to non-Natives. It is important not to blame these Native Americans but to recognize the social forces that affect them, such as the media, extreme poverty, and inadequate education. In light of the fact that most pan-ethnic Native American organizations have issued statements against the mascots, it is offensive for non-Natives to use Native Americans or other people of color to justify the position that the mascots should be retained.

OTHER ISSUES ASSOCIATED WITH THE MASCOTS

Finally, there are several other issues associated with the Native American mascot controversy that need to be addressed. The first issues are tradition and intent. Supporters of Native American mascots regularly point out that they do not intend to offend anyone but to honor Native Americans, and they are just having fun and affirming tradition. It is worth pointing out that not all traditions are good ones. Some examples of bad traditions are racially segregated facilities and the exclusion of women from schools. Many people have benefited from the elimination of such traditions.

It is also crucial to note that intent is not the most important issue here. If a belief or action has problematic consequences (i.e., if it has negative societal effects), then we should eliminate it, regardless of intents. For example, drunk drivers or men who continually comment on the sexual attractiveness of women they work with usually do not intend to harm anyone, and yet the consequences of such actions are often problematic and thus we should work to eliminate these behaviors. Many times, despite our best intentions, when we lack the necessary knowledge, our behavior can be quite harmful to others. Although most people who support Native American mascots do not intend to harm Native Americans, the consequences of the mascots are problematic and therefore the mascots should be eliminated.

The final issue is the small percentage of people who object to Native American mascots. Many supporters of Native American mascots argue that the mascots must not be problematic because only a small number of people object to them. Polls do indicate that if this issue were put to voters, the majority of people in most parts of the United States would vote to retain the mascots (Sigelman, 1998). Yet there are two reasons that the focus on numbers and majority rule is problematic.

First, it is important to note that the majority of people in the United States are uncritical of stereotypes of Native Americans, including the mascots, because of lack of education about Native American issues. Most Americans have had little to no substantial contact with Native Americans, and thus have distorted perspectives that come from television, movies (especially westerns), and tourist traps that feature stereotypes of Native Americans. We have been inundated with stereotypes of Native Americans in U.S. popular culture from birth, so we have come to believe these stereotypes (Green, 1988). It is not surprising that large numbers of people do not understand this issue.

It seems that in areas of the United States where the Native American population is larger and politically active, the non-Native population has a greater understanding of Native American issues because they have been educated by local Native Americans and media coverage of these Native Americans (Davis, 1993). The task of educating the U.S. public or regional populations about Native American stereotypes and lives is a difficult one.

Second, Native Americans represent only about 1% of the U.S. population, so issues they care about (and that most others do not) will not likely win public approval. People who are Jewish and people who travel in wheelchairs also represent a small percentage of the U.S. population, yet this does not mean that others should ignore their feelings and concerns. Even if the percentage of people who are offended is small, others should still try to be sensitive. Part of being a good citizen is trying to empathize with other people, especially those who are different from ourselves. We should attempt to understand why other people are offended by something, but even if we cannot achieve this understanding, the considerate thing to do is to respond to others' concerns.

Those who support the use of Native American mascots often claim that they want to retain the mascots because they "respect" Native Americans. Respect is a meaningless word when the positions of most pan-ethnic Native American organizations are ignored. Real respect is carefully listening to, attempting to understand, and addressing Native American concerns about this issue. On a related note, it is not accurate to say that every possible symbol or mascot will be objectionable to someone. There are many symbols, including most other sport mascots, that are not offensive to any groups of people.

CONCLUSION

In conclusion, equality and justice in society depend on our abilities to empathize with those who are different from us. If we listen carefully to the Native American individuals and organizations that call for an elimination of Native American mascots, it is clear that there are valid reasons why we should work to eliminate these mascots and other problematic images of Native Americans in society. The State of Minnesota has made a coordinated effort to eliminate Native American mascots in its public schools and has been quite successful. The rest of the country needs to follow their lead.

NOTES

This essay was originally published in 2002 in *Multicultural Education, 9*(4), 11–14.

REFERENCES

Bataille, G., & Silet, C. L. P. (Eds.). (1980). *The pretend Indians: Images of Native Americans in the movies*. Ames: Iowa State University.

Davis, L. R. (1993). Protest against the use of Native American mascots: A challenge to traditional American identity. *Journal of Sport and Social Issues, 17*(1): 9–22.

Dorris, M. (1992, April 24). Crazy Horse isn't a good name for a malt liquor. *Star Tribune*, p. 19A.

Green, R. (1988). The tribe called Wannabee: Playing Indian in America and Europe. *Folklore, 99*: 30–55.

Hilger, M. (1986). *The American Indian in film*. Methuen, NJ: Scarecrow.

Lyman, C. M. (1982). *The vanishing race and other illusions*. Washington, DC: Smithsonian Institute.

MacPhie, R. P. (1991, October 25). This "real live Indian" offended by chop. *Star Tribune*, p. 19A.

Ode, I. (1992, January 23). Bellecourt's new AIM. *Star Tribune*, pp. IE–2E.

Rosenstein, J. (Producer). (1996). *In whose honor? American Indian mascots in sports*. (Video).

Shepard, B. (1991, October 26). Letter to the editor. *Star Tribune*, p. 14A.

Sigelman, L. (1998). Hail to the Redskins? Public reactions to a racially insensitive team name. *Sociology of Sport Journal, 15*(4): 317–325.

Smith, D. (1991, November 15). Tomahawk choppers cut us. *Oracle* (Hamline University's student newspaper), p. 5.

Williams, L. E. (1980). Foreword. In J. E. O'Conner, *The Hollywood Indian: Stereotypes of Native Americans in films* (pp. ix–xvi). Trenton: New Jersey State Museum.

5

What the "Fighting Sioux" Tells Us about White People

Robert Jensen

Appeals to the dominant white society to abolish the "Fighting Sioux" nickname and logo typically are framed in terms of respect for the dignity and humanity of indigenous people. That is the appropriate way to address the question, but it has failed—at least, in North Dakota—to persuade most white folks. Today I want to pursue another argument.

I want to suggest to my fellow non-Indian North Dakotans—those of us whose ancestors came from some other continent, primarily those of us who are white and of European descent—that we should support the campaign to change the University of North Dakota name and logo not just because it is offensive, exploitative, and racist (it is all of those things) but also for our own sake. Let us do it for our own dignity. Let us join this struggle so that we can lay honest claim to our own humanity.

I say this because I believe that we give up our dignity when we evade the truth, and we surrender our humanity when we hold onto illegitimate power over others. And I want to argue that is what the nickname controversy is really about—white America refusing to come to terms with the truth about the invasion and conquest of North America, and refusing to acknowledge the fundamental illegitimacy of its power over indigenous people as a result of that conquest. It is about denial of the realities of the past and the present. It is, to follow the analysis of Ward Churchill, about holocaust denial and the consequences of that denial (Churchill, 1997).

THE PAST MATTERS

Let's start with the past, which people often want to avoid. It's history, they say. Get over it—don't get stuck in the past. But this advice to forget history is selective; many of the same folks who tell indigenous people not to get stuck in the past are also demanding that schoolchildren get more instruction in the accomplishments of the Founding Fathers. It is commonly asserted, and undoubtedly true, that Americans don't know enough about their own history (or that of the world). The question isn't whether we should pay more attention to history; the relevant questions are: Who gets to write history? From whose point of view is history written? Which historical realities are emphasized and which are ignored? Let us not take the seemingly easy—but intellectually and morally lazy—path of selectively contending that "history doesn't matter." Everyone knows it matters.

We can begin this historical journey in 1492, with the beginning of the European conquest of the New World. Estimates of the precontact indigenous population vary, but at the time there were approximately 15 million people living north of the Rio Grande, the majority in what is now the United States and perhaps 2 million in Canada. By the 1900 census, there were 237,000 Indians in the United States. That works out to an extermination rate of 97 to 99%. That means the Europeans who came to the continent killed almost all the Indians. It is the only recorded genocide in history that was almost successful. The Europeans who invaded North America, followed by their descendants who colonized the entire continent, eliminated almost the entire indigenous population, and in the process claimed almost the entire land base of those peoples.

But were those indigenous peoples really people in the eyes of the invaders? Were they full human beings? Some Europeans were not so sure. In the Declaration of Independence, one of our founding documents of freedom, Indians are referred to as the "merciless Indian Savages." Theodore Roosevelt, whose name can be found on a national park in this state, defended the expansion of whites across the continent as an inevitable process "due solely to the power of the mighty civilized races which have not lost the fighting instinct, and which by their expansion are gradually bringing peace into the red wastes where the barbarian peoples of the world hold sway" (Roosevelt, 1901).

Among Jefferson's "savages" and Roosevelt's "barbarians" were the fighting Sioux—the Lakota, Dakota, and Nakota, the people who lived in what we now call North Dakota. They fought the Europeans, and they eventually lost. They lost, for example, in the Wounded Knee massacre at the end of the 19th century, when U.S. soldiers opened fire on several hundred unarmed Lakota, killing most of them, mostly women, children, and elderly. That massacre came at the end of what are commonly called the Indian Wars, an ambiguous term for the conflicts between Europeans and indigenous people in North America that helps obfuscate historical reality. Were these wars waged *by* Indians, or *against* Indians? Instead of the Indian Wars, we could be more precise and call them the "European/American wars to exterminate Indians." We could call them part of a holocaust.

But wait, people will say, this ignores the fact that most of the indigenous people died as a result of disease. Today it is no longer considered polite to glorify the murder of Indians and the taking of their land; the preferred route to avoid confronting this holocaust is the disease dodge. But Churchill argues persuasively that the fact that a large number of indigenous people died of disease doesn't absolve white America. Sometimes those diseases were spread intentionally, and even when that wasn't the case the white invaders did nothing to curtail contact with Indians to limit the destruction. Some saw the large-scale death of indigenous people as evidence of the righteousness of their mission: God was clearing the land so that civilized whites could take their rightful place upon it. Whether the Indians died in war or from disease, starvation, and exposure, white society remained culpable.

That's history. It's not the history I was taught growing up in Fargo, North Dakota. But it is a real part of real history. It is every bit as real as the stories of courageous Norwegian farmers who homesteaded through brutal winters. For too long we have tried to keep those two histories separate. It is time to join them, to see that the homesteads were made possible by the holocaust.

Let me be clear: I am not asking anyone who is white to feel guilty about this. I do not feel guilty about this. I feel incredibly pained and saddened by it, just as I feel pained and saddened by other acts of brutality that litter human history. But I cannot take on guilt for events that happened before I was born. Feeling guilt for things outside my control would be illogical.

However, I can—and should—feel guilty about things I have done wrong in my life, over which I do have control. I should feel guilty not simply so that I feel bad but so that change is possible. Guilt is healthy when it leads to self-critique, to moral reflection, to a commitment to not repeating mistakes. We can feel that guilt both individually and collectively. We can see what we have done wrong or failed to do right, both by ourselves and with others. That brings us to the present.

The American holocaust perpetrated by Europeans and their descendants against indigenous people cannot be undone. But we can in the present work to change the consequences of that holocaust. One easy place to start could be eliminating a nickname and logo to which a significant number of Indians object. All that white people would have to do is accept that simple fact, and change the name and logo. It would cost no one anything, beyond the trivial expense of changing the design on some stationary, uniforms, and university trinkets.

But wait, many white people say, isn't systemic poverty on reservations more important than a logo? Of course it is. Are there more pressing problems for Indians than the Fighting Sioux design? Sure. But there is nothing to stop anyone from going forward to address other problems and, at the same time, taking the simple step of changing the nickname and logo. It's not an either/ or choice.

Why do so many people resist that simple change so fiercely? Individuals will have different reasons, of course; I cannot pretend to know what motivates everyone. Many people say it is out of a respect for tradition. But I don't think that's really what is going on. I would like to offer an alternative explanation for why white people will not take such a simple and easy step.

POWER RELATIONS IN THE PRESENT

Let me digress a moment for a story about another question of language that might be helpful. In the 1980s I worked at St. John's University, just down the highway in Minnesota. St. John's is a men's college run by a monastery that had a cooperative relationship with the College of St. Benedict, a nearby women's college run by a convent. As time went on, the level of cooperation between the schools increased, including more joint publications. At one point in the process, staff members at St. Benedict's suggested that in those joint publications we use the term "first-year student" instead of "freshman," for the obvious reason that none of the students at St. Ben's was a "man," fresh or otherwise. It struck me as a reasonable request, a simple thing to do. They weren't asking that we go back and reprint every brochure we had in stock, just that in the future we use the more accurate and less sexist term. I assumed this would not be a problem. But it was a problem for a number of men at St. John's. What a bizarre suggestion, they said. Everyone knows freshman is an inclusive term that means first-year students, male and female. How could anyone bring up such a silly point? I pointed out that to change the term was cost free—all we had to do was switch one term for another. No, they said— there's a tradition at stake, and besides, "first-year student" is clumsy. "But do we really care?" I asked. Yes, many of them did care, quite passionately.

Looking back, I don't think it was a question of tradition or the aesthetics of the terms. It was about power. In the Catholic Church, girls don't tell boys what to do. In the long history of those two colleges, the girls didn't tell the boys what to do. The real issue was simply power. Could the women tell the men what to do? Would the men accept that? Of course, one small request about one term in a brochure was hardly a revolutionary change in the gender practices of Catholicism, the religious orders that operated the colleges, or those institutions. But that wasn't the point. The members of the dominant group were used to being in charge by virtue of who they were, and they were not interested in changing the underlying power dynamics.

Eventually the boys gave up fighting that one, and first-year students at the campuses are referred to today as first-year students. And the women's college over time has continued to challenge the male dominance of the partnership. Everyone is better off as a result, including the boys at St. John's.

Likewise, I think a similar power dynamic is at the core of white resistance to the simple act of dropping nicknames such as Fighting Sioux: Indians don't get to tell white people what to do. Why not? Polite white people won't say it in public, but this is what I think many white folks think: "Whites won and Indians lost. It's our country now. Maybe the way we took it was wrong, but we took it. We are stronger than you. That's why we won. That's why you lost. So, get used to it. You don't get to tell us what to do." I think for white people to acknowledge that we don't have the right to use the name and logo would be to open a door that seems dangerous.

Why should Indians have the right to make the decision over how their name and image are used? Because in the absence of a compelling reason to override that right, a person or group of people should have control over their name and image. That's part of what it means to be a person with full humanity. And in this case, the argument for white people giving Indians that power is intensified by the magnitude of the evil perpetrated by whites on Indians.

To acknowledge all that is to acknowledge that the American nation is based on genocide, on a crime against humanity. The land of the free and the home of the brave, the nation that was born as the vehicle for a new freedom, rests on the denial not only of freedom but of life itself, to a whole group of people—for the crime of getting in the way of what the European invaders wanted for themselves: the land and its resources.

To acknowledge all that is to acknowledge not only that the Fighting Sioux nickname is an obscenity but an artifact of our own barbarism. If Germany had won World War II, it would be equivalent of contemporary Germans naming a university team the Jews and using a hook-nosed caricature. I do not mean that hyperbolically. In heated debates, people often compare opponents to Nazis as an insult. This isn't an insult. It's an accurate comparison. The ideology of racial supremacy underneath the genocide of indigenous people here was not so different from Nazi ideology. Inferior people had to give way so that superior people could make use of land, just as Teddy Roosevelt said. The dominant group wanted something. The subordinated group was in the way. The easiest way to justify that is to define away the humanity of the subordinated group, so a barbaric policy can be seen as natural and inevitable.

To take that simple step—to accord to Indians the basic dignity to control how they are named and represented—is to step onto a road that leads to a confrontation with the mythology of the United States. That can be painful, but not just because of what it forces us to face in the past. The larger problem with stepping onto that path is that it doesn't stop in the past. It leads to something more difficult—the confrontation with the enduring consequences of the genocide. To go down this path forces us to confront the fact that the poverty rate for American Indians (25.9%) is more than double the overall rate (11.3%) and nearly four times as high as the rate for white Americans (7.5%).

Why is that the case? Why, a century after the official end of the Indian Wars, are Indians the poorest racial/ethnic group in the United States? Why is Shannon Country, South Dakota, home to the Pine Ridge Reservation, consistently among the poorest counties in the United States, with a 52.3% poverty rate? What does the massacre at Wounded Knee have to do with the living conditions today of the people on the reservation that includes Wounded Knee?

The past is past, but maybe some of that past also is present. Is white America afraid of looking too much at the past, lest we have to look at the present? Are we afraid of what we might see? What might we learn—about ourselves?

TRADITION OR JUSTICE?

Let me turn to the possible challenges to this position.

Can tradition, the common argument for keeping the Fighting Sioux, trump other considerations? Indeed, tradition makes some people (mostly white) feel good. Does that value to some outweigh the injury to others? Many traditions have fallen by the wayside over time when it became clear that the tradition imposed a cost on some other person or group. It used to be a tradition in some regions for white people to call adult African American males "boy." No big deal, they said; it's just a name. But it was a name that carried a message about power and dominance.

Supporters of the Fighting Sioux might offer a counterargument: In that example all (or almost all) adult African American males objected to the use of the term because it was so obviously a way to denigrate them. But not all Indians object to Fighting Sioux, and there is an argument that such nicknames are meant to honor Indians. So, it is argued, we shouldn't get rid of the nickname.

I do not know of reliable polling data that would tell us how the "average" Indian feels about the name. But, for the sake of argument, let's assume that the vocal opponents of such nicknames and logos are a substantial percentage, but not a majority, of Indians. Let's also assume that the most Indians do not have strong feelings, and that a minority genuinely support such nicknames. Can white people simply say, "Well, see, Indians can't decide, so we'll leave things as they are."

I think that is an attempt to avoid a simple choice. Indians are no more monolithic than any other group; there's no reason to think there would be absolute uniformity of opinion. However, over time many Indians from a number of different backgrounds have developed a clear critique of the use of Indian nicknames and logos, and they have put forward that critique with clarity, honesty, and passion. I find the argument compelling, but even if one doesn't agree, one has to at least acknowledge it is a rational argument and that it is easy to understand why people hold the position. In the absence of a universal demand from indigenous people, but in the presence of a strong argument that many indigenous people support, white people cannot dismiss the issue. It seems to me there are only two possibilities.

The first would be for the North Dakota State Board of Higher Education and the university to acknowledge the long-standing opposition to the team name and change it. The second would be to let the people affected by this— the Indian population of the state and the university—decide the question. In other words, the only dignified and humane positions for white people are to either accept the judgment already rendered by Indians, or, if one believes that judgment is not clear, allow Indians to go forward and make that judgment (without external pressure, such as threats to withdraw funding for Indian programs or students if the decision is to eliminate the name and logo).

I am calling for white people to acknowledge that we have no right to choose how Indians are named and represented. We have no standing to speak on the question. Our place is to shut up and do what we are told. Let me say that again, for emphasis: We white folks should shut up and do what Indians tell us. Let's try it, first, on this simple issue. We might find it is something we should do on a number of other issues.

And if we do that, individually and collectively we will take a step toward claiming our own dignity and humanity. The way in which white America refuses to come to terms with its history and the contemporary consequences of that history has material and psychological consequences for Indians (as well as many other groups). But in a very real sense, we cannot steal the dignity and humanity of indigenous people. We can steal their resources, disrespect them, insult them, ignore them, and continue to repress their legitimate aspirations. We can try to distort their own sense of themselves, but in the end we can't take their humanity from them.

The only dignity and humanity that is truly diminished by the Fighting Sioux is that of white America.

NOTES

This essay was originally a presentation by Robert Jensen at the University of North Dakota on October 10, 2003, sponsored by BRIDGES, a student group that works to remove the university's "Fighting Sioux" nickname and logo.

REFERENCES

Churchill, Ward. (1997). *A little matter of genocide*. San Francisco: City Lights Books.
Roosevelt, Theodore. (1901). *The strenuous life*. New York: Macmillan.

6

Gendered Discourse:
Higher Education, Mascots, and Race

Jennifer Guiliano

Gail Bederman, in her influential 1995 work *Manliness and Civilization: A Cultural History of Gender and Race in the United States, 1880–1917*, explains the growth of college athletics as a development related to late Victorian-era claims to authority based on the physical body and racial superiority. Specifically, "as white middle class men actively worked to reinforce male power, their race became a factor that was crucial to their gender."[1] Sport allowed men to embrace their masculinity on the field and enact displays of physical violence. This violence was juxtaposed with male behavior off the sporting field, which was caught up in the things they had learned on the field, namely respect for rules, order, and control. The masculine ideal was coupled with whiteness as a racial category. Thus, as many historians have proven, the apex of masculinity was white male displays of physical prowess.

How then did sports mascots tie to the white masculine ideal? It would seem logical that the adoption of Indian performance would be antithetical to white masculinity. Yet, as Philip Deloria and others have shown, participants in playing Indian relied upon these rigidified momentary "lapses" in civilized behavior to confirm both psychic and physical superiority in the alienating world of the post–World War I era.[2]

I begin with Bederman and Deloria in order to ground the oft-ignored theorization of the historical links of gender and race between sports, educational institutions, and mascots when considering the contemporary moment. Often scholars (and public discussants) considering the mascot issue fail to connect all education, sports, and mascots fully with race and gender and instead concentrate either on the connection between the affirmation of white racial superiority and educational commercialism or on the claims of racism and traditionalism. Instead, I suggest that even when deploying claims of race and racism they are couched within a gendered language that affirms white male dominance.

One of the most striking features of the November 2003 University of Illinois Board of Trustees meeting was the spatial positioning of the audience. I attended the November meeting out of a deep curiosity caused by the substantial public rumor that newly appointed trustee Francis Carroll would propose the "retirement" of the much-revered and much-despised Chief Illiniwek. Although I, like many of my colleagues in the History Department, was skeptical that Carroll's resolution would come to fruition, I felt that even the possibility of movement regarding the issue could prove pivotal to my critical inquiry into the links between educational institutions and their sports mascots. The local newspaper and television stations staked out campus for the days prior to the meeting after it was confirmed that the Carroll resolution would be on the agenda, and their presence along the back wall of the meeting room offered the sense of heightened suspense that maybe today there would be some kind of action by the board of trustees. Yet what became most enthralling to me was not Carroll's withdrawal of the resolution and the reaffirmation that progress would not be made, it was the audience demographic and seating arrangement. The room was divided into four quarters with aisles dividing each quadrant. Directly inside the door in the upper-right quadrant sat anti-mascot proponents, including a large number of faculty and Native activists. In the bottommost two quarters sat a mix of anti-mascot groups including the Progressive Resource Action Coalition as well as interested community members and administrative officials. Yet it was the fourth quarter, directly in front of me, that presented the realization that the contemporary discourse of the mascot debate was not just an affirmation of whiteness but of a male-gendered whiteness. Of the hundred or so orange-clad students in front of me, an overwhelming number were white men. Belonging to the organizations "Honor the Chief" and "Students for Chief Illiniwek," these orange-clad bodies demonstrated their allegiance to the cause by jumping rhythmically up and down while chanting and deploying the tomahawk chop. Setting aside the disturbing movements mimicking a violent death, I kept focusing on the physical space and the sea of white men. Was the seeming dominance of white men in the pro-Chief alliance significant? Was there a parallel between the pro-mascot movement as a male discursive space and arguments long fronted by colonial historians about the reification of male identity through racialization, conquest, and appropriation?

I left the meeting with a sense that I had just witnessed a physical rendering of the very phenomena Bederman and Deloria had noted in their linkages between sport, masculinity, race, and higher education. I had seen white men shed their own identity by donning garb and performing specialized behavior that would only be legitimate within specific context. And importantly, they did so in a direct appeal to the very bastion of middle-class male identity: the board of trustees at an institution of higher education. The niggling sense that I needed to investigate the historical coupling of higher education, the mascot, gender, and race became even more invasive combined with other public statements offered surrounding the Carroll resolution. The November 18 issue of the *Daily Illini* illustrated the stereotypical ways in which gender was asserted. In response to the statement "Nancy Cantor, the chancellor of the university, has lost control of the issue," university alumnus Matthew Keelan offered the opinion:

> Why does she deserve any control over this issue? She obviously has no respect for the great traditions of the University of Illinois, nor any plans to uphold them. She has her own plans, and I think she should take them somewhere else. Or was that sentence referring to how she lost control, and left crying like a selfish child, when she didn't get her way? Her actions reflect poorly on the University. The tradition of the Chief has always reflected a dignified presence on the University. The University does need to take a stand. A stand to uphold the tradition of Chief Illiniwek. A stand against the political agenda of the misinformed. Take a stand for what is right. Take a stand to protect something which so many people profoundly respect. Hail the Chief.

Keelan strategically opposed the dignity of the "stoic" Chief Illiniwek with Cantor's emotional response. While Keelan explicitly calls Cantor's behavior childish and misinformed, he is also implicitly hyperfeminizing her. Cantor is not just a woman but she is a woman who can't control her emotions. Further, since the university must be a strong traditional (read: masculine) place, Cantor's admission of emotion is a direct affront to men. In many ways, Keelan's feminizing of Cantor parallels what colonial scholars have charted with other gendered colonialism. Keelan's editorial in November became part of an increasingly open charge that university chancellor Nancy Cantor couldn't handle herself, was a neoliberal (which, in the eyes of the writer, was apparently a pejorative term), and was overly emotional in anti-chief stance. As months passed and my puzzling about gender and the mascot grew greater, the gendered nature of the discussion took root in a lecture I offered to students of a U.S. History survey on the gendered and racialized world of the 1920s. In my lecture I talked about the ways in which consumption and race were tied together in postwar America through gendered appeals. Soap ads, sporting goods, cars, and household items all were scrutinized as elements of the increasingly open ties between racialization and commodification. The lecture extended weeks later into my section after my students attended a campus lecture by Julian Bond of the NAACP in com-memoration of the 50th anniversary of *Brown v Board* entitled "The Broken Promise of Brown v. Board."[3] Of the 25 students, an overwhelming number argued that the promise of Brown had not been broken and that public edu-cation has fulfilled its mandate to provide equal access. One of the few lone dissenters offered this statement: "How can we argue that the spirit of Brown and equal rights hasn't been broken when we attend a university that allows a white man to dress up as an Indian and dance around the football field?" A second student responded to the initial question: "It's just like the stuff we talked about in the '20s when people got up on stage in blackface and made fun of African Americans. They're both about racism."

What was so interesting about these statements was not just my happiness that someone in the room had connected Indians as a part of the racialized population but that a student critiqued the mascot as both a racialized and gendered display. It wasn't just whites who dressed up as Indians but it was white men. Even more provocative was the assertion by a male student that "It's just a bunch of guys playing football. Why do people care so much?" and his later belief that if the government and university didn't think it was wrong, why should the students? In this instance, again, the links between sport, higher education, race, and gender were offered up but resolutely un-connected as the discussion quickly deteriorated into students claiming things like "I'm not a racist," "My great-grandmother was Indian and I don't mind the mascot." The more nuanced investigation of the uses of gendered and raced rhetoric then fell to the concerns of authenticity and race.

In many ways, my inquiries into higher education, sport, gender, and race have been sidetracked by the very things my students fell prey to. In a presen-tation to high school students at a local high school that opened with a student asking, "Are you an Indian?" I spent the majority of the time presenting the events of American settlement and colonization just so that I could get them to consider Indians as a racialized group. Much of this is a result, I believe, of the poor understanding of Native American history. Many pro-Chief support-ers articulate a very flat definition of race and racism that is informed by a very minimalist conception of race as either black or white. Indians are neither black nor white and thus cannot be an object of racism, according to them.

I want to tie my grounding of sport and higher education as a white male space to mascot discourse as gendered through a final discursive moment couched in the language of education and race. Our esteemed university president, James Stukel, concluded in public statement that there is

an ominous element of the discourse [that] should alarm anyone who loves and cares about the University of Illinois at Urbana-Champaign. I am referring to the rhetoric of race and the increasing innuendo and bald-faced assertions that those who are not opposed to the Chief are motivated by racism. It is a false and unfair insinuation that inflames an already emotional debate and exacerbates an already intractable situation. In fact, the multitudes of opinions on all sides of the Chief issue are based on principal positions by virtually everyone with a point of view. Certainly there is not one member of the Board of Trustees who is driven by racism in his or her deliberations on this matter. Nevertheless, the rhetoric of race is intensifying. And whether it is intentional or not, it is deceptive and makes it all the harder for opposing sides to come together to resolve the issue.

I end with Stukel's comment not just because of his position as a white male and the head of the university but also because it illustrates the need to consider what it means that there are a sea of white men articulating the pro-mascot position and our university president and board of trustees are such men. At the end of the class discussion that I related to you, the initial student who posed the question of the white men as mascots stayed after to offer her final thoughts to me about the mascot issue. She said,

It's hard to be minority on this campus. It is hard to be black and it's even harder to be Indian. It's hard to be a woman in a classroom often dominated by men. By what's worse than anything is being all three, black, Indian, and female on a campus where white men get to walk around with an Indian head on their clothes and no one even notices.

NOTES

1. Gail Bederman, *Manliness and civilization: A cultural history of gender and race in the United States, 1880–1917* (Chicago: University of Chicago Press, 1996), p. 5.
2. Philip Deloria, *Playing Indian* (New Haven: Yale University Press, 1998).
3. Julian Bond, "The Broken Promise of Brown v. Board." Retrieved from http://www.blackcommentator.com/91/91_j_bond.html

Part II

EDUCATIONAL ISSUES

One of the more troubling aspects of the use of Indianness by sport teams via names, logos, and imagery is its prevalence is schools across the United States. Indeed, the overwhelming majority of Native American mascots have been adopted by educational institutions, where in turn they have become the basis for elaborate halftime rituals, chants, and gestures (like the infamous tomahawk chop). Such use is meant to inspire players through degrading caricatures by overzealous rivals, a range of annual practices (around homecoming, for instance) intended to create a shared identity, and local economies. Sadly, institutions, charged with fostering the development of cultural literacy, critical thinking, and collective memory, have regularly taught lies about Native Americans, recycling stereotypes while reinforcing racial privileges. They have, as Ellen Staurowsky argues in her contribution to this section, miseducated generations of Americans, a perspective echoed by Roy Saigo and the Department of Anthropology at the University of Illinois. Worse, for American Indian students, as Lawrence Baca outlines, schools have become hostile environments, spaces of terror. Importantly, according to Angelina E. Castagno and Stacey J. Lee, schools that encourage students to "play Indian" also create contexts in which others perpetuate fraud by misrepresenting themselves as embodied Indians.

Increasingly, as schools and communities have struggled to transform themselves (often unwillingly), they routinely undertake a difficult journey without a map. The contributions by Terry Grier and David Carl Wahlberg provide useful templates for such processes.

Even before making a change, institutions often worry about alumni giving. In contrast with popular sentiment, Patrick J. McEwan and Clive R. Belfiel assert in their study that such changes do not have an adverse impact on it.

7

A Letter from the Department of Anthropology, University of Illinois, Urbana-Champaign, to the University of Illinois Board of Trustees Regarding the Use of Chief Illiniwek (February 17, 1998)

Dear Members of the Board of Trustees:

We, the undersigned faculty members of the Department of Anthropology, wish to commend the Board of Trustees for agreeing to implement a series of significant, positive steps toward achieving a climate conducive to cultural diversity on the UIUC campus. We note, for example, the important addition of new faculty positions in areas of study such as non-Western and U.S. minority cultures. These developments will enable the University of Illinois to build strength through diversity and will allow the Department of Anthropology to maintain its prominent position in national rankings.

Alongside these positive gains, we note with concern that all the recommendations on inclusivity made to the Board of Trustees have been duly implemented except one: the retirement of the Chief Illiniwek symbol. We understand that the primary reason given for this omission was that the Chief is not a subject of academic concern. We strongly disagree and respectfully request that the Board consider a number of adverse academic effects on the Department of Anthropology that are directly attributable to the ongoing presence of the Chief Illiniwek symbol.

These effects extend into all aspects of our scholarly lives: teaching, service, and research. Several critical areas deserve attention. The Chief: (i) promotes inaccurate conceptions of the Native peoples of Illinois, past and present; (ii) undermines the effectiveness of our teaching and is deeply problematic for the academic environment both in and outside of the classroom; (iii) creates a negative climate in our professional relationships with Native American communities that directly affects our ability to conduct research with and among Native American peoples; and, (iv) adversely affects the recruitment of Native American students and faculty into our university and department.

(i) The presence of the Chief promotes inaccurate conceptions of the Native peoples of Illinois.

It is our duty as teachers at an outstanding, world-class, national educational institution to provide our students with accurate information. As anthropologists we are particularly responsible for providing accurate information regarding cultural identities, symbolic representations, and social processes. Unfortunately, the image of Chief Illiniwek completely misrepresents the American Indian peoples who lived in what is now the state of Illinois. Historical and archaeological records inform us that the Illini were primarily farmers, hunters, and traders who, when first contacted by the French in the mid 17th century, lived in settled villages within a loose political confederacy of twelve tribes. The men did not wear feather war bonnets, and so to represent the Illini with a Plains Indian war bonnet and to dress the mascot in the military regalia of a Sioux warrior is totally inaccurate. It is the direct equivalent of representing Italians or Germans with someone dressed in a Scottish kilt and playing the bagpipes.

In addition, it is frequently claimed that the person portraying the Chief is knowledgeable about Native American cultures, dances, and music. The faculty members in our department whose areas of research and teaching focus specifically upon the music and dances of Native North America find this claim untenable. In marked contrast to indigenous dance forms, the choreographed movements performed by the Chief are a combination of stereotyped gestures and steps taken from the Boy Scout movement and Wild West Shows of the 1920s and 30s, supplemented by acrobatic display. The musical accompaniment is likewise a stereotypic misrepresentation derived from early Hollywood movies.

As an educational institution we do not promote the teaching of "flat earth" theory in geology; why then are we in the business of promoting inaccurate knowledge about Native Americans? As serious scholars and teachers, charged by the State of Illinois to educate its citizens, we find such an inaccurate portrayal embarrassing and opposed to our educational mission of providing students with knowledge that is accurate and true. Armed with accurate information our students would know that, from the Native American perspective, the young man portraying the Chief has not earned the right to wear Lakota Sioux military regalia, just as he has not earned the right to wear a U.S. Marine's uniform and a Purple Heart. They would know that Native American dancing and the wearing of traditional regalia are always connected with spiritual beliefs and practices and so would understand why the Chief's performance as entertainment at a sporting event violates the religious sensibilities of many American Indian people. They would know that American Indians are the only recognized ethnic minority in the U.S. who are still subjected to public stereotyping, and that ethnic stereotyping, however well-intentioned, always misrepresents, and so dishonors, those it portrays.

(ii) The presence of the Chief undermines our teaching effectiveness and is deeply problematic for the academic environment both in and outside of the classroom.

Although it is frequently claimed that the presence of the Chief encourages students to learn about Native American cultures, we find the contrary to be true. The unexamined, sentimental attachment many students hold for the Chief frequently precludes any desire for accurate understanding and thus undermines our teaching effectiveness.

For instance, one unintended consequence of the Chief Illiniwek symbol is that it romanticizes and sentimentalizes indigenous peoples and freezes them in a stereotyped past. It thus ignores the historical record which shows that European intrusions into the Northeast and Midwest resulted in more than two centuries of social turmoil that fueled inter-tribal conflicts as well as conflicts between Europeans and indigenous peoples. Under government pressure to cede large tracts of land to European settlers in the early 19th century, the indigenous people of this region were forcibly removed from their homes and relocated west of the Mississippi River. They were subject to arrest and execution if they attempted to remain in their homelands. The romantic symbol of the Chief betrays a lack of awareness of this history of oppression. This, in turn, provides compelling reasons why most contemporary American Indian people strongly object to the suggestion that they are being "honored" by the Chief.

These historical facts are uncomfortable for many students to contemplate. They contradict core values of this nation as a land of "liberty, freedom, and justice for all." American Indian peoples were excluded from the embrace of these founding principles in the past and are frequently excluded today in ongoing struggles over treaty rights, and economic, educational, and political resources. As educators, we believe that our students are best served by being taught to understand the complexities of all sides of this history, not by being encouraged to ignore it. The image of the Chief actively discourages such inquiry.

We also find that the emotional attachment to the inaccurate and ahistorical image of Native Americans perpetuated by the Chief makes it difficult, if not impossible, for the voices and concerns of contemporary Native American peoples to be heard. It is precisely this fact that leads to the truly ironic situation in which those who insist that they are "honoring" American Indians by their use of this symbol steadfastly deny legitimacy to the strenuous objections being voiced by individuals, by tribal groups, and by major national American Indian institutions. The 1990 census shows that there are over 24,000 American Indians living in Illinois today. There are many thousands more in Oklahoma, Kansas, Iowa, Nebraska, and Wisconsin who are descendants of the former residents of this region. We think that it is incumbent upon this great institution to instigate changes that would make Native American people feel welcome on this campus, and better prepare our students to be responsible and informed citizens of a culturally and historically complex nation.

Anthropology is distinctive as a discipline because, from its very inception, it has confronted the problem of how best to teach people to understand the many and diverse cultures of the world. Several of our students have expressed to us directly their dismay and disappointment that the symbol of their school contradicts what they learn in classes about the harmful effects of racial stereotyping and cultural misrepresentation.

In addition, developing an anthropological understanding involves a capacity for critical self-knowledge. We find that the attachment some students hold for the Chief frequently overrides critical reflection and undercuts our goals as educators to foster cross-cultural understanding. For example, one of our faculty members was verbally attacked and called "an anti-white racist" for citing the example of the Chief in a lecture on racial stereotyping. Another reports that he no longer feels able to bring up the subject in the classroom because it is so divisive. Our teaching assistants have reported similar negative experiences. This is one of the ways in which the Chief Illiniwek symbol negatively affects the very heart of the university community, both inside and outside the classroom. A university, by its very nature, entails a commitment to, and respect for, rational thought. In the present context of institutional reluctance to acknowledge the real harm done by such symbols, we find that the presence of the Chief has become a genuine obstacle to learning for significant numbers of our students and creates an academic environment that is resistant to and dismissive of anthropological understanding.

(iii) The presence of the Chief creates a negative climate in our professional relations with Native Americans.

Not only is the symbol of Chief Illiniwek inaccurate for the Illini, it is also loaded with educational, racial, political, and intellectual implications. Its use has important consequences, both intended and unintended. Among the unintended consequences is the tendency among some Native Americans to dismiss our anthropological research or question our motives simply because we remain part of an institution at which Native American culture is stereotypically displayed in public. We have archaeologists, cultural, linguistic, and biological anthropologists who conduct nationally recognized research with the peoples of the Americas. The presence of the Chief has become a very real impediment to continuing research in Native communities in the U.S., and thus threatens to compromise our ability to enrich our classroom teaching through original research. In turn, this imperils the demanding research and publication record that faculty members are expected to attain to remain in a nationally ranked department.

A related and very serious difficulty concerns our efforts to comply with recent civil rights legislation mandating consultation with Native Americans regarding the accessioning and curation of Native American human remains and archaeological materials at the University of Illinois. Specifically, our department must adhere to the Native American Graves Protection and Repatriation Act of 1990 (Public Law 101–601). Compliance ultimately involves consideration with Native Americans of responsibilities for maintaining archaeological collections and the potential for repatriation of materials that are integral to our educational mission. The process of compliance requires extensive and continuous consultation with Native Americans, and we are finding that the Chief can precipitate negative attitudes on the part of such Native American consultants towards these extremely sensitive negotiations. Retiring the Chief will significantly enhance our chances of reaching mutually positive outcomes in compliance with the Native American Graves Protection and Repatriation Act.

(iv) The Chief adversely affects the recruitment of Native Americans into our department and our university.

Our faculty member whose teaching and research directly involves contemporary Native peoples reports that the Chief Illiniwek symbol is well known in many Native American communities across the country. For example, at a Native American college recruitment event last year, several young Native persons who were well qualified as potential UIUC students expressed their reluctance to consider applying to UIUC. When asked why, they said they expected to find an "anti-Indian," racist climate on this campus to which they were not willing to subject themselves. These potential students reasoned, quite correctly, that an institution cannot use a symbol such as Chief Illiniwek as its sports mascot and at the same time sincerely support a policy of ethnic inclusivity and cultural diversity. As a result of the Chief, such talented individuals have been recruited elsewhere.

CONCLUDING STATEMENT

We have demonstrated how the symbol of Chief Illiniwek affects us academically: it promotes inaccurate knowledge, undermines the effectiveness of our teaching, creates an academic environment dismissive of anthropological understanding and cultural diversity, threatens our professional relationships with Native American peoples, and adversely affects recruitment. The symbol that once created a sense of unity and pride for earlier generations now works in the opposite direction: The Chief has become a focus of division and escalating tension within the campus community and is a source of shame and embarrassment for many students and faculty.

As anthropologists we understand and appreciate the strong attachment many alumni have to the Chief as a symbol of the good times they wish to remember, as a symbol that expresses their desire to feel connected to this landscape and its history, and as a symbol that signifies pride in the tradition of a great educational institution. However, we also believe that our alumni can recognize the significance of social and cultural change and that traditions in and of themselves are not always honorable when times and moral sensibilities change.

Symbols are powerful icons that convey complex messages with lasting impact. It is therefore important to choose symbols with full understanding of the many meanings they may hold. Prior to the civil rights era of the 1960s the use of cultural symbols that harmfully stereotyped ethnic minorities was perceived as unproblematic by people sharing mainstream culture. Our nation's commitment to civil rights during the 1960s revealed the fundamental constitutional flaws of this view. Today, we believe that to acknowledge, understand, and celebrate cultural diversity is not a threat to a unified nation. It is instead the very means by which a vibrant, creative, multi-ethnic society can develop with pride and confidence in the 21st century. The citizens of Illinois have the highest possible standards to attain in meeting this goal, standards defined and embodied by Lincoln himself that obligate us to pursue a more inclusive society with vigor. We are confident those standards are within reach. We are equally certain that courageous leadership from the state's leading academic institution will be necessary to achieve them.

Yours sincerely,

Professors:
Janet Dixon Keller (Chair)   Brenda Farnell
Olga Soffer   Nancy Abelmann
Bill Kelleher   Andrew Orta

F. K. Lehman

Mahir Saul

Helaine Silverman

Arlene Torres

Alma Gottlieb

Paul Garber

Stanley Ambrose

Stephen Leigh

Bruno Nettl

Norman Whitten

David Grove

Linda Klepinger

Alejandro Lugo

Edward Bruner

8

On the Use of American Indian Mascots: A Presentation to the NCAA Minority Opportunities and Interests Committee (January 28, 2002)

Roy H. Saigo

Thank you for this opportunity to talk about the issue of American Indian mascots, logos, and nicknames in college athletics. It is a practice that has generated controversy on campuses across the nation and will continue to do so as long as there are non-Indian teams with names like Warriors, Chiefs, Redmen, Braves, and Savages.

I would like to make it clear that I am not here on my own behalf. I am here representing the many voices that have called on us, as educational leaders, to continue the process of eliminating racism from our colleges and universities.

Believe me, in the past year I have heard all sides of this controversy. I have received impassioned e-mail memos and letters not only from fans of the University of North Dakota but also from many others asking why I am wasting my time on an issue that's none of my business.

I have heard and read messages that claim that this is a trivial issue, or that such nicknames bring honor to American Indians.

However, I also have talked with and heard from many American Indians as they have shared with me the hurt and degradation they and their children feel when they see caricatures of American Indian persons, culture, and spiritual symbols.

They and other advocates of change on our campus and in our community question how others would feel if faced with such demeaning depictions of themselves as humans.

When I became president of St. Cloud State University a year and a half ago I realized that the demonstrations and emotional turmoil over this issue had been steadily escalating over the past several years.

I knew this was a topic that deserved a broad forum for discussion and resolution. I also knew that this was a controversy that many other campuses were coping with.

So, last winter our campus hosted the Midwest Forum on American Indian Mascots to allow regional schools the opportunity to share their challenges and explore solutions.

Last March, in response to all the concerns and proposals I heard, I drafted resolutions first to our regional athletic conferences and then to Division II President's Council Chair Patricia Cormier, asking that the issue be raised for discussion.

This Fall the MOIC [NCAA Minority Opportunities and Interests Committee] responded positively to this initiative.

As you know, many colleges and universities have retired their Indian-related mascots, logos, and athletic team names. Stanford and Dartmouth did this 30 years ago, in response to student actions. Colgate, Marquette, and Minnesota State–Mankato are other examples.

Quinnipiac University in Connecticut is the most recent school, with the board of trustees voting this past December to replace the "Braves" nickname with a yet-to-be-determined choice.

In making the announcement, Vice President for Academic Affairs Lynn Bushnell stated:

> Although fond of the tradition we've had for 50 years, the university community clearly recognized the difficulties of using a name that has the potential to misrepresent and denigrate an entire group of people. And, despite our clear intention to honor and remember the Native Americans once known as the Quinnipiaks, to do so only through athletics was found to be no longer appropriate.

The QU news release went on to identify some of the strongest factors that motivated their change.

They—like many others—squarely identify this as an educational issue.

Despite the hundreds of high schools and colleges that have made the change in recent decades, at least 42 American colleges and universities still have retained their Indian symbols. Some of these schools have compromised in some way, such as by dropping offensive mascots or replacing them with a nonracial or nonhuman mascot.

For instance, Minnesota's Winona State University retained the name "Warriors" but now uses a classical Greek soldier as their logo.

Just recently, San Diego State University—the Aztecs—announced plans to revamp their dancing "Monty Montezuma" mascot. Monty will be replaced by a "historically accurate" character who will serve as a "university ambassador."

The most interesting compromise might be that of Indiana University of Pennsylvania, who retained the nickname "Indians" for its athletic teams, but the team symbol is an animal, the black bear.

Some of you—and I know many of our colleagues—may be wondering, "What's the harm in this?"

Today I would like to share some examples of the harm.

I ask you to put yourselves and your own family members in the place of Indian parents, children, and college students, and imagine what it would be like to experience what they experience.

I ask you to consider the testimony and requests of individual American Indians, tribal governments, and American Indian organizations.

I encourage you to review the reasoning behind decisions that other institutions and organizations have made on this topic.

I hope that you will be persuaded by the will of the American people as expressed in the 1974 Civil Rights Act and in the recent, strong statements of the United States Commission on Civil Rights.

In April of 2001 the Civil Rights Commission issued a statement calling for a halt to the use of Native American images and nicknames as sports symbols. In the words of the commission:

> The stereotyping of any racial, ethnic, religious or other groups when promoted by our public educational institutions, teach all students that stereotyping of minority groups is acceptable, a dangerous lesson in a diverse society. Schools have a responsibility to educate their students; they should not use their influence to perpetuate misrepresentations of any culture or people.

This statement echoes again the theme that this is a highly appropriate issue for all educational institutions.

As for the assertion that mascots bring honor to American Indians, student Dan Lewerenz of the *Kansas State Collegian* newspaper voiced an articulate answer in a 1995 editorial:

> Suppose Kansas City had chosen to honor Jackie Robinson by naming their baseball team the Negroes. Diehard fans would come in blackface, and plastic spears would be sold by the thousands so fans could do the Hottentot chop. . . .
>
> What's the difference between the reality of teams with American Indian mascots and the imaginary Kansas City Negroes?

Does that example offend you? I find it very uncomfortable, but I think it makes a strong point about society's differential sensitivity to specific examples of racism.

We teach future citizens and leaders. What we tolerate and teach in our colleges and universities sets a tone of acceptance or nonacceptance in society at large.

In his editorial, Lewerenz went on to answer those who ask, "If it's such a big deal, why did nobody care until now?"

His reply was,

> People have cared about and protested the use of Indian mascots for decades. Certainly more people are paying attention to the issue now, but to assert that nobody cared until now is like saying nobody minded slavery until the outbreak of the Civil War.

Many people *do* care and care deeply about this issue. While St. Cloud State University does not have an American Indian mascot, we do compete in athletics with a university that does. When its teams come to our campus, we are faced with upholding the principle that our campus has long asserted: that we decry any form of racism.

And many, many people do believe that the issue of American Indian mascots in college athletics *is* one of full-fledged, anachronistic, institutionalized racism.

This issue cannot be trivialized as simply a matter of "political correctness." Rather it truly is an *educational* issue. It is directly related to the key role of a public university in supporting social justice, equality, and educational opportunity.

Our society has phased out many other discriminatory customs and laws that once were considered acceptable but now are considered shameful. I believe this evolution will and should continue.

African Americans no longer are required to ride in the back of the bus, and we no longer read "Little Black Sambo" to our children.

Asians are no longer openly depicted as buck-toothed individuals whose loyalties to America are suspect.

Yet the racist practice of stereotyping American Indians as cartoon characters and subhuman creatures continues. It is a deep wound, as it also trivializes and misrepresents Indian cultural and spiritual symbols.

American Indian mascots perpetuate stereotypes and lock American Indians into stagnant roles as seen by others of the dominant culture, *not* themselves. This is similar to how the old Aunt Jemima "mammy," black lawn jockey, and minstrel-show images perpetuated stereotypes of African Americans—stereotypes our society now sees as too demeaning.

What do the Indian mascot stereotypes teach?

According to many American Indians, those who argue to retain Indian mascots, or to regard them as harmless, don't realize the depth and breadth of the harm they do.

No matter how noble the official statements about their mascots sound, colleges and universities can't control behaviors that arise from the use of Indian mascots. American Indian mascots provide numerous occasions for racist and derogatory "collateral damage" to occur. Some of this damage already has been mentioned above: the impact it has in the classroom.

Some of the ugliest damage, however, occurs through "behind-the-scenes" events that add to a hostile environment for American Indian students, non-Indian students of conscience, and faculty and staff members on our campuses. These events may be subtle, but often they are vicious, such as racial taunting and acts of aggression.

Collateral damage also occurs when a school's mascot is depicted in a hostile or disgusting manner.

For example, the University of North Dakota "Fighting Sioux" mascot has been portrayed in sex acts with the North Dakota State University "Bison." (Incidentally, this is the "after" version of a "before-and-after" exchange. The "before" version was equally offensive. You can imagine what was depicted in the cutout area on the bison's back.)

Is this "honoring" American Indians?

The "Fighting Sioux" mascot also has been shown with x's in his eyes, indicating drunkenness, along with other exaggerated stereotypical features initiated at the will of UND students, alumni, and fans.

And then there is the marketing.

Many Indians are horrified by the disembodied head logos, as they resemble advertisements posted at stores that collected Indian heads as bounties during the days of political control by genocide. So, what can the NCAA do?

According to its mission and stated values, the NCAA seeks to "foster individual empowerment and personal well-being"; to "promote respect, communication, and teamwork"; and to "encourage diversity."

I do not believe that continuing the use of American Indian mascots fits with that mission. I urge you to continue with an in-depth study of this issue and to seek understanding of the American Indians' point of view.

To assist in your work, I highly recommend that you view the acclaimed PBS videotape *In Whose Honor?* It presents this issue much more powerfully than I can.

It isn't easy to foster change, especially when many wonder why there is a *need* to change something. It is hard to shake the status quo. However, we are hardly starting "from scratch." Rather, this is an intermediate stage in an ongoing continuum, and we are, at this moment, significant players.

In recent decades we have witnessed tremendous evolution in issues of civil rights and social justice. I believe that 20 years from now the use of Indian mascots in college athletics will be on that long list of insensitive practices that Americans no longer abide.

While you may not agree with our campus's role as a catalyst for this particular issue, we will continue to encourage open and broad discussion on this and other important issues.

In closing, I'd like to share a piece of my mail with you. I recently received a poignant letter from a father whose 11-year-old son, an American Indian, was picked on physically and verbally by other students when he openly objected to the use of Indians as mascots and logos. He wrote:

> White students, parents, administrators, and teachers fail or refuse to understand or accept the fact that use of Indians as mascots is offensive. Racism stems from the lack of understanding, lack of knowledge, and lack of respect. Many white people say it's "honoring" the Native Americans, but it is no honor when we are listed among animals and are abused daily in our lives. We are people, *not* mascots. And it hurts.

We are educators. We touch the future.
Thank you again.

9

American Indian Imagery and the Miseducation of America

Ellen J. Staurowsky

During the summer of 1998, the New York State Department of Education initiated an inquiry into the use of Native American mascots by schools for the purpose of determining if the practice is offensive and should be stopped. The study undertaken at the direction of the State Education Commissioner Richard Mills was in response to an appeal filed by Robert Eurich, a taxpayer from Orange County (NY). In 1996, Eurich sought to have the "Red Raiders" mascot eliminated from Port Jervis High School because he alleged it violated his civil rights and those of students attending the school (Associated Press, 1998a; Russin, 1998). Although Commissioner Mills dismissed Eurich's appeal, he did recognize the "seriousness of the issue the petitioner raises and that other districts statewide engage in similar practices" (Associated Press, 1998a, p. 1A).

The New York State Department of Education is one among many policy-making bodies to address the appropriateness of the use of American Indian mascots, symbols, and iconography in school settings. During the past three years, the issue has manifest itself from border to border and coast to coast in numerous discussions, debates, and disputes (Willman, 1997; "Hearing held," 1998). Saliently, the issue has even attracted the attention of the United States Department of Justice (USDOJ). The February 1999 investigation by the USDOJ at Erwin High School in North Carolina marks the first occasion when Native American images have been examined by a federal agency for the purpose of determining if the symbols contribute to a racially hostile learning environment (Pressley, 1999).

These incidents reveal the complicated dynamics that are invoked and/ or provoked when educators and communities attempt to discuss this issue.

Schools throughout the state of Minnesota and institutions such as Cornell, Marquette, Miami University of Ohio, St. John's, Stanford, and Syracuse (Lapchick, 1996; Staurowsky, 1996) have found reasons to stop the practice of using American Indian imagery for sport teams. However, the potential for discussions on this issue to become volatile is evident as well.

Indicative of the palpable sense of the need for reinforcement when it comes to handling this issue, Superintendent Church of the Afton (NY) School District said she would welcome a directive from the state as a means of avoiding contentiousness at the local level. Church's prediction that constituencies may register a range of reactions to the prospect of eliminating American Indian mascots can be gauged from the immediacy of response generated when the proposed New York State Department of Education study was made known to the public. The mere announcement of such a study evoked definitive positions by educational decision makers before the investigation ever got under way. Several athletic directors from Section IV in central New York, where 13 school districts are known as Indians, Chiefs, Senecas, Blackhawks, and Warriors, were quick to note that their school names were a "source of pride" and "a reflection of our area" (Russin, 1998a, p. 1A). About the study, one local sportswriter in Ithaca, NY, recognized two years ago as one of the most "Enlightened Cities" in the United States, editorialized:

> I guess if I lived on a reservation and a high school was nicknamed the "Iroquois Pale Faces" I would be offended. . . . But that's not the perspective I'm working from. Nope, this is the all common-sense channel. . . . There is absolutely nothing wrong with Indian-related names. (Russin, 1998b, p. 1A)

For the remainder of this article, I will focus on the cultural fallout confronted when addressing the issue of American Indian imagery as it has become infused into and perpetuated by school districts and communities. The complex racialized fabric of attitudes and beliefs fostered in adults and children through the reliance on American Indian mascots as the centerpiece of school, community, and team identities will be unraveled. The end result will be the identification of critical areas of inquiry that educators should address with themselves, their students, their families, and their communities about the continued use of these symbols.

Central to the argument presented in this article is an acknowledgment that few Americans, whether educators or representatives from any other sector of the population, have had the opportunity to acquire the depth of knowledge or understanding about this nation's history relative to American Indians that allows for a responsible consideration of this issue. A close examination of the dialogue surrounding American Indian imagery in sport reveals that people who we typically think of as the beneficiaries of systematic and complete schooling consistently mistake "common sense" (a set of common understandings that permit consensus based on accurate information) for "nonsense" and yet feel confident and empowered even in their lack of knowledge. This realization is compelling because it raises questions about the very essence of the educational process that good teachers care about the most, that being educational integrity and accountability.

AMERICAN INDIAN MASCOTS AS SYMPTOMATIC OF CULTURAL ILLITERACY

At a theoretical level, school systems in the United States are vested with the responsibility of cultivating the intellectual skills in citizens essential for functioning productively and meaningfully within a human and humane society. A critical tool in realizing this goal is cultural literacy, a means by which the vast differences in individual and group experiences and knowledge can be bridged and accommodated in a democratic, pluralistic society. Although the central importance of cultural literacy in education is undisputed, how cultural literacy is conceptualized and achieved is very much up for debate. In his treatise on the failure of schools to create a literate society, Hirsch (1987) urged a return to commonly shared content areas as the basis for mutual understanding and societal stability. He argued that there is a need for the identification and implementation of a core curriculum that would be delivered uniformly to students throughout the United States so as to ensure that all students received a baseline level of knowledge.

One need only watch a "Jaywalking" segment on the *Tonight Show* as interviewees struggle to correctly identify the number of states in the Union or testify to the small number of Americans who vote to appreciate at some level the argument Hirsch (1987) makes. His fundamental premise is particularly relevant to the issue of understanding the dialogue that emerges surrounding American Indian imagery, however, for two reasons. First, Hirsch's conceptualization of cultural literacy and how to achieve it is reflective of a dominant value system that has been operating in education for a considerable portion of this century. As a corollary, because his conceptualization is anchored in an ethnocentric perspective that fails to adequately provide for American Indians, an examination of his approach explains the gaps that occur between Native American parents and their allies who advocate for change within schools and those who actively or passively resist change when it comes to the matter of mascots.

To elaborate, Hirsch (1987) contends, perhaps rightfully so, that the "civic importance of cultural literacy lies in the fact that true enfranchisement depends upon cultural literacy" (p. 92). He continues by suggesting that the illiterate and semi-literate (the poor and the marginal) will be doomed to poverty and to the powerlessness of incomprehension if they are not taught the markers, such as certain areas of literature and standard English, that would otherwise connect those disadvantaged groups to the power structure of the dominant society.

Inasmuch as Hirsch's (1987) perspective on this matter reveals how power structures may work and how access to power is achieved through education (ideas that are contested in and of themselves), his position also discloses the kind of cultural blind spots that discussions surrounding American Indian mascots ought to illuminate but consistently do not. Illustrative of this point is Hirsch's response to concerns about how nationwide requirements would be identified and defined. Referencing an American tradition of pluralism, Hirsch observes that "Because our country started out with a powerful commitment to religious toleration, we developed habits of cultural toleration" (p. 94).

Hirsch's (1987) logic, although sustainable when linked to the dominant culture, falls apart when placed in the context of white–Indian relations. The United States has not historically afforded American Indians any degree of religious freedom, and genocide can hardly be thought of as cultural toleration.

As a departure gate for expounding on what is needed with regard to cultural literacy, an American tradition of pluralism offers a model that simply does not work when it comes to either the historic or present-day treatment of American Indians by educational systems. This notion of the American melting pot, however, structurally undergirds much of public education and educational theory as seen in Hirsch's (1987) work and others like it. As Pewewardy (1997) explains, "American schools have been designed to either destroy Indian culture and tribal language or graduate Indian students with a Eurocentric value system which is individualistic, competitive, and materialistic" (p. 17A). In the process, schools have often destroyed the possibility of non-Indians appreciating the influences and forces that have shaped their own lives.

Confronting the myth of the American melting pot and its integration into approaches to cultural literacy sheds new light on discussions about the practice of schools using American Indian imagery. It highlights the fact that these images emanate out of communities that have, for the most part, been woefully undereducated about the stereotypes they have chosen to represent their schools.

This can be tested using a modification of Hirsch's (1987) model of a common list of things that all Americans should know. Would Americans' view the stereotypical fierce and fighting male Indian warrior in the same light if they were fully aware of how the characterization of American Indians as "savages" in the Declaration of Independence affected the shaping of the policies the United States government adopted relative to the nation's First People? How might those images be viewed differently if thought was given to the connection between the actions of the principal writer of that document, Thomas Jefferson, who is credited with setting the framework for Indian removal in motion in 1803, and the fate of American Indians since that decision was made (Ellis, 1997)? How curious that the foe most feared and hated has been transformed by the dominant culture into the ultimate symbol of victory. To valorize the image of the "fighting Indian" without soberly recognizing the degree to which the United States sought to summarily conquer and control that very entity has created what Pewewardy labels "dysconscious racism" (as reported in Schroeter, 1998).

WHITE ASSUMPTIONS AND CULTURAL LITERACY

The distortions in logic that permeate justifications for American Indian imagery reflect what feminist researchers Maher and Tetreault (1997) call "white assumptions" which influence and mold the construction of knowledge as it is produced and resisted in classroom and school settings. Assumptions of whiteness circulate undetected throughout discussions and debates about the continued use of American Indian imagery. For example, rarely do educators preface discussions about this topic with an acknowledgment that these images are white inventions adopted by white educational power structures.

Despite public opposition by almost every Native American organization in the United States, some of which include the National Congress of American Indians, the National Indian Education Association, Advocates for American Indian Children, the National Coalition for Racism in Sport and the Media, and the Society of Indian Psychologists, patterns of non–Native American responses to formal requests by Native Americans for the elimination of mascots and imagery have frequently taken the form of denial, defensiveness, or dismissiveness (Brady, 1999; Pressley, 1999; Staurowsky, 1998). It is not uncommon that appeals for the eradication of stereotypical images, on the grounds that their elimination would abate forces that undermine the self-esteem and self-image of Native Americans, are met with allegations that these appeals are shallow attempts at "political correctness" ("Hearing held," 1998; Russin, 1998b; Yarbrough, 1998). As Colgan (1997) wrote in a letter to the editor of *JOPERD* about the issue of eliminating the use of American Indian mascots, "It is sad the way groups of citizens search so diligently to find something to be disgruntled about" (p. 4). Yarbrough (1998) extends this one step further by equating all examinations of these issues to exercises in "political correctness," as if to suggest that there is no value in revisiting old assumptions with renewed insight or seriously assessing the educational welfare of all students.

What some educators and citizens appear unable and/or unwilling to grasp at a macro-level is the fact that this dynamic of American Indians explaining why something is offensive while non-Indians actively or passively choose not to respond or respond contrarily is the most persistent theme underscoring Indian–non-Indian relations. Locust (1988) argues that the fundamental differences between American Indians and non-Indians foster the discriminatory treatment American Indian students experience in school through a lack of appreciation for their belief and value systems. This is seen in the continuing use of eagle feathers, dancing, music, and chanting in association with American Indian mascots. On repeated occasions, attempts have been made to educate the public about the sacredness of these symbols and ceremonial practices (Rosenstein, 1997). And yet, a large portion of the public appears to believe that their right to use these symbols in frivolous, casual ways at the ballpark or an athletic contest is a matter of personal opinion. In this instance, the sanctity of a culture is not sufficient cause to protect certain revered symbols from being worn inappropriately, merchandised, or desecrated in some other manner. This practice cuts in two directions by violating Indian taboos and customs while also contributing to the collective ignorance of masses of Americans at the same time.

In his work on cultural literacy, Ferdman (1990) explored the process of becoming and being literate in a multi-ethnic society. According to Ferdman, literacy is culturally framed and variable. As a consequence, literate behavior may be defined differently from culture to culture. This conception offers a way for educators to rethink the issue of American Indian mascots, which has become so deeply imbedded in the average American's psyche due to the official sanction of institutional authority, collective ownership, and mass identification.

What this examination of race and cultural literacy reveals is a significant flaw in the way cultural literacy has traditionally been conceptualized by many influential educators and internalized by the majority of Americans throughout most of the twentieth century. Whereas Hirsch (1987) cautions that cultural illiteracy may impoverish and relegate certain groups to the "powerlessness of incomprehension," cultural illiteracy is not located solely or entirely among the marginalized. Impoverishment, in turn, need not be thought of only in economic or class terms. To grasp this point is to become aware that the non-Indian power structure has acquired its privileged status through its own intellectual impoverishment, selective incomprehension, and moral compromise. In order for genuine understanding to occur, one needs to consider that members of the *culturally illiterate* group in these discussions about American Indian imagery are non-Indians. Hirsch's tenet that true societal enfranchisement is achievable only when one is culturally literate needs to be modified. For the majority, being culturally illiterate is sometimes acceptable, expedient, and profitable, particularly when it comes to American Indians.

As educators, if we begin to conceptualize the use of American Indian imagery as a form of cultural illiteracy that has historically benefitted the dominant group to the detriment of American Indians, the path is cleared to more fully appreciate the impact this long-standing practice has had in the shaping of a hostile cultural and classroom climate for American Indians and an intellectually numbing environment for both Indians and non-Indians alike.

A HOSTILE CULTURE AND CLASSROOM CLIMATE FOR AMERICAN INDIANS

In 1997, President Clinton established a Race Initiative Advisory Board for the purpose of promoting a national dialogue on race issues, to increase an understanding of the history and future of race relations, to identify and create plans to calm racial tension, and to promote increased opportunity for all Americans to address crime and the administration of justice (Gray, 1998). The findings from a presidential report entitled "One America: The President's Initiative on Race" showed that Native Americans experience more pronounced levels of racism in the form of economic and physical abuse than any other identified group. Further, Native Americans were found to manifest the "highest instances of suicide, the lowest life expectancy, the highest levels of infant mortality, and the highest rates of unemployment nationwide" (Gray, 1998). Despite acknowledging that the United States' record of mistreatment of Native Americans required acts that would ameliorate the neglect and isolation that Indians feel, the president did not appoint a Native American to his team of advisors (Associated Press, 1998c). President Clinton's omission or oversight in naming a Native American to the advisory board caused considerable consternation within the Native American community.

In a meeting with nine tribal leaders in Denver in March of 1998 to discuss the absence of a Native American on the board, the tribal leaders called the omission unconscionable and unacceptable (Griego, 1998, p. 1). Appreciation for the sentiment felt is revealed in Scott's (1998) response to the lack of awareness demonstrated by the White House when she wrote:

> How can this government hope to address a problem as deep and pervasive as racism without providing an opportunity for equal representation to the people

most directly affected by racism for over 200 years. . . . No face more directly reflects the evils of racism, institutionalized and otherwise, than the face of Native peoples. . . . This country has only to look at its own history if it wishes to see where racism, unchecked, leads. Is it possible that this government fears to look too deeply into the mirror of its own beginnings? (p. 2)

It is possible that what is at work here is a clash between the fantasy, fictionalized Indians many non-Indians pretend to be during Halloween and while they are masquerading as Warriors and Indians and Renegades and Chiefs at the local level and the dilemmas encountered when real Indians raise issues that demand something that goes beyond pretense. Pewewardy (1994, 1997) connects the dots between the failure of American institutions (education, government, religion, the criminal justice system, health care, media, entertainment, sport) in general to comprehend lived American Indian experience and the reduction of American Indian life to little more than a singular stereotype of a mythical be-feathered fighting figure.

Pewewardy (1994, 1997) describes the practice of using Indian mascots as symbolic representations of teams and anchors for community identity as "cultural violence" which serves to distort the perceptions of both Indian and non-Indian children. The end result has been three-fold. Indian children have been left with "deep emotional scars" and what Locust (1988) refers to as "wounds of the spirit" as evidenced in Native American children having the highest dropout rates, the highest suicide rates, and the lowest academic achievement levels of any minority group (Ambler, 1997; Harjo, 1996; James, Chavez, Beauvais, Edwards, & Oetting, 1995; Lee, 1992; Wood & Clay, 1996). Non-Indian children have been raised as what I would call cultural narcoleptics, permitted to sleep the sleep of the uninformed and unknowing. For all children, Indian and non-Indian alike, the use of American Indian imagery introduced and replicated over and over in lieu of a comprehensive and extensive examination of the historical and social antecedents of Indian and non-Indian relations contributes to the miseducation of masses of Americans and a generalized level of ignorance. This realization signals a need for educators to struggle with areas of inquiry that frequently go unaddressed or unexamined.

CRITICAL AREAS OF INQUIRY OFTEN UNADDRESSED OR UNEXAMINED

In any given time period, an analysis of various meanings associated with familiar institutional practices reflects the changes that cultures undergo as they evolve. The orchestration of major societal reversals on perspectives regarding women's right to vote (Sherr, 1994), slavery (Coakley, 1998), and the capability of older citizens as seen most recently in John Glenn's flight into space (Jackson, 1998) attest to the contested nature of seemingly intractable ideas and the potential for change. The educational importance of examining Native American mascots stems from the fact that such topics allow for a similar revisitation of the power of words, symbols, and images. By subjecting these terms to critical analysis, three areas of inquiry that educators might do well to explore become apparent: the prevalence of American Indian imagery, the cultivation of an educational facade, and the progressive miseducation of Americans.

The Prevalence of American Indian Imagery

Within the mass produced and commodified world of American capitalism, images associated with American Indians have long been the choice of twentieth-century advertisers seeking to contrast the primitive ways of the unsophisticated and uneducated with the civilized fortunes of the well-to-do (Staurowsky, 1998). One need only span the shelves of grocery stores to find "Land o' Lakes" butter with an "Indian" maiden on the label; survey vehicles in an auto mall to discover that "Cherokees," "Winnebagos," and "Pontiacs" are routinely available to buy or lease; or rifle through the Liz Claiborne collection to come upon the "Crazy Horse" line of women's clothing (Bordewich, 1996; Brouse, 1998; Coombes, 1996). The disproportionate degree to which American Indian imagery has been used in promoting the interests of corporate America is replicated in schools as well.

According to Pressley (1999), more than 2500 schools in total still employ these images. As an identifiable category, images that depend on some aspect of perceived American Indian culture and tradition are more popular by a wide margin than any other single group of ethnic symbols selected to represent athletic teams and educational institutions. Despite this remarkably high level of representation, there is little if any genuine curiosity expressed by educators regarding the disparity between the prevalent use of this imagery and the small percentage of American Indians within the population.

Whereas the average American tends to view these images as benign or innocuous, scholars suggest that this imagery taps into deep-seated Eurocentric cultural forms that enact and replay old conflicts between Indians and non-Indians. It is the case that the prevailing stereotypes of warring, wild Indians in paint, feathers, and buckskins or loincloths replicate images popularized by Wild West Shows and World's Fair exhibitions from nearly a century ago and the more recent western film genre of the latter part of the twentieth century (Churchill, 1992; Coombes, 1996). As signifiers of the superior level of sophistication and accomplishment achieved by the "colonizers" then and now, the "primitive" images of American Indians have marked the growth of a capitalist consumer culture and in the process have created a degree of "cultural saturation" that does not encourage racial sensitivity. As Bordewich (1996) notes, Americans are more comfortable with fictional Indians than with real Indians.

In addressing the alarming level of unquestioning acceptance of these images by Americans, Kenneth S. Stern, the American Jewish Committee's expert on anti-Semitism and extremism remarked that "The use of mascots is a reflection of the limits of dehumanization our culture will allow. . . . It deeply concerns me that many people of goodwill find these dehumanizing portraits unremarkable" (as reported in "American Jewish Committee," 1998, p. 11).

American Indians as the "Face" of Education: The Cultivation of an Educational Façade

For those who seek to defend American Indian mascots, notions that these images are rooted in conscious decisions to celebrate virtues of Indian character, to honor an admirable people, and to memorialize a forgotten people are recurrent themes. In defending the representation of an Indian as a mascot for Menomonie (WI) High School, a 16-year-old football player told the Wisconsin Senate Education Committee that "We incorporate words like dignity, strength, honor, pride, and we really give a lot of respect to the tradition " (as reported in "Hearing held," 1998, p. 2). Similarly, advocates for the "Braves" mascot at Birmingham (CA) High School reported taking pride in the logo, regarding it as a positive symbol because it best represented "the land of the free and the home of the brave" (as reported in Willman, 1997). The incongruity in these statements deserves to be challenged at several levels.

Whereas the perspectives expressed are moving, they are nonetheless rhetorically and contextually empty. To project dignity, honor, respect, strength, and pride onto a manufactured image while simultaneously displaying an inability to accord those very same things to living Indians seeking to be heard speaks volumes about just how great the level of miseducation is on this topic. To comfortably assert that the symbol of the American Indian is a logical and consistent image with "the land of the free and the home of the brave" ignores the legacy of genocide, forced assimilation and acculturation, and repeated mistreatment to which American Indians have been and continue to be subjected to today (Brown, 1991; Churchill, 1997).

From a Native American perspective, Pewewardy (1997) asks, "Where is the honor in being introduced as the 'savages' at football games?" (p. 17A).

As educational institutions and educators come to grips with the issue of American Indian mascots, recognizing that there is an untidy and prickly thicket of contradictions that must be removed becomes part of the task of reeducation this requires.

American Indian Imagery as Tools for Teaching Racism

In articulating a reason why Indian schools choose Indian people as mascots, Veilleux (1993) observed that the preference is "based upon their misinformed stereotypical notion that our Indian ancestors were warlike, bloodthirsty, wild savages" (p. 6). If American Indians harbor these misperceptions, how pronounced are the effects of these images on non-Indians?

There can be little doubt that the racism reflected in the pages of the Naperville (IL) High School yearbook in 1987, which chronicled "87 Uses for a Dead Redskin," demonstrates that a school mascot can be a powerful tool in the miseducation of students on matters of race (as reported in Veilleux, 1993). The process through which distorted "race logic" (Coakley, 1998) becomes learned is outlined by Veilleux, who notes:

> The purpose of a mascot in an athletic competition is to serve as a focal point or "target" for competing teams and their fans to express allegiance to the home team or opposition to the visiting team. When the "target" or mascot is representative of a race of people such as American Indians, it becomes a racial issue. (p. 7)

Although frequently acknowledged within educational circles in general that stereotypes form the bedrock of prejudice and racism, schools have been extremely slow to accept responsibility for miseducating students through the continued use of American Indian imagery as the most visible symbols of their enterprise.

CONSIDERATIONS FOR PHYSICAL EDUCATORS AND SPORT SCIENTISTS

In an age when schools are making concerted efforts to teach tolerance and to grapple with issues of diversity, it behooves educators to accept the challenge posed by President Clinton upon meeting American Indian leaders in the summer of 1998, when he remarked that Americans need to "fess up" to the mistreatment of American Indians. For physical educators, coaches, athletic administrators, and sport scientists, part of "fessing up" involves the prospect of confronting and owning our shortcomings. This is never an easy undertaking but it is the thing that is most necessary if our students are to be best served. For many of us, myself included, we've grown up with our own community and personal identities linked to these images. This issue asks for our introspection, our courage, and our insight in facing the flaws and faults in our own education. If the students whom we care about are to have the best chance of apprehending the complex history that contributes to their world view, we, as their teachers, must be as culturally literate as possible.

In conclusion, professionals from the allied fields of sport science and physical education are perhaps positioned better than anyone else to provide leadership on this issue, given the integral role we play in facilitating athletic opportunities for students. By calling for the elimination of stereotypes in the form of American Indian images, we can contribute positively to the education of all of our children, Indian and non-Indian alike.

NOTE

This article is a reprint of the original article that appeared in *Quest, 51,* no. 4 (November 1999): 382–392.

REFERENCES

Abram, S. (1997, October 28). More than a mascot: Schools: When a Native American group urged Arcadia High to stop using the Apache as a symbol, official made it an educational issue to be studied—and decided by—the Student Council. *Los Angeles Times,* p. 2B.

"Alumni lose battle to save Indian mascot." (1998, April 7). *New York Times,* p. 22A.

"Alumni sue over Indian mascot." (1998, January 8). *Sacramento Bee,* p. A5.

Ambler, M. (1997, Spring). Without racism: Indian students could be both Indian and students. *Tribal College, 8*(4), 8–11.

"American Jewish Committee leader calls Indian mascots 'dehumanizing.'" (1998, March 31). *Native American, 15*(1), p. 11.

Associated Press. (1998a, July 9). Use of Indians as mascots to be subject of an inquiry. *New York Times,* p. 8B.

Associated Press. (1998b, July 9). State will review Indian mascots. *Ithaca Journal,* p. 1A.

Associated Press. (1998c, July 9). Race forum takes on Indian neglect: Clinton admits past ignorance. *Ithaca Journal,* p. 1B.

Bordewich, F. (1996). *Killing the white man's Indian: Reinventing Native Americans at the end of the twentieth century.* New York: Doubleday.

Botstein, L. (1990, Spring). Damaged literacy: Illiteracies and American democracy. *Daedalus, 119*(2), 55–84.

"Chief Osceola and Renegade." (1998, November). Florida State University Homepage. Retrieved from http://www.fansonly.com/schools/fsu/trads/fsu-trads-osceola .html/

Churchill, W. (1997). *A little matter of genocide: Holocaust and denial in the Americas 1492 to the present.* San Francisco: City Lights Books.

Coakley, J. J. (1998). Sport in society: Issues and controversies (6th ed.). Boston: Irwin McGraw-Hill.

Colgan, C. J. (1997, August). Mascots reflect strength, power. *JOPERD, 68*(6), p. 4.

"Commencement '98." (1998, May 29). *Chronicle of Higher Education*, p. A8.

Connelly, M., Corbellini, C., & Grant, C. (1995). *A survey of Native American mascots in sport organizations.* Unpublished report submitted as a requirement for the Ithaca College Sports Information class, Spring, 1995.

Davis, L. (1993). Protest against the use of Native American mascots: A challenge to traditional American identity. *Journal of Sport and Social Issues, 17*, 9–22.

Dill, J., Yona, N., & Hicks, J. (1998). American Indians and President Clinton's Initiative on Race. *Minorities Job Bank*. Retrieved from http://www.minorities-jb .com/native/initial.htm/

Ellis, J. J. (1996). *American sphinx: The character of Thomas Jefferson.* New York: Alfred Knopf.

Ferdman, B. (1990, May). Literacy and cultural identity. *Harvard Educational Review, 60*(2), 181–204.

"Florida State University Seminole Boosters—Trademarks—Spearpoints." (1998, November). Florida State University homepage. Retrieved from http://www.polaris .net/fsuboost/trademarks.htm/

Gray, L. (1998). Clinton report on race says Indians suffer more: Report not the first to point at dismal record. *Oklahoma Indian Times*. Retrieved from http://www .minorities-jb.com/native/clintonreport10.html/

Griego, T. (1998, March 24). Indian leaders meet with board: White House's failure to name tribal leader to race panel discussed. *Rocky Mountain News*. Retrieved from http://www.insidedenver.com/extra/race/o324rsid3.html/

Harjo, S. (1996, Summer). Now and then: Native Peoples in the United States. *Dissent, 43*(3–184), 58–60.

"Hearing held concerning schools' Indian nicknames at school." (1998, January 30). *Ojibwe News, 10*(16), p. 2.

Helfand, D. (1998, January 8). Birmingham booster sues L.A. Unified over Indian mascot ban. *Los Angeles Times*, p. 5B.

Helfand, D. (1998, January 8). Suit targets schools' ban on Indian mascots. *Los Angeles Times*, p. 5B.

Hirsch, E. D. (1987). *Cultural literacy: What every American needs to know.* Boston: Houghton Mifflin.

"History of the Marching Chiefs." Florida State University homepage. Retrieved from http://www.marchingchiefs.fsu.edu/history.htm/

Jackson, D. (1998, November 16). The sky not is the limit. *Newsweek*, p. 20

Jaimes, M. A. (1992). Introduction: Weapons of genocide. In W. M. Churchill (Ed.), *Fantasies of the master race: Literature, cinema, and the colonization of American Indians*. Monroe, ME: Common Courage Press.

James, K., Chavez, E., Beauvais, F., Edwards, R., & Oetting, G. (1995). School achievement and dropout among Anglo and Indian females and males: A comparative examination. *American Indian Culture and Research Journal, 19*(3), 181–206.

Keohane, S. (1998). A presidential sham. *Minorities Job Bank*. Retrieved from http://www.minorities-jb.com/native/initia2.html/

Lampros, A. (1997, August 15). Indian mascot issue tossed back to Galt Students. *Sacramento Bee*, p. B1.

Lapchick, R. E. (Ed.). (1996). *Sport in society: Equal opportunity or business as usual?* Thousand Oaks, CA: Sage.

Lee, C. D. (1992, February). Literacy, cultural diversity, and instruction. *Education and Urban Society, 24*(2), 279–291.

Lick, D. W. (1993, May 18). Seminoles—heroic symbol at Florida State. *USA Today.*

Lindelof, B. (1997, November 3). Galt students to pick new Indian mascot logo. *Sacramento Bee*, p. B1.

Locust, C. (1988, August). Wounding the spirit: Discrimination and traditional American belief systems. *Harvard Educational Review, 58*(3), 315–330.

Maher, F. A., & Tetreault, M. K. T. (1997, Summer). Learning in the dark: How assumptions of whiteness shape classroom knowledge. *Harvard Educational Review, 67*(2), 321–349.

Markon, J. (1998, July 9). School mascot probe/State looks at American-Indian references. *Newsday*, p. A22.

McCaffrey, S. (1998, July 9). State probes schools' use of Indian mascots. *Buffalo News*, p. 10A.

Pewewardy, C. (1994). Re-education will improve portrayal of Native-Americans. *Indian Country Today, 13*(33), A6.

Pewewardy, C. (1997, January 15). Commercial and intellectual exploitation of Native peoples. *News From Indian Country, 11*(1), 17A.

Poland, P. (1998, April). Controversy brews into court case over mascots. Retrieved from http://www.Angelfire.com/biz/RobertWard/index.html/

Pressley, S. A. (1999, Feb 17). Use of Indian Mascots Brings Justice Dept. to N.C. Town. *Washington Post.*

Robinson, H. (1997, November 23). GHS board adopts new mascot; Lawsuit threatened. *Sacramento Bee*, p. N1.

Rodriguez, R. (1998, June 11). Plotting the assassination of Little Red Sambo: Psychologists join war against racist campus mascots. *Black Issues in Higher Education, 15*(8), 20.

Rolo, M. A. (1998, June 30). Marked media. *Circle, 19*(6), 7.

Rosenstein, J. (Producer). (1997). *In Whose Honor? Indian Mascots and Nicknames in Sport*. Video.

Russin, D. (1998, July 9). Mascot change would cost schools. *Ithaca Journal*, p. 2A.

Russin, D. (1998). Sensitivity needed with mascots, but logic should prevail. *Ithaca Journal*, p. 1B.

"School expels parents for selling banned logo shirts." (1997, September 27). *Los Angeles Times*, p. 2B.

Schroeter, E. (1998, March 31). Native educators address mascots, esteem and culture. *News From Indian Country, 12*(6), 10A.

Scott, C. (1998). The race initiative: 6 degrees of separation: The presidential racial advisory commission or what's wrong with this picture? *Minorities Job Bank*. Retrieved from http://www.minorities-jb.Com/native/sixdegrees.html

"Seminoles Traditions—Seminole Scouts Club." (1998, November). Florida State University homepage. Retrieved from http://www.fansonly.com/schools/fsu/trads/fsu-trads-scoutclub.html/

"Seminoles Traditions—The War Chant." (1998, November). Florida State University homepage. Retrieved from http://www.fansonly.com/schools/fsu/trads/fsu-trads-chant.html/

Staurowsky, E. J. (1996, Winter). Tribal rights: An exercise and sport sciences professor analyzes the widespread use of Native American mascots. *Ithaca Quarterly*, p. 19–21.

Staurowsky, E. J. (in press). An act of honor or exploitation: The Cleveland Indians' use of the Louis Francis Sockalexis story. *Sociology of Sport Journal*.

Veilleux, F. (1993, May). Educational institutions promote racist attitudes. *Circle, 14*(5), 6.

Willman, M. L., & Becker, T. (1998, April 7). District ban on Indian nicknames upheld. *Los Angeles Times*, p. 1B.

Willman, M. L. (1997, September 26). "Brave" Boosters may defy board on mascot ban. *Los Angeles Times*, p. 8B.

Windle, L. (1998). When your voice isn't heard, it tends to get louder: A first-person account of the Denver Advisory Board on Race meeting 3/23/98. *Minorities Job Bank*. Retrieved from http://www.minorities-jb.com/native/denverrace.html/

Wood, P. B., & Clay, W. C. (1996, September). Perceived structural barriers and academic performance among American Indian high school students. *Youth and Society, 28*(1), 40–61.

Yona, N. (1998). Realization or rhetoric—commentary and dialogue on racism and the Indian people. *Minorities Job Bank*. Retrieved from http://www.minorities-jb.com/native/rhetoric7.html/

Zatzman, D. (1997, September 20). Group rallies for Birmingham mascot. *Los Angeles Times*, p. 3B.

10

Native Images in Schools and the Racially Hostile Environment

Lawrence R. Baca

In the great spectrum of race relations in America, we can say without equivocation that American Indians[1] are treated differently than other minority races. For example, negative images of American Indians are accepted where comparable images for other racial and ethnic groups are not. The Frito Bandito is gone, the image of Little Black Sambo is gone, and yet, hundreds of comparable false, stereotyped, and offensive images of American Indians continue to exist. In 2002, a popular clothing manufacturer produced a T-shirt with Asian caricatures on it and the saying "Two Wongs don't make it White," and because of protests by Asian Americans and others about the stereotype, the shirt and its offensive images were gone within days of arrival at the stores—removed by the manufacturer.

In Washington, D.C., in 1999, an employee of the city government was removed from his position by the mayor for using the word "niggardly" in a discussion with a Black employee. Nigger, a word so infamous that it is often referred to on the national television news as the "N" word, and niggardly have no relationship to each other in their root or in their meaning. But the power of the "N" word is such that a sound-alike word resulted in a formal complaint being filed, and the employee against whom it was filed was disciplined for the proper use of a proper English-language word.[2] Also in 2002, Trent Lott resigned as Speaker of the House of Representatives because of criticism he received for implying that he supported Strom Thurman's segregationist views. In the same city, the local National Football League team is the Washington Redskins. Many of us who are Indians consider the word *Redskin* to be the Indian Country "R" word. The patent and trademark hearing board has ruled that "redskin" is a pejorative that cannot be patented.[3] Two states (California and Utah) have ruled that the "R" word is too offensive to be allowed on automobile license plates. But the team continues to use the name. Fans continue to wear jackets, hats, and T-shirts with a racial pejorative on them, and this is generally accepted by the public. Imagine a T-shirt or jacket with a pejorative against any other race or ethnic group—nigger, wop, kike, slope, spic—being allowed at the work place or at a public school. The good news is that you probably cannot imagine this. Better still, you do not have to because it is not going to happen to another race or ethnic group. Indians are treated differently.

In the national effort to eliminate the use of stereotyped and caricatured American Indian images, American Indians are using logic, education, and the law to bring about change. In this article, I will address the one area where the law may provide an avenue to seek relief from these practices in educational institutions. I should state, however, that as of this writing, there has been no successful administrative or court challenge to the use of faux and caricatured American Indian images in schools under these statutes. As one of my colleagues has noted, the law with respect to negative American Indian images has not advanced to the same level that it has with respect to other racial or ethnic minorities.[4] I will address the analysis that I think is most fruitful and the difficulties of its success. Those difficulties might be encapsulated in the words "White folks just don't get it."

THE RACIALLY HOSTILE ENVIRONMENT ANALYSIS

One way to look at the negative effects that stereotyped images of American Indians have is to apply a racially hostile environment analysis. The essential core of this analysis is in the term "hostile environment," which was first developed in the context of the workplace. The analysis readily flows over into the educational arena and is of particular concern here. Remember that when the Supreme Court struck down the concept of separate but equal, it did so first in education. Although I am offended by the image of Chief Wahoo of the Cleveland Indians baseball team and the name of the Washington Redskins, I do not have to go to the stadium and subject myself to them. And although that image and name prevent me from attending a game or truly enjoying one if I did, I ascribe a lesser importance to that than the same imagery at an elementary or secondary school or college. Education is more important than my right to partake of a place of public accommodation. As an adult, I can chose to not go. The choices of a child in elementary or secondary school or even those of a college-age student are not so clear. Whereas the images and names of some sports teams do, in my mind, violate my right to full and equal enjoyment of the baseball or football stadium, I have greater concerns about the effects of negative Indian imagery on children in our schools.

Title VI of the 1964 Civil Rights Act provides, "No person in the United States shall, on the ground of race, color, or national origin, be excluded from participation in, be denied the benefits of, or be subjected to discrimination under any program or activity receiving Federal financial assistance." Every federal agency that provides funding to other entities writes regulations that the fund recipient must agree to abide by or lose their funds. The Department of Education has written regulations that provide that no recipient can cause or allow a racially hostile environment.

The context in which these cases will arise is when, in the case of an elementary or secondary school student, a parent will complain that the school is creating or maintaining a racially hostile environment that prevents his or her children from fully participating in the educational program. The leading and most thoroughly researched article in this area is "Native American Mascots, Schools, and the Title VI Hostile Environment Analysis," by Daniel J. Trainor (1995). Let me note without equivocation that the article is written with its primary purpose being to defend the continued use of the mascot Chief Illiniwek at the University of Illinois. While Trainor argues quite persuasively that American Indian mascots should be removed from elementary and secondary schools, he then boldly, and incorrectly, argues that they should not be removed from colleges and universities. While he correctly notes that the analytical framework must be adjusted to the age and experience of the student, his basic and most flawed position is that you simply cannot have a racially hostile environment at the college or university level because the Indian students who are offended by the mascot will know about it in advance and will not apply to go to the school in the first place.

He is half right. The Indians who are offended will not come because there is a racially hostile environment that prevents them from applying. Trainor is so adamant about defending the University of Illinois that he misses his own point. The very knowledge that prevents them from coming to a school with a racially offensive mascot is knowledge of an environment of racial hostility in which they find that they will not be able to enjoy the full educational benefits of the educational program offered.

The racially hostile environment analysis established by the Office for Civil Rights (OCR) can be summarized as follows: Is there harassing conduct at the school, (whether physical, verbal, graphic, or written) that is sufficiently severe, pervasive, or persistent so as to interfere with or limit a student's ability to participate in or benefit from the services, activities, or privileges it provides? The regulations provide that a school may not effectively cause, encourage, accept, tolerate, or fail to correct a racially hostile environment of which it has actual or constructive notice.

To establish a violation, OCR must find, based on the totality of the circumstances, that (a) a racially hostile environment existed, (b) the school had actual or constructive notice of the racially hostile environment, and (c) the school failed to respond adequately to redress the racially hostile environment. It is also important to note that an alleged harasser need not be a school agent or employee. Liability under the Title VI regulations is premised on a school's general duty to provide a nondiscriminatory educational environment.

In determining whether the racial harassment is sufficiently severe, pervasive, or persistent, OCR will examine the context, nature, scope, frequency, duration, and location of racial incidents. It is unlikely that casual or isolated racial incidents will be found to create a hostile environment. OCR looks at a sliding scale of the combination of the severity of the incidents and the pervasiveness or persistence of the events. A single highly charged incident could be given the same weight as more pervasive or persistent conduct that is less severe. OCR notes that it is also important to consider the number of harassers involved and their relationships to the victim.

To determine severity, OCR will consider the nature and location of the incidents and the size of the educational institution. Incidents of lesser severity or a smaller number of incidents can create a racially hostile environment in the smaller locality of a primary school as opposed to the larger environment of a college campus. An event that occurs in a public place on campus will be received differently than the same event in a private locale. It does not matter whether the instances of harassment are directed at the complainant; even those directed at others are considered in determining whether a hostile environment exists.

OCR will apply a variation of the reasonable person standard to determine that the harassment is severe enough to adversely affect the enjoyment of some aspect of the educational program. The question, then, is whether the environment would affect a reasonable person of the same age and race as the victim. OCR believes that the conduct in question must be judged from the perspective of a person of the same race as the victim. Where elementary-school-aged students are involved, the standard as applied to a child must take into account the age, intelligence, and experience of children of the same age and race.

And, finally, OCR does not require the harassment to result in a tangible injury to the victims of the harassment. It only requires that the harassment negatively affect the enjoyment of an educational program offered by the fund recipient.

So, how are Indian complainants losing cases under this standard? School officials create and maintain the images. They know of their existence. School officials may mistakenly believe that these images are benign, but once an Indian parent or child comes forward and says that they are not, the school has knowledge of the offense. And what about the scope, frequency, and duration? No matter how minor the school officials attribute the harm of racial caricatures, they are so pervasive that their presence is overwhelming. And they are always present throughout the school year. Failure of non-Indians to accept that these images interfere with the child's ability to participate in the educational programs allows for the continued use of American Indian mascots. It is the overwhelming presence of these images that has numbed non-Indians into accepting these images as neutral, if not positive, images. At schools named to honor Black leaders, the students do not dress in "African dress"—whatever they may think that to be—and engage in what they believe to be African dance rituals at halftime of school sporting events.

WHITE FOLKS JUST DON'T GET IT

The most famous, or infamous, of the OCR's Indian mascot investigations is that of the University of Illinois. Charlene Teters, a Spokane woman, was recruited to come to the university. When she arrived, Teters found that she and her young children were assaulted by the persistent presence of what she calls "the severed head" of Chief Illiniwek, known locally as "the Chief." Likewise, she found the antics and faux Indian dance of the student who portrays "the Chief" at school events to be insulting and offensive to Indian people and Indian culture. Teters began a many-year-long protest of the denigration of Indian culture. During her many protests about "the Chief," Teters has been called vile names, has had trash and other objects thrown at her, and has even been spit on by supporters of "the Chief."

Teters also filed a complaint with the OCR at the United States Department of Education. OCR accepted her complaint and conducted an investigation. The eventual finding was in favor of the university. The OCR stated in its letter that the incidents of hostility were not severe enough or pervasive enough to rise to the level of a hostile environment. They also found that the incidents of physical and verbal assaults were not necessarily associated with the mascot but may have been a result of the protest. There seemed to be an overreliance on a necessity for incidents of physical hostility associated with the mascot.

Therefore, I ask the question, What about the hostility against the mind? In *Brown v. Board of Education* (1954), the Court focused on the nature of the separation of the races as the primary evil of the doctrine of separate but equal. The Court noted that even if schools were equal, the separation of the races, especially with the imprimatur of the state, would have negative effects on young Black children.

> To separate them from others of similar age and qualifications solely because of their race generates a feeling of inferiority as to their status in the community that may affect their hearts and minds in a way unlikely ever to be undone.

The Court found that the separation was a badge of inferiority to "the colored race."

> The impact is greater when it has the sanction of the law; for the policy of separating the races is usually interpreted as denoting the inferiority of the negro [*sic*] group. A sense of inferiority affects the motivation of a child to learn.

Let us compare this notion of being treated differently to the experience of the American Indian child at a school that maintains an American Indian mascot. The Indian child who attends a school with an American Indian mascot theme is confronted with false and offensive images constantly from the moment of arrival to the bus ride home. Let us assume that a severe event of a racially harassing nature, such as a Black man hung in effigy in the middle of a campus or a swastika burned into the lawn of a Jewish fraternity house, although it may not be a physical confrontation, can be likened to a punch in the nose—a blow that knocks someone to the ground. Now let us assume that the false image of your race posted on campus is a racially harassing event no more severe than a touch of a finger on someone's shoulder. Imagine that you go to your place of employment and a coworker touches you on the shoulder as you get out of your vehicle. Another touches you on the shoulder as you get to the front door of your building, and another touches you as you get into the elevator. Your colleague touches you as you arrive at your desk, when you go to the coffee room, and again when you return. Imagine that this behavior is done only to members of your race. No single touching is itself a severe harassing event, but the cumulative touchings would drive most people to strike out or stop coming to work. Most of us would reach the point very quickly where we are not capable of fully participating in or enjoying the benefits of our workplace in this environment, even though we are receiving mere touches.

Now think about the reality for the Indian child who attends school where there is an American Indian mascot. The child arrives at school, and when the child gets off of the bus, he or she is confronted with the 22-foot-tall statue of an American Indian, usually in some form of "warrior" dress, such as a loincloth and nothing more. The "warrior" will wear one or more feathers and most likely hold a spear, club, or tomahawk. The Indian child walks into the school and sees a painting of this same image on the wall outside the principal's office or perhaps a caricature with a large belly and an overexaggerated nose, often with a bent feather in a headband. The child goes to class and sees the faux image on the classroom wall and on schoolbook covers. When the child goes to the gym, the same ubiquitous, but not real, Indian is painted on the floor, and non-Indian students run back and forth over the face bouncing a basketball. If the child attends a school sporting event, it is likely that a White student will dress up in some form of Indian "costume" and perform fake ritualistic dances for the fans. These events occur daily, weekly, hourly. These images are omnipresent in the life of the Indian child while the child attends school. She does not see any other race singled out for this kind of caricature treatment. And, these images are all done with the acquiescence and the imprimatur of the state. In *Brown*, the court specifically noted that the very nature of separation of the races, which was the badge of inferiority of the Black race, was made even more severe because it was done with the sanction of the state. Here, the characterizations, the faux imagery, the secular use of religious iconography are only those of American Indians, and they are sanctioned by the state. The Indian child internalizes that her race is treated differently and that she is looked on by her classmates as different. That difference is not a uniqueness that causes others to want to be your friend or to learn from your cultural worldview, but rather, it is more often a point of mockery and, perhaps, open ridicule. The stereotypes that trap Indian people and culture in a pre-Columbian amber also represent the failure to recognize the continued existence of Indians as living cultures and peoples. The Indian child recognizes that using the Indian race as a mascot is a badge of inferiority. And equally important is the ease with which one culture becomes safe to mock and caricature when others are not. The images are ubiquitous, they are omnipresent, and they are so pervasive as to become white noise or wallpaper to the non-Indian. To the Indian child, they are an insidious invasion of his or her educational experience.

Non-Indian children also receive a subtle message. In their subconscious, they note, "My culture is not caricatured. My religious heritage is held with respect, such that our iconography will not be used in a secular manner at my school. No person of another race will paint their face white and engage in imitations of what they associate with my race. Therefore, my culture must be superior." These may be subtle messages, but they are powerful messages.

According to statistics generated by the United States Department of Justice, an American Indian is four times more likely to be the victim of a violent crime by a person not of his or her race than any other racial or ethnic group. Likewise, Indians are victims of hate crimes at a rate that is far out of proportion to their numbers in the population at large. The prevalence of fake and negative images of American Indians is a contributing factor to these crime rates. The ability to objectify an entire race of people and to amalgamate them under the singular false image of the dancing, prancing, tomahawk-chopping, savage warrior contains within it the ability to physically assault the individuals to whom one ascribes these characteristics. When a people are only stereotypes, they are not real.

Today, education is perhaps the most important function of state and local governments. Both compulsory school-attendance laws and the great expenditures for education demonstrate our recognition of the importance of education to our democratic society. It is required in the performance of our most basic public responsibilities, even for service in the armed forces. It is the very foundation of good citizenship. Today it is a principal instrument in awakening the child to cultural values, in preparing the child for later professional training, and in helping the child to adjust normally to his or her environment.

Whether it is being denied a seat at the restaurant of our choice or failing to receive a loan at the bank, what the American population at large has failed to accept is that the stereotypes created by school and professional sports mascots carry over into the everyday lives of American Indians.

NOTES

This article was originally published in 2004 in the *Journal of Sport and Social Issues, 28*(1): 71.

1. I use the terms "American Indian" and "Indian" interchangeably in this article. Historically inaccurate though the terms may be, Indian is the term used in the Constitution and, therefore, it is the "legal name" of those peoples indigenous to the 48 connected states of the United States.

2. The employee was later reinstated when common sense prevailed.

3. In 2003, the U.S. District Court overturned this decision, finding that there was not sufficient evidence presented at the initial trial to demonstrate that the trademarks were disparaging.

4. It is also unfortunate that no studies have been undertaken with respect to how stereotypes and negative images affect the academic performance of American Indian children.

REFERENCES

Brown v. Board of Education, 347 U.S. 483 (1954).

Civil Rights Act, Title VI. (1964).

Trainor, D. J. (1995). Native American mascots and the Title VI hostile environment analysis. *University of Illinois Law Review,* 1995, 971.

11

Native Mascots and Ethnic Fraud in Higher Education: Using Tribal Critical Race Theory and the Interest Convergence Principle as an Analytic Tool

Angelina E. Castagno and Stacey J. Lee

Within higher education, policies regarding racial diversity are among the most complicated, divisive, and contradictory. On the one hand, we have observed that institutions of higher education have made efforts to recruit and retain students of color, and most universities advance the rhetoric of celebrating multiculturalism. Still, there is evidence that little has been done to change the core culture of universities, to obtain equitable representation of students and faculty of color, or to improve campus climate. In this article we examine one university's policies regarding racial diversity, particularly with regard to Indigenous[1] students. As with other institutional policies, this university's policies both advance and limit racial equity and social justice. The university's policies reflect an attempt to celebrate multiculturalism without fully challenging the culture of whiteness. This article is framed around the following questions: What does the interest convergence principle tell us about diversity-related policies in institutions of higher education? And, how do one university's policies related to Indian mascots and ethnic fraud impact campus climate and the experiences of Indigenous students? Our central argument is that when situated within a tribal critical race theory framework (Brayboy, 2005a), the interest convergence principle can help to explain both progressive policies around race as well as policies that preserve the status quo.

RESEARCH METHODS AND CONTEXT

This article is based on research the first author carried out over the 2002–2003 academic year at Midwestern University[2] (MU) (Castagno, 2003, 2005).

89

As a qualitative study designed to explore the experiences of Indigenous women at a large, predominantly white university, this research consisted of ethnographic interviews with 12 self-identified Native women undergraduate and graduate students,[3] semi-structured interviews with five Native faculty and staff who work closely with the student community, participant observations at various American Indian and diversity-related events on campus, and document analysis. In conversations with Indigenous students and staff, concerns were raised regarding a number of university policies. In an effort to examine some of these particular policies, we reviewed official institutional documents, memos, and published policies. This article takes a subset of the findings from the larger study in order to analyze the ways the interest convergence principle can help make sense of ethnic fraud and Indian mascot policies in institutions of higher education.

Midwestern University is a public Research I institution located in a mid-sized city in the Midwestern United States, with students of color making up less than 10% of the over 40,000 student population. Approximately 0.5% of the students at Midwestern University self-identify as American Indian or Alaska Native. In addition to struggling with the recruitment of students of color, Midwestern also struggles to retain students of color who do enroll. Although the 6-year graduation rate for white students is 77%, it is only 52% for students of color as a whole group, and 42% for Indigenous students specifically.

Midwestern University has long enjoyed a reputation for being socially and politically progressive. At the same time, however, the fact that 90% of the students are white has contributed to an image that Midwestern is a "white school." As at other institutions with predominantly white populations, the dominant culture of Midwestern reflects the culture of whiteness—that is, whiteness sets the tone for what is considered to be "normal" and shapes conversations around racial diversity (Lee, 2005). Overt expressions of racial hostility do occur on the Midwestern campus, but these are relatively rare. Rather, most expressions of racism are more subtle and largely invisible to whites. Commenting on the culture of Midwestern, one Indigenous woman remarked, "because [Midwestern] is supposed to be so liberal, it's like undercover racism." The culture of whiteness at Midwestern leaves Native American students feeling socially isolated. Indigenous women frequently tell stories of being ignored or stereotyped by non-Native students. One woman asserted, "There are so many things out there that are anti-Native or anti–people of color and it's kind of, as much as I would never not admit to being Native hellip. It's hard to sometimes. Sometimes I just feel like it's everybody versus me."[4] These experiences are a poignant reminder of the historical legacy of institutional racism veiled behind a rhetoric of meritocracy, colorblindness, and equal opportunity within institutions of higher education (Allen, 2005; Anderson, 1993).

INTEREST CONVERGENCE AND TRIBAL CRITICAL RACE THEORY AS A THEORETICAL FRAMEWORK

We structure our analysis using the interest convergence principle because it allows us to both explain the social phenomenon at hand and to critique Mid-western's persistent failure to work toward greater equity and social justice. The interest convergence principle is part of a larger body of work called criti-cal race theory (CRT).[5] While there is a fairly substantial body of CRT work in the field of education, this work primarily utilizes the counter-storytelling methodology rather than taking up specific analytic principles as tools for making sense of data. As DeCuir and Dixon (2004) argue:

> In this particular historical moment when attacks on remedies for education inequity, such as affirmative action, are on the rise, it is essential that we utilize the full power of CRT, including Whiteness as property, interest convergence, and the critique of liberalism. (p. 30)

We take this call seriously and focus on the explanatory power of interest con-vergence to analyze and understand the contradictory policies and practices of universities regarding race and racial diversity.

The interest convergence principle is found throughout Derrick Bell's (1979, 1980a, 1980b, 1987) writings, and as Taylor (1999) has noted, the interest convergence principle has its roots in the Marxist theory that the bourgeoisie will tolerate advances for the proletariat only if those advances benefit the bourgeoisie even more. Simply put, this principle states that people believe and support what benefits them, so the majority group toler-ates advances for racial justice and greater equity only when such advances suit the self-interests of the majority group. Bell (1979, 1980a, 2004) uses the *Brown v. Board of Education* (1954) case to illustrate the interest convergence principle. He explains how the interests of whites to promote the United States as a democratic nation abroad and to uphold the freedom of the black soldiers who had defended the country in WWII converged with the interests of blacks to have access to equal educational opportunity. The result was a unanimous ruling in support of school desegregation in the mid 1950s.[6] Bell (1979, 1987, 1989) further argues that whites will not support civil rights policies that appear to threaten their superior social status. Again referring to the civil rights era, Bell (1979) notes, "Most Northern Whites do not oppose desegregation in the abstract. What they resist is the price of desegregation" (pp. 11–12). In other words, any progress toward greater social justice must not be seen as a "major disruption to the 'normal' way of life for the majority of Whites" (DeCuir & Dixon, 2004, 28). Thus, although the converging of interests sometimes results in movement toward greater equity, this movement stops when the price of the change becomes too high for the dominant group.

Although the interest convergence principle originated in critical race theory, we are situating it within a tribal critical race theory (TribalCrit) framework because TribalCrit provides a more culturally specific and, hence, accurate perspective on issues relating to Indigenous people and communities (Brayboy, 2005a). CRT grew out of a black–white binary understanding of race that fails to capture some important issues and nuances applicable to the experiences of other racialized groups. TribalCrit, on the other hand, includes tenets and principles that are culturally specific to Indigenous people and communities. The TribalCrit tenets that are most relevant for our purposes here include the idea that colonization is endemic, Indigenous people are not just racialized but also occupy a unique political status within the United States, and that policies and practices aimed at tribal nations are generally rooted in assimilationist and white supremacist goals.[7] Tribal nations have a unique history and a unique political relationship with the federal government, and both of these factors must be central to analyses of educational policies and practices involving Indigenous students (Brayboy, 2005a; Tsosie, 2000).

In this article, then, we use the analytic lens of interest convergence within a tribal critical race theory perspective to examine race in higher education and particularly the policies and practices impacting Indigenous students at a predominantly white university in the Midwestern United States. We illustrate how an interest convergence theoretical frame helps explain the "logic" behind institutional policies and practices from the point of view of the university and the problems of these same policies and practices from the point of view of Indigenous people in the academy. Situating interest convergence within a TribalCrit perspective allows us to highlight and make sense of the nuances particular to the experiences of tribal nations and Indigenous students.

An examination of Midwestern's rhetoric surrounding race reveals that their policies and practices reflect their perceived interests. At a recent campuswide "summit" to discuss the progress and direction of the university's diversity initiatives, the provost asked the rhetorical question, "Why diversity?" That is, why is the university concerned with issues of diversity overall and, particularly, the recruitment and retention of students of color? He answered this question by explaining how the institution "owes it to the state" to serve its diverse constituents, has an educational obligation to produce qualified citizens for the diverse workforce, and then concluded with "in short, it makes us a better and more competitive university."

Just as the provost used this last statement to sum up his thoughts (and one would assume the institution's position) regarding MU's concerns with diversity initiatives and increasing racial equity, this statement also illustrates our primary argument. Using the interest convergence principle, we argue that institutions of higher education allow and even work actively toward a particular form or level of diversity, but they plateau at a level beneath true equity. Once racial remedies no longer hold value or benefit the institution itself, the status quo is maintained. The concern is rooted in the institution's self-interest of being a "better and more competitive" institution rather than in a social justice rationale. This is, of course, explainable in that the institution most likely views issues of diversity and multiculturalism from its own perspective (as we all do), but it is crucial to point out that this is a perspective of power and, particularly, of whiteness.[8] If efforts for diversity are entirely driven by the needs of the institution, we will continue to have a situation that favors those in charge. Furthermore, while it is true that diversity may make the institution more competitive, it does not necessarily follow that a diverse institution will either address all the concerns faced by students of color or work toward greater equity and social justice.

While the principle of interest convergence could prove useful in analyzing a number of diverse policies and practices in higher education, in this article we focus specifically on two institutional policies that directly affect Indigenous students and faculty at Midwestern University. In what follows, we use an interest convergence and TribalCrit theoretical framework to analyze MU's policy regarding Indian mascots and the absence of a policy regarding ethnic fraud. We follow Taylor's (1999) recommendation that in order to really assess whether interest convergence is at work, we must provide a "tally of Black gains versus those of Whites; or more precisely, what interests of Blacks were allowed as long as White interests were also promoted" (p. 195). In the end, our use of the interest convergence principle allows us to make sense of the university's position while also critiquing that position for failing to embrace and act upon the interests of Indigenous people and, thus, failing to uphold social justice as an institutional priority.

INTEREST CONVERGENCE AND INDIAN MASCOT POLICIES

Many elementary, secondary, and postsecondary schools and a handful of professional athletic teams across the country have Indian mascots, names, and logos. The use of Native mascots, team names, and logos sparks heated debate in many communities throughout the United States. While the arguments in favor of such mascots generally revolve around the long-standing identity of a particular team and the way in which such teams are "honoring" Indigenous people, the most common arguments against the use of Native mascots include that Indigenous people should have control over societal definitions of themselves; that most sports-related representations misuse cultural symbols and practices for entertainment purposes; and that they represent racist stereotypes of Indigenous people as either noble or bloodthirsty savages, a historical race that only lived in the past, and a homogeneous group of people (King, 2004; Staurowsky, 2004). The number of schools that have Native mascots has dropped significantly over the last 30 years in response to calls from the United States Commission on Civil Rights and countless Native communities and organizations, but according to various sources, there are still 2,000–2,500 schools that have Native mascots (Clarkson, 2004). The continued acceptance of these mascots highlights one way in which schools are constructed as white public spaces and the lengths to which people will go to protect such spaces (Farnell, 2004). The emotional and economic investment in these spaces and their associated privileges is further evidenced by white people who either claim Indian identity themselves in the process of defending the use of Indian mascots or actively seek an Indigenous person who will support their cause (Springwood, 2004; Strong, 2004).

At Midwestern University, many Indigenous people express strong opposition to the continued use of Indian mascots, names, and logos. Although MU does not have a Native mascot, it does regularly play against other schools with Native mascots, and many non-Native students on campus wear clothes displaying various Native mascots. One Indigenous woman who is a student at Midwestern shared the following:

> One time, I was sitting in this big lecture and I totally needed to pay attention because I just wasn't understanding what the professor was talking about and this guy comes and sits in front of me, and he has on his hat backwards with like, the [Cleveland] Indian's logo and I just stared at it and I was getting real mad. I was like, "Who does he think he is, sitting in front of me. Like of all the people to sit in front of, he comes to sit in front *me*." I was just like, no. I got so upset. I was just sitting there and I was kind of laughing at the same time because I was so mad, it was just funny. But I didn't even pay attention in class. I was just like, man, when it starts to affect like, my academic career, it needs to stop.

This student found Indian logos so offensive that their public display interrupted her ability to learn in the classroom. In a similar vein, another woman said, "Imagine if we took a cross and started dancing around with it hellip like in response to eagle feathers." Although it is common for Indian mascots to wear feather headdresses and dance around the basketball court at halftime to entertain the crowd,[9] this student asks us to imagine the public outcry if a mascot were to take a large crucifix, which is a symbol with similar cultural and ceremonial value among many white Americans, and dance around with it for entertainment purposes.

These issues hit particularly close to home for Indigenous students at Midwestern because one of its conference rivals, the University of Illinois at Urbana-Champaign (UIUC), has a "chief" as its mascot, and the Midwestern student newspaper regularly publishes articles in defense of UIUC's mascot. The Indigenous community on campus also regularly writes letters to the editor about the inappropriateness and offensiveness of such mascots and, more importantly, of such articles being printed in the campus newspaper. When UIUC came to Midwestern for a men's basketball game in the spring of 2003, the Native student group on campus sponsored a well-attended teach-in and protest the evening of the game.

Midwestern University has a policy regarding Native American logos, mascots, and names that was developed in the early 1990s in response to pressure from Indigenous faculty, staff, and students. After another university's "scalping braves" mascot came to campus for a men's basketball game, many Midwestern community members asked the Athletic Board to ban all athletic competition against any team that used American Indian mascots or team names. The Great Lakes Intertribal Council, which represents most major tribal nations in the area, also requested the ban. After months of committee meetings and discussions between various constituents, the Athletic Board and the university administration adopted a policy that "discourages all teams from bringing their American Indian mascots to [Midwestern] athletic facilities," "discourages planned events using an American Indian mascot, symbol, names and activities if that use is disrespectful," discourages the sale of athletic wear with Indian mascots or logos on campus, and refuses to schedule with teams using such mascots "unless the team is a traditional rival or a conference member."

In order to use the interest convergence principle for analyzing this case, we must ask ourselves what are the interests of the institution, what are the interests of the Indigenous community, and where do they converge? It is important to note, first, that Midwestern University adopted some policy regarding the Native mascot issue. By adopting a policy at all, the institution has acknowledged that this is an important issue. By responding in some manner to the concerns raised by the Indigenous community over the use of Native mascots on campus, the university stands to gain the support of Native people both on campus and throughout the state, they are able to demonstrate publicly that they are a progressive university that "cares" about social justice issues, and they can "prove" that they are a responsive institution that takes the concerns of all of its "clients" seriously. On the other hand, the Native community's interests lie both in the reduction of harmful and offensive stereotypes and misinformation and in the possibility of greater autonomy in determining cultural representations of themselves. Because the institution has something to gain by adopting a policy in response to concerns over Native mascots, their interests converge with the interests of those who first brought forth the concern in the first place.

Unfortunately, however, the adopted policy fails to go far enough in eliminating Native mascots on campus and, therefore, in meeting the needs of the Indigenous community. The policy consists of weak language that "discourages" rather than "prohibits" the use of Native mascots on campus and the sale of athletic wear with Native logos. What does it mean for an institution to simply "discourage" such behavior? Unfortunately, the policy evades this question and leaves the issue open to different interpretations. What is clear, at least, is that in discouraging behavior, the institution has no responsibility or accountability to demand any real change. The interest convergence principle helps us make sense of this policy by highlighting how the institution is willing to make concessions toward greater social justice but only up to the point at which it stands to lose something. An even clearer example of the interest convergence principle at work in this policy is the concession that the Athletic Board will not schedule games with teams that have Indian mascots unless the team is a traditional rival or a conference member. Here the institution clearly recognizes and honors the interests of the Native community on campus by refusing to schedule games with some teams who have Native mascots, but the institution is even more protective of its own interests by still scheduling games with teams with whom they have "long-standing commitments"—a clear demonstration of advancing social justice only up to the point at which it is no longer convenient or in the best interests of the institution.

The potential losses to the university are significantly increased if the policy would have been stronger; that is, had the university prohibited the use of mascots and the sale of athletic wear with Native logos and refused to schedule any games with teams with Native mascots, they would most likely also experience a loss of revenue from missed games, alumni discontent, and disapproval from other conference schools. In the end, then, this policy likely leaves Indigenous people feeling like their interests are being neither heard nor protected by the institution—and indeed, perhaps they are not. The investment on the part of the university in protecting its own interests is certainly neither new nor surprising. TribalCrit reminds us of the long history of colonization and assimilatory policies aimed at tribal nations in the United States, and Midwestern's mascot policy continues in this tradition by controlling and disseminating images of Indigenous people and co-opting sacred symbols and practices for entertainment purposes.

INTEREST CONVERGENCE AND ETHNIC FRAUD

Ethnic fraud is another contentious issue within Indigenous communities and has many implications for institutions of higher education, particularly around admissions, scholarships, and faculty hiring. Ethnic fraud is the deliberate falsification or changing of ethnic identities in an effort to secure personal advantage in the form of, for example, scholarship funds, admission to special programs, research considerations, or faculty positions at mainstream universities (Gonzales, 2001; Pewewardy, 2004). Ethnic fraud is a significant concern among Indigenous communities because tribes are sovereign nations with the sole right to determine their own constituents, and any other institution or group of people who attempts to define membership in tribal nations violates this precedent (Churchill & Morris, 1992; Morris, 1992). TribalCrit reminds us that the relationship between tribal nations and the U.S. is one of "government to government" in nature. Rebecca Robbins (1992) makes this abundantly clear:

> Insofar as the federal government is constitutionally prohibited from entering into treaty relationships with any entity other than another fully sovereign national government, it follows that each treaty entered into by the United States with an Indian nation served the purpose of conveying formal federal recognition that the Indian nation involved was indeed a nation within the true legal and political meanings of the term. Further, given that these treaties remain on the books and thus are binding upon both parties, it follows that North American indigenous peoples continue to hold a clear legal entitlement—even under U.S. law—to conduct themselves as completely sovereign nations unless they themselves freely determine that things should be otherwise. (p. 90)

Given the sovereign status of tribal nations, it should be undisputed that they have the sole right to determine membership within their nations (Jaimes, 1992). Unfortunately, however, a number of institutions and government entities have infringed upon this right by failing to guard against ethnic fraud among Indigenous students, faculty, and staff.

Institutions of higher education show blatant disregard for tribal sovereignty when they base hiring, admissions, and funding decisions on the self-identification of American Indians and Alaska Natives rather than on some verifiable proof of tribal enrollment. As Grande has argued,

> Claiming one's ancestral background is not, in and of itself, problematic, but when such claims are opportunistically used to cash in on scholarships, jobs, set-aside programs, and other affirmative economic incentives, it becomes a highly questionable practice—particularly when such "fraudulent Indians" quickly discard their new identity as soon as it no longer serves them. (Grande, 2000, 352; see also Machamer, 1997)[10]

It is important to note that Indigenous people and communities hold differing opinions regarding "ethnic fraud"; some believe that only individuals can and should determine their self-identification, while others believe that tribal governments ought to determine the criteria through which individuals can identify with a particular tribal nation.

This range of opinions was present among the Indigenous women at Midwestern, and the women who said they were more assimilated and less tribal-culturally connected adamantly opposed policies requiring proof of tribal affiliation, while women who were far more tribal-culturally connected supported such policies. After sitting through a focus group during which the vast majority of the women were less tribal-culturally connected and all agreed that Midwestern should not adopt a policy guarding against ethnic fraud, the one woman present who had grown up and attended schools on a reservation told the first author in an individual conversation that "It does matter." She elaborated by talking about how historically "reservation Indians" have been denied many opportunities available to Native people who are more assimilated into the mainstream and if there are only so many resources available for Indigenous people, they should not be taken by people who "use their Native identity" to claim the limited resources when they really are not "part of any community." Much like this woman's views, a number of Indigenous scholars and activists believe ethnic fraud is a national problem in higher education (Pewewardy & Frey, 2004).

Although not all Indigenous people agree on the degree to which self-identification policies should be usurped by proof of tribal enrollment policies, at least some universities are beginning to recognize the problems with self-identification. For example, the American Indian and Alaska Native Professors' Association has a policy statement on ethnic fraud that encourages universities to follow the example of the University of Oklahoma and the University of Washington who have formal verification policies adopted by university administration. At Midwestern University, a group of faculty, staff, and students presented information to the provost and vice chancellor for student affairs in Fall 2002 requesting that Midwestern implement a policy requiring proof of tribal affiliation from students who self-identify before allocating limited financial resources to such students. They presented the University of Oklahoma's policy and argued that, first, the institution must recognize tribes as sovereign nations with the sole right to determine their own constituents, and second, that given limited financial resources set aside for Indigenous students, the institution ought to ensure such funds are distributed appropriately. According to one staff member intimately involved in this process, the university was extremely resistant to the idea, and in a written statement in December 2002, the provost wrote, "At present, we do not think it is within the purview of the state hellip or the university to establish the bureaucracy and procedures to identify members of American Indian tribes."

As with the mascot example, the interest convergence principle can help make sense of the institution's reluctance to adopt a policy that would guard against ethnic fraud. The interests of Native people and the institution converge in the sense of wanting to recruit more Indigenous people to the university: Both want improved recruitment and retention of American Indian and Alaska Native students. But the cost to the university of implementing a policy guarding against ethnic fraud is simply too high. In the case of admissions, the institution clearly has a vested interest in not requiring proof of tribal enrollment because that would decrease the number of people they can "count" as Native and, therefore, as students of color. Given that the numbers of Indigenous students at Midwestern University are already disproportionately low in comparison to the state's population and number of reservations and given that the university has made the recruitment of underrepresented students a fundamental goal of its campus-wide diversity plan, an enrollment verification policy would set the university back even further in terms of its stated goals. Indeed, as one Indigenous women student at MU explained:

> The university wants to keep the numbers up. I don't think they care how or whatever. But I think [the American Indian student services] office called and at one point questioned the number of people who check the box and then kind of disappear off the face of the earth. And I think they were going to try to implement something like hellip [where you have to] show you have some tie to your community hellip. The university was very opposed to that idea. I think with [the diversity plan], I think they just want the numbers to be as high as possible. (emphasis added)

Although ethnic fraud is a concern at the level of admissions, it is far more crucial when it comes to allocating limited financial resources such as scholarships and awards to Indigenous students. Like many universities around the county, Midwestern has a number of scholarships and programs that "foster diversity"—that is, funds that target and assist underrepresented groups of

students on campus. Two of these scholarships that target American Indian
and Alaska Native students are controlled and disseminated by Indigenous
people themselves, and all the other funds (which, needless to say, total significantly more money) are controlled by other groups of people and often
target all students of color. Interestingly, the two scholarships disseminated
by Indigenous people themselves do require verification of tribal enrollment
or affiliation with a federally recognized tribe. Indigenous people who are
enrolled in tribal nations have an interest in advancing such a policy because
they believe that the limited resources should be going to appropriate people.
However, none of the other scholarship funds that are controlled by others and
target all students of color at MU require self-identified Indigenous students
to demonstrate proof of tribal enrollment. As with the admissions example, the
interests of the institution and Indigenous people converge around financially
supporting a more diverse student body. But they diverge about the particularities of allocating the money, with the result being institutional practices
that are not in the best interests of culturally connected and tribally enrolled
Indigenous people—which, in turn, fails to support the self-determination and
sovereignty goals of tribal nations.

Concern over ethnic fraud is an important issue in terms of faculty hiring
at mainstream colleges and universities. Though he does not explicitly name
his framework as such, Pewewardy (2004) essentially makes an interest convergence argument in his discussion of faculty hiring:

> If the institution does not ask for tribal documentation or does not support the
> call for implementing a policy on ethnic fraud, then it is allowing the charade to
> continue, because often it has much invested in the fraud and exposure would put
> the institution in jeopardy. Both the institution and the individual benefit from this
> arrangement. The school gets diversity credit and satisfies the affirmative action
> office. The institution employs someone who is most unlikely to challenge the
> status quo. They acquire the quota without the problems. And, the individual has
> a better chance of getting the faculty position, research grant, committee assign-
> ment, or awards that she or he is seeking in higher education. (p. 202)

In other words, by not requiring prospective faculty to demonstrate proof of
tribal enrollment, the university benefits by getting to "count" more of its
faculty as Native, and the new hires who would otherwise not be considered
"targeted minorities" benefit by being eligible for particular funds, positions,
and recognitions. On the other hand, this harms both tribal-culturally connected faculty members because of stiffer competition and tribal nations who
have few, if any, members represented on university campuses.

A less obvious way self-identification policies serve the interests of the
university is illustrated by Pewewardy's statement above, that "the institution

employs someone who is most unlikely to challenge the status quo." In this context he is referring specifically to the status quo regarding the policy, but a number of Native students at Midwestern allude to the idea that the university prefers Indigenous students who will be supportive of the status quo in general. By admitting and then financially and socially supporting Native students who are more assimilated and have minimal ties to Indigenous communities, world-views, and cultures, the university engages in a kind of preventative practice that guards against it being subject to severe critique and, therefore, called upon to change. Many of the most publicly active Indigenous women students at Midwestern come from predominantly white communities with minimal ties or knowledge of their tribal nations. For Indigenous women who come to Mid-western with weak tribal-cultural ties, the university generally facilitates their increased awareness and knowledge of Native cultures, histories, and peoples. These women speak positively about their experiences on campus and their "newfound identities." One woman, for example, explained, "Since coming here, my Native identity has really taken center stage because I grew up in such a white setting. You kind of grow up and conform to those sets of values hellip. So, I think since coming to campus I've grown much more comfortable and further into my Native identity." Many women shared this sentiment and explic-itly cited the "cultural diversity," "big events," and "Native clubs and activities" as contributing to their perception of Midwestern as a diverse institution that facilitates their cultural learning and identity. Not insignificantly, these events and activities reflect a fairly superficial approach to multicultural education that does nothing to challenge or change the core culture of the institution. De-spite the limitations inherent to this approach to multicultural education, these women are generally impressed—or at least content—with the educational and cultural experiences offered at Midwestern University. Importantly, it is these women's opinions that the institution promotes in order to validate its efforts toward multicultural education.

Although many Native women from predominantly white communities who have minimal tribal-cultural ties find the university to be a place of increased opportunities for interacting with other Indigenous people and for gaining cultural knowledge, Native women who come to the university with much stronger tribal-cultural connections find the university to be a place of limited cultural expression and growth. Their time at Midwestern gener-ally results in the marginalization or bracketing of their Indigenous cultural knowledge and practices. One woman described how "you could feel like you have to lose your identity in order to fit in," and another woman said,

I don't think it was a decision that I made. It was just that, whether I wanted to do it or not, I was going to naturally conform into this environment because hellip [the kind of environment I was] used to being in just wasn't available here. So it's kind of difficult to kind of stay grounded in your culture in the university where it's just basically nonexistent.

These women who are more tribal-culturally connected and critical of the institution speak about how issues of race, power, and culture are rarely talked about or even acknowledged among the majority of students, faculty, and staff at Midwestern. One women said, "It's like they want us to be here but they don't want us to be of color."[11] These women's concerns reflect the fact that superficial approaches to multicultural education leave the culture of whiteness unchanged. These concerns, however, go largely unheard by the institution.

This brief discussion of the different experiences of both less and more tribal-culturally connected women and how they are differently positioned within the university highlights how the absence of a policy protecting against ethnic fraud contributes to the likelihood that less tribal-culturally connected women will be more numerous, publicly active, and thus visible within the campus community.[12] Since these women are generally supportive rather than critical of the institution, MU can cite their voices as evidence of progress toward cultivating a more welcoming and diverse campus community. So the interest of the university in maintaining the status quo and the interests of those who cannot prove tribal enrollment also hit a point of convergence around self-identification policies. Overriding self-identification policies with enrollment verification policies would likely lead to many fewer "official" Indigenous students and faculty, protest among those who feel the institution should not require them to prove their identity, and potentially more intense pressure from the smaller group of tribally enrolled students and faculty for a university that is responsive to their needs. A policy guarding against ethnic fraud would potentially facilitate greater equity in the distribution of funds, jobs, and resources. But, because the price is too high for the university to require proof of enrollment, self-identification policies remain intact.

LIMITATIONS OF THE INTEREST CONVERGENCE PRINCIPLE

Our analysis suggests that universities like Midwestern are willing to embrace policies that reflect a superficial approach to multicultural education, an approach that acknowledges and even celebrates cultural diversity. Policies that actually challenge the status quo and reflect a critical approach to multicultural education, however, are neither considered nor adopted. Importantly,

Indigenous women's experiences of being stereotyped and feeling socially isolated demonstrate the limitations of superficial approaches to multiculturalism. Although we have focused on two particular policies that primarily impact Indigenous students and faculty at Midwestern University, it is important to recognize that the interest convergence principle can also be used as an analytic tool for examining other policies and practices in institutions of higher education.

But interest convergence analyses are not without their limitations and, in particular, they present a dilemma for those of us with anti-racist and social justice agendas. On the one hand, the interest convergence principle exposes the selfishness behind many policies and practices that may advance greater racial equity—this is the bad news interest convergence analyses bring. On the other hand, perhaps some good news lies in the idea that if those of us working for greater social justice can convince those with power that certain policies and practices that bring about greater equity are also in their own best interests, then we may have found a promising strategy for social change. Unfortunately, however, such strategies are limited by their reliance on liberal assumptions about the process of social change. Thus, although interest convergence helps make sense of the policies and practices outlined in this article, CRT and TribalCrit remind us that greater racial equity and social justice will not be achieved within this liberal framework of individual property rights, a focus on equality, and colorblindness.

Critical race theory, in fact, poses a widespread critique of liberalism's slow pace for social change and emphasis on sameness and equal treatment (Delgado & Stefancic, 2001; Dixson & Rousseau, 2006). Within the field of education, access to the same schools, for example, is not enough to redress past injustices when racism, tracking, and white privilege continue to disadvantage students of color. CRT also critiques liberalism's emphasis on rights because rights are usually procedural rather than substantive and because rights are almost always restricted when they conflict with the interests of those in power (Bell, 2004; Delgado & Stefancic, 2001; Ladson-Billings, 1998)—as is clear in the passing of the USA Patriot Act (2001), for example. Since civil rights are intimately connected to individual property rights, change is too slow to be effective, and white people have largely benefited from the construction of whiteness as the ultimate property (Harris, 1995; Ladson-Billings, 1998). Thus, as Ladson-Billings and Donnor (2005) recently reasserted, CRT's emphasis must be on taking issue with liberalism's willingness to "only go so far" in the struggle for greater equity and social justice. In a similar vein, tribal critical race theory highlights the patterns of colonization and assimilation that have resulted from well-intentioned liberal "friends of the Indians" (Brayboy, 2005a). Throughout history (and in the present day), the liberal-minded democratic principles of freedom and equality have often stood as obstacles to tribal nations' pursuits of sovereignty and self-determination. Keeping these limitations in mind may help us think through alternative strategies for achieving equity and social justice in our institutions of higher education.

In sum, we have argued that the interest convergence principle helps make sense of not only Midwestern University's partial action regarding Indian mascots but also their inaction regarding ethnic fraud among Indigenous students and faculty. Though we can find some justification of these policies and practices from the perspective of the institution, interest convergence also allows us to critique them on the grounds that they are primarily in the interests of the institution and, fundamentally, of white supremacy. Tribal critical race theory pushes us to recognize how these policies and practices are part of a legacy of racism and colonization—a legacy that unfortunately will not be disrupted by relying on the good intentions of those in positions of power.

NOTES

The authors thank the anonymous reviewers and Bryan Brayboy for feedback on earlier drafts of this article. This article was originally published in *Equity and Excellence in Education, 40*(1) (January 2007), 3–13.

1. Throughout this article we use the terms "Indigenous," "Native," "American Indian," "Indian," and "Native American" interchangeably to refer to the peoples indigenous to what is now the United States. Scholars, educators, and other Indigenous people have not come to an agreement over the use of these terms, and we do not use specific tribal affiliations (the generally preferred practice) in an effort to protect the identities of the women who participated in this study.

2. All proper names have been changed to protect the anonymity of the participants in this study. Although ideally we would like to name Midwestern University in order to "out" the institution with respect to what they are and are not doing around diversity and social justice, IRB protocol does not permit us to do so.

3. This research was originally designed to explore the experiences of Indigenous women on a predominantly white campus. The research design focused on self-identified Native women because the first author was interested in the range and variation of experiences among this diverse group of women, and because this is currently the way Midwestern University identifies American Indian and Alaska Native students. We recognize, of course, the irony in this aspect of the research design given our examination of ethnic fraud in this article.

4. This is an illuminating example of the racial battle fatigue that often results from the countless experiences of racial microaggressions at "liberal" universities such as Midwestern. Although overt forms of racism are rare on these campuses, research has

shown the multiple and varied ways students of color are marginalized and assaulted in predominantly white communities (Solórzano, 1998; Solórzano, Ceja, & Yosso, 2000).

5. Because of space limitations, we are unable to elaborate on CRT here, but we offer this brief explanation: Critical race theory begins with the notions that racism is ordinary (Delgado & Stefancic, 2001), and that race still matters in contemporary U.S. society (West, 2004). It recognizes, however, that differential racialization processes and experiences of racism certainly exist within and between groups (Delgado & Stefancic, 2001). Proponents of CRT argue that it is a tool for uncovering racial subordination and the marginalization of people of color and that in adopting a CRT frame, researchers necessarily are called to expose and challenge the racism inherent in everyday social life (Lynn, Yosso, Solórzano, & Parker, 2002; Parker & Lynn, 2002; Villenas & Deyhle, 1999). The main goals of CRT include presenting narratives and storytelling as valid forms of data and legitimate approaches through which to understand race and racism, eradicating racial subjugation while recognizing that race is a social construct that has very real impacts on people's lives, challenging dominant ideologies and working towards social justice, and making connections between race and other axes of oppression (Ladson-Billings, 1998; Solórzano & Yosso, 2002).

6. More recently, Guinier (2004) has argued that interest convergence is limited in its ability to explain the partial progress towards racial equity because of its sole focus on the interests of powerful white elites and blacks. In doing so, interest convergence theory has overlooked other positionalities (e.g., social class, geography) that affect perceived interest divergences between and among groups. For example, Guinier highlights the fact that working-class whites resisted desegregation efforts and were also the ones to be directly affected by desegregation. While this is a helpful contribution to our understanding of efforts at greater racial equality, our work—like Bell's original focus in developing interest convergence—highlights the relationship between the interests of the powerful white elites and the interests of a group of color.

7. In order to keep our argument as straightforward as possible, we do not elaborate on the other aspects of tribal critical race theory. For a full description of this theoretical framework, see Brayboy, 2005a. It is also worth noting that other scholars have extended CRT into LatCrit, FemCrit, and AsianCrit in order to highlight the particularities of other groups.

8. While definitions of whiteness abound among scholars, we mean here to reference ways institutions, structures, and social relations are organized such that white people consistently benefit at the expense of people of color.

9. For more on the history of dancing for the entertainment of white audiences, see Browner, 2002, and Farnell, 2004.

10. The issue of opportunistically claiming Native identity has become increasingly complicated as there appears to be a growing industry of DNA testing companies who purport to inform individuals of their racial and ethnic background (TallBear, 2005). There also is some evidence that people may be using these products and services with the sole purpose of claiming "benefits" (e.g., affirmative action scholarships) set aside for members of racialized groups. A white business executive from Maryland with two adopted sons had his children's DNA tested and found them

to be 9% American Indian and 11% Northern African; in explaining his decision to have his sons' DNA tested, the father said, "Naturally when you're applying to college you're looking at how your genetic status might help you" (Harmon, 2006, p. A1).

11. Although there is a growing body of research that examines Indigenous students' experiences in institutions of higher education (Brayboy, 2004, 2005b; Castagno, 2005; Fixico, 1995; Garrod & Larimore, 1997; Huffman, 1991, 2003; Kirkness & Barnhardt, 1991; Mihesuah & Wilson, 2004; Pavel, 1998; Pewewardy & Frey, 2004; Tierney, 1992, 1993; Wright & Tierney, 1991), we do not explicitly engage with this literature here because doing so would detract from our primary purpose of illustrating how differently positioned Native women experience Midwestern University and how that variability is in the best interest of the institution. In other words, while most published studies examine the personal experiences of Indigenous students, we are primarily concerned in this article with institutional policies as they relate to Indigenous students.

12. Brayboy (2004) uses the concept of visibility in order to analyze Indigenous students' experiences at Ivy League universities. He offers an important and useful explanation of visibility and invisibility, but we are using the term here to mean simply that less tribal-culturally connected women are positioned by the institution as more visible because institutional leaders like what these women have to say.

REFERENCES

Allen, W. (2005). A forward glance in a mirror: Diversity challenged—Access, equity, and success in higher education. *Educational Researcher, 34*(7), 18–23.

Anderson, J. (1993). Race, meritocracy, and the American academy during the immediate post–World War II era. *History of Education Quarterly, 33*(2) , 151–175.

Bell, D. (1979). Bakke, minority admissions, and the usual price of racial remedies. *California Law Review, 76*, 3.

Bell, D. (1980a). Brown v. Board of Education and the interest-convergence dilemma. *Harvard Law Review, 93*, 518.

Bell, D. (1980b). *Race, racism, and American law* (2nd ed.). Boston: Little, Brown.

Bell, D. (1987). *And we are not saved: The elusive quest for racial justice.* New York: Basic.

Bell, D. (1989). The final report: Harvard's affirmative action allegory. *Michigan Law Review, 87*, 2382.

Bell, D. (2004). *Silent Covenants: Brown V. Board of Education and the Unfulfilled Hopes for Racial Reform.* Oxford: Oxford University Press.

Brayboy, B. (2004). Hiding in the ivy: American Indian students and visibility in elite educational settings. *Harvard Educational Review, 74*(2), 125–152.

Brayboy, B. (2005a). Toward a tribal critical race theory in education. *Urban Review, 37*(5), 425–446.

Brayboy, B. (2005b). Transformational resistance and social justice: American Indians in Ivy League universities. *Anthropology and Education Quarterly 36*(3), 194–211.

Brown v. Board of Education. (1954). 347 U.S. 483, 74 S.Ct. 686, 98 L.Ed. 873.

Browner, T. (2002). *Heartbeat of the people: Music and dance of the northern pow-wow.* Urbana: University of Illinois Press.

Castagno, A. (2003). *(Re)contextualizing Indian higher education: A qualitative study of Indigenous women at a predominantly white university.* Unpublished master's thesis, University of Wisconsin, Madison.

Castagno, A. (2005). Extending the bounds of race and racism: Indigenous women and the persistence of the black–white paradigm of race. *Urban Review, 37*(5), 447–468.

Churchill, W., & Morris, G. T. (1992). Key Indian laws and cases. In M. A. Jaimes, Ed., *The state of Native America: Genocide, colonization, and resistance* (pp. 13–21). Boston: South End Press.

Clarkson, G. (2004). Using Indian mascots continues racial harm. *Detroit News.*

DeCuir, J., & Dixon, A. (2004). So when it comes out, they aren't that surprised that it is there: Using critical race theory as a tool of analysis of race and racism in education. *Educational Researcher, 33*(5), 26–31.

Delgado, R., & Stefancic, J. (2001). *Critical race theory: An introduction.* New York: New York University Press.

Dixson, A., & Rousseau, C. (Eds.). (2006). *Critical race theory and education: All God's children got a song.* New York: Routledge.

Farnell, B. (2004). The fancy dance of racializing discourse. *Journal of Sport and Social Issues, 28*(1), 30–55.

Fixico, D. (1995). American Indians (the minority of minorities) and higher education. In B. Bowser, T. Jones, & G. A. Young (Eds.), *Toward the multicultural university* (pp. 103–124). Westport, CT: Praeger.

Garrod, A., & Larimore, C. (1997). *First person, First Peoples: Native American college graduates tell their life stories.* Ithaca, NY: Cornell University Press.

Gonzales, A. (2001). Urban (trans)formations: Changes in the meaning and use of American Indian identity. In S. Lobo & K. Peters (Eds.), *American Indians and the urban experience* (pp. 169–185). Walnut Creek, CA: Altamira.

Grande, S. (2000). American Indian identity and intellectualism: The quest for a new red pedagogy. *International Journal of Qualitative Studies in Education, 13*(4), 343–359.

Guinier, L. (2004). From racial liberalism to racial literacy: Brown v. Board of Education and the interest-divergence dilemma. *Journal of American History, 91*(1), 92–118.

Harmon, A. (2006). Seeking ancestry, and privilege, in DNA ties uncovered in tests. *New York Times*, A1.

Harris, C. (1995). Whiteness as property. In K. Crenshaw, N. Gotanda, G. Peller, & K. Thomas (Eds.), *Critical race theory: Key writings that formed the movement* (pp. 276–291). New York: New Press.

Huffman, T. (1991). The experiences, perceptions, and consequences of campus racism among Northern Plains Indians. *Journal of American Indian Education, 30*(2), 25–34.

Huffman, T. (2003). A comparison of personal assessments of the college experience among reservation and nonreservation American Indian students. *Journal of American Indian Education, 42*(2), 1–15.

Jaimes, M. A. (1992). Federal Indian identification policy: A usurpation of Indigenous sovereignty rights in North America. In M. A. Jaimes (Ed.), *The state of Native America: Genocide, colonization, and resistance* (pp. 123–138). Boston: South End Press.

King, C. (2004). This is not an Indian: Situating claims about Indianness in sporting worlds. *Journal of Sport and Social Issues 28*(1), 3–10.

Kirkness, V., & Barnhardt, R. (1991). First nations and higher education: The four R's—respect, relevance, reciprocity, responsibility. *Journal of American Indian Education, 30*(3), 1–15.

Ladson-Billings, G. (1998). Just what is critical race theory and what's it doing in a nice field like education? *International Journal of Qualitative Studies in Education, 11*(1), 7–24.

Ladson-Billings, G., & Donnor, J. (2005). Waiting for the call: The moral activist role of critical race theory scholarship. In N. Denzin & Y. Lincoln (Eds.), *Handbook of qualitative research* (3rd ed.). Thousand Oaks, CA: Sage.

Lee, S. (2005). *Up against whiteness: Race, school, and immigrant youth.* New York: Teachers College Press.

Lynn, M., Yosso, T. J., Solórzano, D. G., & Parker, L. (2002). Critical race theory and education: Qualitative research in the new millennium. *Qualitative Inquiry, 8*(1), 3–6.

Machamer, A. (1997). Ethnic fraud in the university: Serious implications for American Indian education. *Native Bruin, 2,* 1–2.

Mihesuah, D., & Wilson, A. eds. (2004). *Indigenizing the academy: Transforming scholarship and empowering communities.* Lincoln: University of Nebraska Press.

Morris, G. T. (1992). International law and politics: Toward a right to self-determination for indigenous peoples. In M. A. Jaimes (Ed.), *The state of Native America: Genocide, colonization, and resistance* (pp. 55–86). Boston: South End Press.

Parker, L., & Lynn, M. (2002). What's race got to do with It? Critical race theory's conflicts with and connections to qualitative research methodology and epistemology. *Qualitative Inquiry, 8*(1), 7–22.

Pavel, D. M. (1998). *American Indians and Alaska natives in postsecondary education.* Washington, DC: U.S. Department. of Education Office of Educational Research and Improvement, National Center for Education Statistics.

Pewewardy, C. (2004). So you think you hired an "Indian" faculty member? The ethnic fraud paradox in higher education. In D. Mihesuah & A. Wilson (Eds.), *Indigenizing the academy: Transforming scholarship and empowering communities* (pp. 200–217). Lincoln: University of Nebraska Press.

Pewewardy, C., & Frey, B. (2004). American Indian students' perceptions of racial climate, multicultural support services, and ethnic fraud at predominantly white universities. *Journal of American Indian Education, 43*(1), 32–60.

Robbins, R. (1992). Self-determination and subordination: The past, present, and future of American Indian governance. In M. A. Jaimes (Ed.), *The state of Native*

America: Genocide, colonization, and resistance (pp. 87–121). Boston: South End Press.

Solórzano, D. (1998). Critical race theory, race and gender microaggressions, and the experience of Chicana and Chicano scholars. *Qualitative Studies in Education, 11*(1), 121–136.

Solórzano, D., Ceja, M., & Yosso, T. (2000). Critical race theory, racial microaggressions, and campus racial climate: The experiences of African American college students. *Journal of Negro Education, 69*(1/2), 60–73.

Solórzano, D. G., & Yosso, T. J. (2002). Critical race methodology: Counter-storytelling as an analytical framework for education research. *Qualitative Inquiry, 8*(1), 23–44.

Springwood, C. (2004). "I'm Indian too!" Claiming Native American identity, crafting authority in mascot debates. *Journal of Sport and Social Issues, 28*(1), 56–70.

Staurowsky, E. (2004). Privilege at play: On the legal and social fictions that sustain American Indian sport imagery. *Journal of Sport and Social Issues, 28*(1), 11–29.

Strong, (2004). The mascot slot: Cultural citizenship, political correctness, and pseudo-Indian sports symbols. *Journal of Sport and Social Issues, 28*(1), 79–87.

TallBear. (2005). *Native American-DNA.com: Marketing indigeniety?* Presented at the American Anthropological Association's 104th annual conference, Washington, DC.

Taylor, E. (1999). Critical race theory and interest convergence in the desegregation of higher education. In L. Parker, D. Deyhle, & S. Villenas (Eds.), *Race is hellip race isn't: Critical race theory and qualitative studies in education* (pp. 182–201). Boulder, CO: Westview.

Tierney, W. (1992). *Official encouragement, institutional discouragement: Minorities in academe—The Native American experience.* Norwood, NJ: Able.

Tierney, W. (1993). The college experience of Native Americans: A critical analysis. In L. Weis & M. Fine (Eds.), *Beyond silenced voices* (pp. 309–324). Albany: State University of New York Press.

Tsosie, R. (2000). Sacred obligations: Intercultural justice and the discourse of treaty rights. *UCLA Law Review, 47*, 1615.

USA Patriot Act. (2001). *Uniting and strengthening America by providing appropriate tools required to intercept and obstruct terrorism.* Washington, DC: Pub. L. No. 107–56, 115 Stat. 272.

Villenas, S., & Deyhle, D. (1999). Critical race theory and ethnographies challenging the stereotypes: Latino families, schooling, resilience, and resistance. *Curriculum Inquiry, 29*(4), 413–445.

West, C. (1998). Race matters. In M. Andersen & H. Collins (Eds.), *Race, class, and gender: An anthology* (5th ed., pp. 122–125). Belmont, CA: Wadsworth.

Wright, B., & Tierney, W. (1991). American Indians in higher education: A history of cultural conflict. *Change, 23*(2), 11–18.

12

Mascots and Meaning: How One District Worked Through the Emotional Issue of Changing Team Logos

Terry Grier

It started with a memo in 2002. The State Board of Education strongly encouraged all North Carolina school districts to consider the educational and psychological effects of using American Indian mascots. With the Native American dropout rate at twice the state average, the state board worried that the use of these mascots could be one of the reasons. More than 60 North Carolina public schools had Indian mascots, including three in my district, Guilford County. Guilford has 68,200 students, 372 of whom are Native American.

The state board asked us to review our use of Indian symbols and to educate our staff on how these symbols affect all students at the one elementary school and two high schools that used Native American mascots. As a result, the elementary school's student council voted to change their mascot to the "Bears."

Staff members at both high schools said they were sensitive to the issue, but neither school wanted to change long-standing tradition. The entire process that evolved over the next 18 months was emotionally trying for our school board, staff, and school communities. While the decision was not unanimous, the board and staff united to make the process inclusive and successful.

Here's how we did it.

STATING THEIR CASE

We started by hosting discussions between the Guilford Native American Association and the two high school PTAs. Everyone was cordial, but both sides were passionate about their views, and no one seemed willing to budge.

The issue created discussion among some board members and high school alumni, then became lost in the day-to-day events of a large urban school district.

Then, in November 2003, the issue surfaced again during the National Indian Education Association's annual convention, which was being held in Greensboro. Monroe Gilmour, coordinator of the North Carolina Mascot Education and Action Group, sought an update on our position on removing Native American mascots from our schools. He had spoken with the principal at one of the high schools with a Native American mascot and planned to send a letter that would question the practice. Gilmour also asked me to share the letter with the school board.

If the intention is to honor Native Americans, the letter asked, why are only the mascots—not the schools themselves—named after Indian leaders? Why aren't other racial groups scrambling to be so honored? The Guilford County Blacks? The Guilford County Whites? Why do those mascot names sound ridiculous but not the Guilford County Indians?

After receiving the letter, a board member asked Gilmour to speak at a board meeting. Gilmour told the board that Indian mascots—even the so-called dignified ones—are the modern-day equivalents of the blackface minstrel imagery found at Sambo's restaurants.

Following the presentations and drawing from information provided by the staff, the board voted to begin the process of eliminating Native American mascots. To ease the process, the board decided to hold meetings with the leadership teams of the two high schools.

CONTROVERSIES ERUPT

The board's action made headlines in the media and resulted in numerous letters to the editor, editorials, and commentaries on both sides of the issue. Our website was deluged with e-mails, the majority of which supported keeping the mascots and logos.

Members of the North Carolina Mascot Education and Action Group and the Guilford Native American Association, however, repeatedly told us that they perceived the use of Indian mascots, logos, caricatures, and similar images by our schools as a clear form of institutional racism. They asked how long white children would want to stay in a school where they were laughed at and mocked.

When we held our meetings with representatives from the two high schools, members heard a different point of view. The first group indicated that the Indian mascot had been used in earlier community schools as a way to honor the relationship between the area's Native American and Quaker settlers.

The group representing our second high school took a different approach.

Seeming resigned to the loss of their "Indian with a headdress" logo, they lobbied the board to keep their "Red Raider" mascot. In fact, representatives from both schools were passionate in supporting their mascots.

Following the meetings, the board continued to receive e-mails, letters, and telephone calls from the community. A Guilford County commissioner even got involved, lobbying in support of the mascots.

At a heavily attended board meeting, community representatives again spoke during the public comment portion of the agenda. The board then reviewed three mascot policies developed by the board attorney but could not decide which was the most appropriate.

Then, the board took the unusual action of directing me to meet with representatives from the two high schools and the Guilford County Native American Association. After that, the board asked me to write a policy for board review.

A NEW POLICY

At the next regularly scheduled board meeting, I presented the board with this policy:

> All mascots, nicknames, and descriptors, including drawings, symbols, or similar identifiers, used by a school's extracurricular clubs or sports teams or by schools' curricular clubs, organizations, or activities shall ensure respect for cultural differences, values, and attitudes of all peoples. The Guilford County Board of Education prohibits the use of American Indians or any other existing race or ethnic group as a mascot, nickname, descriptor, or similar identifier of any extracurricular sports team or club, curricular club, organization, or activity that may be offensive to existing races or ethnic groups.

The board approved the policy on a nine to one vote, and it was listed on our website for 21 days of public comment before appearing on the agenda for a second reading and final approval.

At the second meeting, the staff reported that it would cost approximately $185,000 to retire the Native American mascots and logos from the two high schools. This number would be significantly reduced because one school's band was scheduled for uniform replacement (at district expense) during the coming year. After a lengthy discussion, the board passed the policy, but amended it to delete the term "American Indians."

ACCEPTING NEW MASCOTS

Following 18 months of small group meetings, board meetings, board re-treats, e-mails, telephone calls, letters, letters to the editor, editorials, and commentaries, we managed to satisfy the original request of prohibiting the use of Native American mascots or logos by sports teams. But now the policy had a much broader reach, extending the prohibition to include any race, cul-ture, or ethnic group as a mascot.

The central office and school staffs worked hard to implement the new pol-icy before the 2004–05 school year started. The first step was to work with the two high school communities. Most students, faculty members, and school supporters understood the rationale behind the board's decision, but many felt that removing their mascot amounted to punishing them now for wrongdoing that had happened in the past—behavior that was no longer accepted.

Realizing that new athletic and band uniforms had to be purchased, basket-ball courts refinished, and school signage redesigned, school principals were faced with the political and emotional challenge of helping move their school families toward developing new symbols to represent their schools.

Although in both schools the immediate reaction of several students, alumni, and booster club members was not supportive, one high school kept its "Red Raiders" mascot but changed its logo from a Native American wearing a headdress. The other high school changed its mascot from "The Indians" to "The Storm."

LESSONS LEARNED

Guilford County now has no schools using Native American mascots. Since we started in this process, however, we have learned a number of valuable lessons.

They include:

Recognize the link. Symbols are extremely important to individuals and organizations. They provide a link between the past, present, and future. Dis-trict leaders and policymakers should not discount the depth of feelings that individuals and groups have toward school mascots and logos.

Listen to both sides. Individuals on both sides of the issue feel passionate about their views. It is extremely important for school leaders and policy-makers to listen to both sides before making decisions. Regardless of their positions, all parties deserve to be heard and treated with dignity and respect.

The principal is key. The degree of success in implementing any school-wide change hinges on the leadership provided by the school principal. The principal of the school that changed its team from "The Indians" to "The Storm" brought his community together by continuing to hold informational sessions and educating his staff, student body, and community.

Pay homage to the past. The staff decided to retire—rather than abolish—the schools' Native American mascots. At separate ceremonies, students, staff, and alumni witnessed the induction of the mascots into each school's Athletic Hall of Fame. It was very important to bring an honorable closure to symbols of the past and, at the same time, introduce the new symbols of the future.

13

Strategies for Making Team Identity Change

David Carl Wahlberg

The number of intercollegiate athletic teams with Native American logos, nicknames, and mascots continues to decrease as institutions make changes from such identities, and no new universities assume Indian identities. The 27 schools in this research study group that eliminated Native American sports identities illustrate this trend toward elimination. The trend is further illustrated by the 14 institutions of 33 the NCAA asked to conduct self-studies on their use of Native American identities that changed sports identities of their own volition by the time the self-studies were due. Pressure on the remaining schools to make similar changes will predictably continue from social action groups, the NCAA's decision of August 2005, state and federal departments of education, and the court system. Legal challenges—notably one that seeks to deny the Washington Redskins trademark protection on the grounds that the name violates trademark law by disparaging Native Americans—are ongoing (Rosner, 2002). Additionally, regional accrediting agencies, while yet to take sanctions against schools with Indian sports names, have taken an interest in how schools use Native American identities. The North Central Association of Colleges and Schools term the lack of progress on the issue at the University of Illinois "an embarrassment" (Newbart, 2004, p. 6) in Illinois' accreditation report, and the same association urged the North Dakota State Board of Higher Education to reconsider its order requiring the University of North Dakota to maintain its Fighting Sioux identity (University of North Dakota, 2004).

As pressure continues on schools with Native American sports identities to stop using such logos, nicknames, and mascots, the process of orchestrating a voluntary change for those university administrators who choose to champion change will pose a daunting task. This research demonstrates that schools which have changed their Indian mascots (1) have not to a great extent seen the threatened abandonment of fans and financial supporters, (2) that the change allowed these universities to reach a conclusion to their identity crisis, and (3) that senior public relations practitioners at these schools overwhelmingly encourage identity change. This research has also demonstrated that the change was often difficult, as shown in this survey response: "The process was handled very badly over a decade ago, and we still get echoes of unhappiness over the way the debate/decision was conducted." One public relations practitioner, who suggested that just as change makes some constituents happy, change would also make some unhappy, calls for decisive leadership, "Someone or some entity must be willing to take the heat that will inevitably come."

Another practitioner offered that dialogue helps the campus community adjust to the need for a change and the change itself, and that these dialogues include fundamental elements of campus identity, "Discussion needs to be held around the values of the institution, mission of the institution, and culture of the institution."

Changing campus attitudes can be a large undertaking. Rather than have a university's central administration mandate an immediate change of athletic identity, one survey respondent supported a longer process saying, "The campus climate has to be ready for a change."

BEING A PART OF THE TEAM

The preceding comments underscore the need for a thoughtful process to initiate a change. This process can begin by understanding why such a large gap exists in the perspectives of those who support making a change and those who wish to maintain existing team identities. One means to understand that gap is to understand that, to many university stakeholders, the debate over sports identities is deeply personal.

Social identity theory holds that individuals derive much of their self-esteem from their memberships in social groups (Tajfel & Turner, 1979). Dietz-Uhler and Murrell (1999) note that group identification can be so important to some that any threat to their group will elicit a strong sense of defensiveness. Group members may assume that actions taken by their group are correct (Turner & Oakes, 1989) and that members of a group seek to derive positive esteem from their group membership and, so, favor their own group over others (Dietz-Uhler & Murrell, 1999, p. 16). The more elite the group, the greater the personal satisfaction a member feels he or she receives through the association. An alumnus of the University of North Dakota exhibited this sense of elitism in a letter to the editor of a North Dakota newspaper defending the university's Fighting Sioux identity, "now that the American Indian tribes of North Dakota have been successful in bringing down the most famous institution in the state" (Ridgeway, 2005, p. A17).

Team identification is an extension of social identity theory. Team identification involves the extent to which a fan feels a psychological attachment to a team (Wann, 1997; Wann & Branscombe, 1993). Scientists from a number of disciplines have sought to measure levels of team identification to better understand the behaviors of sports fans (Wann & Pierce, 2003). Fans who highly identify with a sports team exhibit a number of self-serving biases, including being more positive about the team's past and present performances (Wann & Dolan, 1994). Fans with high levels of team identification were willing to attribute their team's success to internal factors and losses to external factors (Wann & Dolan, 1994), and even willing to consider illegally assisting their team (Wann, Hunter, Ryan, & Wright, 2001). Laverie and Arnett (2000) found that college boosters place more value on being a fan than do university faculty and staff.

In short, highly identified fans do not objectively perceive issues affecting their team. Further, perceived threats to the in-group (team) from out-groups become personal threats to the highly identified team supporter. Cognitive dissonance is a psychological phenomenon that refers to the discomfort felt at a discrepancy between what a person already knows or believes and new conflicting information or interpretation (Atherton, 2004). Assertions that a team nickname is racist can be met with disbelief and discomfort if in-group members do not perceive the group's norms and individual beliefs as racists. The team identity "Indians" or "Braves" has a positive meaning in the mind of the sport fan who is highly identified with that team. This team identity of Brave or Sioux is discrete from the actual tribe of people who are usually not members of their team's social group. That a team's identity is something dishonorable is untenable to highly identified fans because their self-concept is built, in part, on their membership in something they perceive as highly honorable. The issue brings personal discomfort (cognitive dissonance) because their social status cannot be both honorable and dishonorable. The identity their team has appropriated is their own now, and that identity is good. That others see their social group in another manner is both a group and personal challenge. Groups resist proposed changes to their group identity because they believe the group is good and correct. "To not fight it is saying that somehow we were wrong. I don't think a university as great as this, the alumni would put up with something so wrong," said University of North Dakota athletic director Tom Buning (Kolpack, 2005, p. D1).

Concern over the development of social identity in young Native Americans is cited by the American Psychological Association (2005) in a resolution calling for the retirement of American Indian sports mascots. Using the perspectives of social identity theory can help university administrators and crisis managers understand the very personal nature of team identification and provide clues on how to facilitate the discontinuation of a Native American sports identity.

Crisis managers seek to reach the resolution stage of a crisis so that organizational resources can be directed to meeting other organizational goals. In suggesting strategies for making change and reaching a resolution to a sports identity crisis, I make the following assumptions:

1. The trend toward the elimination of Native American sports identities in intercollegiate athletics will continue with pressure coming from within universities and from external sources (including accrediting agencies, sports associations, legal challenges, and governmental entities).
2. The August 2005 decision by the NCAA renews the opportunity for schools to reflect on past decisions.
3. Changing athletic identities can be difficult but, as shown in this research, has yet to result in a widespread loss of public support for those schools that have already made such a change.
4. While changing athletic identities is difficult, making the change brings the issue to a conclusion. In contrast, those universities that resist change and allow the ongoing debate to serve as a public challenge to the social legitimacy of their organization threaten to devalue in-group membership. Assumption 1 posits that universities may initiate athletic identity change internally or others may mandate identity change. Note that an outside mandate is largely hypothetical since no accrediting agency or athletic association has yet taken such a definitive step. Still, such agencies can use a variety of means as incentives rather than mandates to achieve the end of making change, as the NCAA did in August 2005 when the association mandated changes at the events it controls (playoffs) while noting universities had the authority to adopt whatever mascot they choose.

STRATEGIES FOR MAKING CHANGE

The research questions in this study provide answers to university crisis managers attempting to resolve the contradiction of Native American sports identities that are seen by some constituents as honorable and positive, but by others as racist and vestiges of a discredited sense of the superiority of white culture. The application of the lens of social identity theory provides insights into why this contradiction can be so difficult to resolve. Based on the information gathered in this research on 27 universities that have already made identity changes, I suggest three strategies for university administrators to facilitate a name change. The strategies seek to create change and acceptance of the change while minimizing the alienation of important university constituencies.

- Take initiative.
- Institute reflective process.
- Accept not all will agree.

Take Initiative

The trend is clear: American universities are abandoning Native American identities. While moral arguments can be subjective, educators nonetheless have a special imperative to do the right thing. Professional sports teams may have profit as their highest reason for being, but universities do not. The appropriation of a minority culture's identity for the benefit of a majority culture is a kind of theft, even when the motives are not vindictive. Further, as Pewewardy writes (2000, 2001), educators have an obligation to challenge stereotypes. Native American mascots have their roots more in a mythical perception of the Old West and Americana than in any reality. Further, even "authentic" Indian mascots that are claimed to honor Native Americans exist first as a means of building public support for an athletic program, and only secondarily, if at all, as an extension of the cultural and educational programming of a university. The mascots were not created as an exercise in intercultural education, but rather athletic competition. The idea that they honor Native Americans came only as an afterthought to justify their existence.

Universities should not wait to be mandated to do the right thing. They can, instead, take the moral high ground and initiate change. The process they begin will offer challenges. Talk radio, letters to the editor, controversy, threats, and heated debate will likely ignite. So be it. Doing the right thing is not always popular.

From the standpoint of being more effective agents of change, taking the initiative to change an athletic mascot rather than to continue to fight change could decrease constituent resistance to the change. Research on fan identification reveals fan perceptual bias in favor of their team and against those viewed as opponents. If outsiders mandate an unpopular change, it will predictably be viewed with greater hostility than if their social group chooses the change, as illustrated by this newspaper editorial: "By trying to coerce UND [University of North Dakota] into making such a hot-button change, the NCAA inspired not cooperation, but backlash" (Dennis, 2005, p. D1). If a change is perceived to be rooted in the idea that outsiders see one's social group as having negative (racist) characteristics, then the root is a threat to group cohesion. If, on the other hand, change comes from the group itself, the threat is lessened. The "eureka moment" described in this research for a football coach reluctant to change at Adams State College came when respected members of the athletic program spoke of their personal hurt from the team's use of a Native American identity, not because an outside speaker contradicted a personally held construct by calling evil what the coach believed to be good. Further, delaying change because not all Native American opinions are the same is a roadblock to reflective discourse. Florida State University, for example, has the support of the Seminole tribe of Florida in its use of the Seminoles' identity, but was asked by the Seminole tribe of Oklahoma to stop.

A 2002 *Sports Illustrated* poll found that 81 percent of Native Americans who live outside traditional Indian reservations and 53 percent of Indians on reservations did not oppose Native American sports images. That poll was contradicted one year later by *Indian Country Today* that reported that 81 percent of its respondents found the images objectionable (Fears, 2005).

To delay decision making until all Native American voices are the same is condescending. All Native Americans no more think alike than all Native Americans live as Sioux warriors in tepees and dress in buckskins. The 2002 *Sports Illustrated* survey showed widespread Native American support for the use of Native American sports identities, but most national Native American organizations oppose the use of collegiate Indian sports mascots. Universities should take responsibility for their own actions and not delay reflective thought on this issue. See the appendix for a listing of American Indian organizations opposed to the use of Native American Indian athletic identities, as compiled by one anti-Indian mascot organization.

Institute Reflective Process

Universities are complex organizations with many stakeholders, often having differing expectations of an institution. The nature of institutions of higher education is to gather data, conduct analysis, and challenge assumptions. Initiating successful organizational change is legitimized by a lengthy and thoughtful process. President Charles Kupchella at the University of North Dakota created such a one-year process before he would make a final decision on the continued use of the Fighting Sioux nickname. The process included consultations with tribal governments, alumni groups, and on campus forums.

The process became moot when the governing State Board of Higher Education ordered the university to maintain its Sioux identity after receiving an e-mail from Ralph Engelstad, a wealthy alumnus, threatening to withdraw a $100 million gift of an ice hockey arena if the nickname was changed (for more detailed descriptions of these events at the University of North Dakota, see Vorland, 2000; Brownstein, 2001; LaPoint, 2004; and Wahlberg, 2004). Similarly, Marquette University discontinued its Warriors name and logo in 1994 only to have the issue resurface ten years later when an alumnus and board officer offered $1 million with another anonymous $1 million match for a return to the nickname.

The University of North Dakota initiated a broad-based inclusive process to study the university's Fighting Sioux identity. President Kupchella displayed the burden of leadership by reserving the final decision for himself, even wearing a shirt imprinted with "I'll decide" at one forum (Swanson, 2000, para. 1).

Open-ended comments from survey respondents in this research reiterate the need for an effective decision-making process: "How this is handled is very important. To many at the university and alumni of it the mascot is the single most memorable icon for the university. Whether this should be or not, it almost certainly is."

The diverse nature of university constituents means the task of involving people in a name change process will involve on and off campus groups, including these constituencies identified by one respondent: "Have all key groups, alumni, and others participate in selecting a new mascot." Another respondent said the change was an occasion to overhaul their entire athletic marketing program.

The main reasons we were successful in our change were: (1) we had a very large, representative group that helped us gain buy in; and (2) we packaged it as an entire identity change for our athletics department, not just a new mascot. We developed an entire graphics package for our athletics department (something we'd never had before).

Accept Not All Will Agree

While this research shows that the 27 universities in this study group did not experience downward trends in football game attendance or charitable donations, circumstances unique to each campus may produce different outcomes. What would have happened at the University of North Dakota if the State Board of Higher Education had not complied with a donor's demand that the university keep its athletic identity? Would a $100 million dollar hockey arena have been allowed to decay in the North Dakota winter, as Engelstad threatened? Will $2 million in proposed gifts at Marquette University evaporate because the university will not return to the Warriors identity?

Is offending a single or a few rich donors worth the cost to institutional integrity, as happened at the University of North Dakota when a columnist wrote, "Say this for the University of North Dakota, if it's going to sell its soul, $100 million is a good price to fetch" (Grow, 2001, para. 1). University administrators need to accept that not everyone will agree on decisions about athletic identities, but that as stewards of their institutions, they have a responsibility to make decisions and these decisions will be the mark of their institution's social legitimacy. Said one survey respondent, "Although it was a controversial decision, the university's understanding of the issues involved and its willingness to make a difficult decision so early in the debate over Indian mascots was a defining moment for Stanford."

FINAL THOUGHTS

The emotional and personal nature of the debate over the use of Native American sports identities in collegiate sports makes it more difficult for administrators to determine the best course of action when confronted with challenges to revered sports identities. The loss of support from important constituencies is a serious threat to an institution's ability to achieve its goals. This research attempted to separate subjective versus objective information to aid in decision-making. I cannot prove that the use of Native American identities in collegiate sports is right or wrong, but by looking at what happened at 27 universities that have already made such a change, I have sought to factually address the threatened loss of fan and donor support if a university proposes the elimination of an Indian sports identity.

Using football fan attendance records for five-year periods before and after name changes, I found no generalizable pattern to show a loss of fans. Using donation records for five-year periods before and after name changes, I found no generalizable pattern to show a loss of financial support from donors. Accessing the opinions of senior public relations practitioners at these 27 universities, I found consistent support for the changes and the belief that the change ended their sports name controversies.

If one purpose for scientific inquiry is the establishment of predictability, then this research establishes that universities considering the retirement of their Native American sports identities will predictably enjoy similar patterns of continued fan support. This support may be threatened, though, if institutional change is mandated by outsiders and seen as a threat to in-group identity as a challenge to group norms, rather than internally motivated and an affirmation of group norms. Universities that continue to resist sports identity change may find their biggest failure is that their actions prolong their time of chronic crisis and mire their institutions into prolonged crisis where their social legitimacy is challenged, where their university becomes increasingly isolated from peers, and where divisions require the allocation of time and energy that might otherwise be used in support of the achievement of organizational goals. Further, the barrage of accusations that the university is supporting racism saps institutional dignity and the self-perceived elite status that individuals seek in their group memberships. If the accusations reduce the university's elite status, then the value of being a member of that in-group is, likewise, diminished and so, too, can be the desire to display team bumper stickers, attend alumni events, and write checks in support of the organization.

The NCAA action of August 2005 has given universities an opportunity to revisit their uses of Native American sports identities. Some will choose to resist change through legal or NCAA procedural means. These organizations will delay reaching Fink's stage of crisis resolution as the matter drags on and evolves, opposing sides dig in deeper, and the matter becomes more divisive, pitting institutional constituents against each other and making a final outcome even more difficult to achieve.

But those organizations that have continued Native American sports identities also have another choice; that of using the NCAA's decision as the latest reason to reopen the door to making a change, one that is internally directed and, thus, less threatening than one mandated. The trend is clear: American universities are discontinuing the appropriation of Native American identities. Universities can resist this outcome, as has been done for more than 40 years, or universities can accept the outcome and end a divisive debate that divides rather than unites campuses.

REFERENCES

American Psychological Association. (2005). *APA resolution recommending the immediate retirement of American Indian mascots, symbols, images, and personalities by schools, colleges, universities, athletic teams, and organizations.* Retrieved October 19, 2005, from www.apa.org/releases/ResAmindianMascots.pdf

Atherton, J. S. (2004). *Teaching and learning: Cognitive dissonance and learning.* Retrieved August 2, 2005, from http://www.learningandteaching.info/learning/dissonance

Brownstein, A. (2001, February 23). A battle over a name in the land of the Sioux. *Chronicle of Higher Education.* Retrieved June 17, 2004, from www.chronicle.com

Dennis, T. (2005, October 2). Our opinion: NCAA should hold hearings in North Dakota [Editorial]. *Grand Forks Herald,* p. D1.

Dietz-Uhler, B., & Murrell, A. (1999). Examining fan reactions to game outcomes: A longitudinal study of social identity. *Journal of Sport Behavior, 22*(1), 15–27.

Fears, D. (2005, August 14). Indian mascots: Matter of pride or prejudice? *Washington Post,* p. A3.

Grow, D. (2001, January 17). Money apparently matters in Indian nickname dispute. *Star Tribune.* Retrieved November 14, 2004, from www.startribune.com

Kolpack, J. (2005, August 13). Nickname ban will keep Sioux AD busy. *Forum,* p. 1D.

LaPoint, J. (2004, November 5). The little rink on the prairie in North Dakota. *New York Times.* Retrieved June 2, 2005, from www.nytimes.com

Newbart, D. (2004, August 24). Accreditation body says Chief is embarrassing. *Chicago Sun Times,* p. 6.

Pewewardy, C. D. (2000). Why educators can't ignore Indian mascots. Retrieved January 6, 2005, from www.aistm.org.fr.groups.htm

Pewewardy, C. D. (2001). Educators and mascots: Challenging contradictions. In C. R. King & C. F. Springwood (Eds.), *Team spirits: The Native American mascots controversy* (p. 272). Lincoln: University of Nebraska Press.

Ridgeway, L. (2005, October 8). Tribes bring down a great university [Letter to editor]. *Forum,* p. A17.

Rosner, S. R. (2002). Legal approaches to the use of Native American logos and symbols in sports. *Virginia Sports and Entertainment Law Journal, 1*(2), 97.

Swanson, I. (2000, January 28). Kupchella to form panel to study nickname. *Grand Forks Herald.* Retrieved June 3, 2004, from www.grandforks.com

Tajfel, H., & Turner, J. (1979). An integrative theory of intergroup conflict. In W. G. Austin & S. Worchel (Eds.), *The social psychology of intergroup relations* (pp. 61–76). New York: Academic Press.

Turner, J. C., & Oakes, P. (1986). The significance of the social identity concept for social psychology with reference to individualism, interactionism, and social influence. *British Journal of Social Psychology, 25,* 237–252.

Vorland, D. (2000). *The Fighting Sioux team name and logo at the University of North Dakota.* Grand Forks: University of North Dakota.

Wahlberg, D. C. (2004). Ending the debate: Crisis communication analysis of one university's American Indian athletic identity. *Public Relations Review, 30,* 197–203.

Wann, D. L. (1997). *Sport Psychology.* Upper Saddle River, NJ: Prentice Hall.

Wann, D. L., & Branscombe, N. R. (1993). Sports fans: Measuring degree of identification with the team. *International Journal of Sport Psychology, 24,* 1–17.

Wann, D. L., & Dolan, T. J. (1994). Influence of spectators' identification on evaluation of the past, present, and future performances of a sports team. *Perceptual and Motor Skills, 78,* 547–552.

Wann, D. L., Hunter, J. L., Ryan, J. A., & Wright, L. A. (2001). The relationship between team identification and willingness of sports fans to consider illegally assisting their team. *Social Behavior and Personality, 29*(6), 531–536.

14

Native American Mascots and Alumni Giving

Patrick J. McEwan and Clive R. Belfield

> As long as alumni are opening their wallets because [Chief Illiniwek] dances at football, volleyball and basketball games, the Board of Trustees won't let the Chief go.
>
> —Editorial page of the *Daily Illini*, February 19, 2001

Since the 1960s, at least 42 colleges and universities have eliminated Native American nicknames, symbols, or athletic mascots, ranging from Chief Moccanooga to the Savages. At least 43 others maintain their names, often in the face of costly debates. An alumnus at the University of North Dakota threatened to withhold $100 million if the university abandoned its "Fighting Sioux" name (Brownstein, 2001). At the University of Illinois at Urbana-Champaign, administrators spent more than $300,000 to promote a dialogue about the merits of "Chief Illiniwek," but the controversy persists (Wagner, 2001; Wise, 2003).[1] There are similar controversies at other colleges and universities (a complete list of institutions is provided in table 14.5).[2]

Campus debates often hinge on two issues. The first is whether Native American nicknames damage the educational experience of Native American students, an opinion expressed by a range of organizations, including the U.S. Commission on Civil Rights.[3] The second is the revenue impact of changing a school's nickname or symbol. The conventional wisdom is that donations will fall dramatically, particularly from alumni, although the anecdotal evidence disagrees on this point (Connolly, 2000; Spindel, 2000). The second issue—the topic of this paper—can be viewed a peculiar facet of a larger question: What are the determinants of former students' charitable giving to their alma maters?

127

Previous research has found links between alumni giving and numerous personal and institutional characteristics.[4] These include individual income (Clotfelter, 2003; Okunade & Berl, 1997); past fraternity membership (Harrison, Mitchell, & Peterson, 1995); and overall academic quality (Baade & Sunderberg, 1996; Leslie & Ramey, 1988).[5] A recent study, using student-level data from multiple institutions, found that self-reported measures of satisfaction with past educational experiences are especially important determinants of donation (Clotfelter, 2003). It is plausible that memories of school nicknames and symbols are entwined with warm opinions of previous educational and social experiences. (In fairness, there are students—perhaps Native American—for whom exactly the opposite is true.) Students would then interpret a nickname's removal as a signal that the same experience is no longer being provided.

The net effect on alumni giving is an empirical question. It is challenging to answer because one must identify a counterfactual estimate for how schools' alumni donations would have evolved if they had not dropped a nickname or athletic symbol. In this paper, we address the challenge by compiling up to 32 years of data on alumni donations in 83 colleges and universities with Native American nicknames. In the period covered by our data, 34 schools dropped a nickname. We identify the effect on donations by comparing the change in donations in those schools to changes in schools that did not drop a nickname, using a two-way fixed effects model. A variety of additional empirical specifications probe the robustness of the results.

In general, the results suggest that dropping a Native American nickname leads to declines in the percentage of alumni who donate, particularly among bachelor's institutions. However, there is little effect on total donations, and it appears that the size of the average donation—among alumni who donate—may rise slightly. Although difficult to corroborate without micro data, a plausible interpretation is that alumni who stop giving are among the smallest donors to begin with—perhaps drawn from younger cohorts. The pattern of results is also consistent with the notion that some increased their donations to compensate for non-givers. Overall, the results suggest that revenue impacts will be minimal, and that schools might fruitfully center their debates on the educational impact of Native American nicknames.

DATA

Table 14.5 identifies 85 colleges or universities with Native American team names or mascots, focusing upon accredited institutions that offer four-year degrees or higher. Since there is no definitive list of such institutions, it was constructed by referencing a number of sources (a full list of sources is available from the authors). We first consulted general accounts of the controversy (e.g., Spindel, 2000) and web pages that compile lists of college team names.[6] We verified this information by consulting schools' web pages. In cases in which nicknames or symbols were changed, we located press releases to verify the date. When such information was unavailable or conflicting, we contacted schools' athletic or public relations offices.

In this paper, the elimination of a Native American nickname or symbol is defined as the treatment. Overall, 42 institutions have been treated since the late 1960s, though at an accelerating pace. In the first two decades of the sample, 13 schools had dropped nicknames; in the 1990s, the number increased to 21. As Table 14.1 indicates, the institutions in our sample grant a range of degrees (bachelor's, master's, and doctoral) and are both privately and publicly managed. In several cases, noted in table 14.5, schools dropped the use of a logo or other imagery but maintained a Native American nickname. Later results will explore the sensitivity of results to the exclusion of such "weakly treated" schools.

For each of the previous schools, we extracted data on annual alumni donations between 1969 and 2000 from the Voluntary Support of Education (VSE) survey, conducted by the Council for Aid to Education. The empirical analyses will focus upon three dependent variables: (1) the percent of alumni who donate in a given year (*Alumnipercent*); (2) the total amount of alumni donations (*Alumnitotal*), adjusted to 2000 prices with the Consumer Price Index; and (3) the average donation among those who donated, also in 2000

Table 14.1.   Schools with Native American Team Names, by Type

	Never Dropped	Ever Dropped	Total
Doctoral			
Public	9	6	15
Private	0	5	5
Masters			
Public	13	9	22
Private	5	9	14
Bachelors			
Public	1	2	3
Private	15	11	26
Total	43	42	85

prices (*Alumniavg*). The VSE data further report the bachelor's, master's, or doctoral status of each institution, as well as its public or private status. Each institution's official affiliation to a religious denomination was constructed by consulting school web pages. Finally, we extracted each institution's self-reported expenditures and endowment from the VSE data.

Overall, 83 of the institutions in table 14.5 had at least one observation in the VSE data between 1969 and 2000.[7] The average school reports data in 22 of 32 years. Using table 14.5, we constructed a dummy variable (*Dropname*), equal to one in the first full year after the name or symbol was dropped, and in all years thereafter.[8] It is equal to zero in previous years, and in all years for untreated schools.

Table 14.2 reports the sample descriptive statistics. On average, just over 20% of alumni make a donation. The means of the monetary donation variables appear skewed by several doctoral universities, notably Stanford University. Upon dividing the sample by the type of institution, one notes that bachelor's institutions report a higher percentage of alumni donors than doctoral institutions, although the average size of each donation is somewhat lower than doctoral universities. Overall, 44% of the observations correspond to schools that ever dropped a nickname between 1969 and 2000 (*Everdropname*), while 16% correspond to treated observations (*Dropname*).

Table 14.2.　Descriptive Statistics

	Full sample				*Doctoral*	*Masters*	*Bachelors*
	Mean (S.D.)	*Min.*	*Max.*	*N*	*Mean (S.D.)*	*Mean S.D.)*	*Means (S.D.)*
Alumnipercent	20.03 (13.34)	0.00	100.00	1657	17.85 (13.30)	14.76 (10.61)	25.97 (13.18)
Alumnitotal*	3.75 (12.80)	0.00	209.90	1793	11.95 (23.46)	0.64 (0.89)	1.28 (2.17)
Alumniavg	436.05 (697.91)	0.00	19533.71	1680	663.71 (1196.51)	251.03 (308.44)	455.04 (422.67)
Dropname	0.16	0.00	1.00	1793	0.34	0.13	0.08
Everdropname	0.44	0.00	1.00	1793	0.64	0.42	0.32
Doctoral	0.25	0.00	1.00	1793	1.00	0.00	0.00
Masters	0.36	0.00	1.00	1793	0.00	1.00	0.00
Bachelors	0.39	0.00	1.00	1793	0.00	0.00	1.00
Private	0.64	0.00	1.00	1793	0.34	0.51	0.96
Religious	0.46	0.00	1.00	1793	0.19	0.35	0.74
Expenditures*	93.85 (173.35)	1.32	2074.06	1718	288.98 (257.23)	41.58 (33.61)	16.46 (11.89)
Endowment*	96.06 (443.95)	0.00	8886.00	1710	322.77 (842.06)	11.82 (19.07)	26.34 (42.80)

Note: Variable is divided by 1,000,000.

EMPIRICAL APPROACH

The principal goal is to estimate the impact of dropping a Native American name or symbol on measures of alumni donations. The basic specification for doing so is a two-way fixed effects model of the following form (in this case, using *Alumnipercent* as the dependent variable):

$$Alumnipercent_{it} = \delta \, Dropname_{it} + \mu_t + \alpha_i + \varepsilon_{it} \qquad (1)$$

where school i's value of *Alumnipercent* at time t is a function of *Dropname*. The μ_t and α_i are year-specific and school-specific fixed effects, respectively, while α_i is an idiosyncratic error term. We will first estimate least-squares regressions with the dependent variable in its original units, and then its natural log.

The coefficient of interest is δ, the estimated impact of dropping a name. In Equation (1), δ is identified by comparing changes in donations between treated and untreated schools. Its causal interpretation rests upon the assumption that changes in untreated schools provide a counterfactual estimate of how treated schools would have fared in the absence of the treatment. This is not the case if unobserved factors within schools affect the likelihood of dropping a mascot in addition to alumni donations (i.e., $coc(Dropname_{it}, \varepsilon_{it}) \neq 0$). ". For example, it is possible that a "progressive" administrator is more inclined to drop a Native American name and also more likely to work hard at fund-raising. To address possibilities such as this, we will also report estimates from specifications that further include linear time-trends for each institution, as well as time-varying variables that might affect the willingness of alumni to donate (such as schools' current endowments and expenditures). We will also estimate models in a range of subsamples to probe the robustness of the results.

RESULTS

Main Results

Figure 14.1 provides some preliminary evidence, by graphing the mean of each dependent variable across time. Separate means are calculated for "ever-treated" schools (solid lines) and "never-treated" schools (dashed lines). In the absence of any treatment effect, one would expect the two lines to move roughly parallel to one another. In the presence of an effect, one would expect that any distance between higher (treated) and lower (untreated) groups would close, especially in the 1990s when most nicknames were dropped.

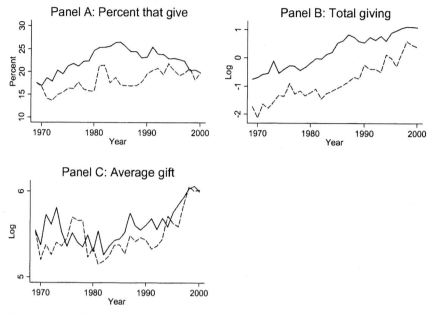

Figure 14.1. Alumni giving in schools with Native American team names. *Note:* **Solid lines include schools that have ever dropped a team name or mascot; dashed lines include schools have never dropped one. The** *y* **axis of Panels B, C, and D graph the mean log of each monetary value, in 2000 prices.**

That pattern is evident in panel A, the percentage of alumni who donated. In early decades there is a gap of 5 percentage points which closes substantially, particularly after the mid-1990s. There is no obvious pattern in panels B and C, in which means in each year are taken over the natural log of each variable.

Table 14.3 reports a series of regression estimates for each dependent variable. Each cell reports a regression coefficient (and its standard error) that correspond to the three dependent variables and several alternate specifications. Let us first consider the results for *Alumnipercent*. Column (1) reports estimates of Equation (1) that include school-specific and year-specific fixed effects. The coefficient implies that dropping a name lowers the percentage of alumni who give by 1.2 percentage points. Further controlling for school-specific time trends yields a more substantial effect of 3 percentage points. The addition of other controls does not alter the fundamental conclusion, although the number of observations is reduced due to missing data.

The same specifications are repeated in columns (4)–(6) using the natural log of the *Alumnipercent*.[9] All coefficient estimates are negative. The magnitude is only appreciable (and significant at 10%) upon controlling for school-specific trends. It suggests that dropping a name leads to a decline of

Table 14.3. Effects of Dropping Native American Team Names on Alumni Giving

	Linear Dependent Variable			Log Dependent Variable		
	(1)	(2)	(3)	(4)	(5)	(6)
Alumnipercent	-1.24*	-3.00***	-3.97***	-0.01	-0.10*	-0.16***
	(0.67)	(0.71)	(0.79)	(0.06)	(0.06)	(0.05)
N	1655	1657	1484		1780	1582
R^2	0.73	0.80	0.81	0.68	0.78	0.80
Alumnitotal	-1.39	-3.02***	-3.61***	-0.07	0.02	0.01
	(0.96)	(0.94)	(1.06)	(0.08)	(0.08)	(0.08)
N	1793	1793	1588	1780	1780	1582
R^2	0.72	0.90	0.90	0.87	0.90	0.90
Alumniavg	-107.34*	-119.78*	-84.01	-0.02	0.10	0.14*
	(61.89)	(70.37)	(67.58)	(0.06)	(0.08)	(0.08)
N	1680	1680	1502	1674	1674	1498
R^2	0.34	0.39	0.42	0.67	0.72	0.74
Year fixed effects?	Y	Y	Y	Y	Y	Y
School fixed effects?	Y	Y	Y	Y	Y	Y
School time trends?	N	Y	Y	N	Y	Y
Additional controls?	N	N	Y	N	N	Y

Notes: Each cell reports a coefficient from a separate regression. *** indicates statistical significance at 1%; ** at 5%; and * at 10%. Robust standard errors are in parentheses. Additional controls include the log of a school's expenditures and the log of its endowment.

approximately 10% in the percentage of alumni who donate (given a sample mean of 20, this implies an effect of 2 percentage points), which is consistent with previous estimates. As before, the effect becomes even larger and more statistically significant upon controlling for endowment and expenditures.

The results for *Alumnitotal* are less robust. The linear specifications in columns (1)–(3), especially those controlling for time trends, imply that total donations decline substantially, by more than $3 million, an implausibly large magnitude given the small size of alumni donations in the non-doctoral institutions in the sample. These estimates are subject to particular influence by institutions with changes that are large in absolute terms (even if they are small relative to an institution's initial donations). Expressing the variables as natural logs diminishes the influence of such observations. Indeed, none of the estimates in columns (2)–(6) are statistically distinguishable from zero.

The final estimates pertain to the average donation among alumni who donated (*alumniavg*). Focusing on columns (4)–(6), the coefficient estimates from semi-log regressions provide weak evidence that the average donation might increase, with estimate implying gains of some 10%. However, only the estimate in column (6) is statistically significant, and marginally so.

Thus far, the results tell a more nuanced story than a uniformly negative response by alumni. On average, it appears that proportionally fewer alumni make a donation, with little impact on total donations. One hypothesis, consistent with this evidence, is that younger cohorts of alumni in each school withheld relatively small donations. These cohorts have the lowest incomes among alumni, and prior research with micro data has suggested that income is an important determinant of giving behavior (e.g., Clotfelter, 2003). The average donation among alumni givers could even rise—as our estimates weakly imply—if "small-givers" withhold their support or if alumni with divergent preferences increase the size of their donations. In the absence of micro data on each institution's potential donors, these hypotheses cannot be tested further.

One might suspect that some institutions dropped a nickname because they had little reason to expect an alumni giving response (and, conversely, that some institutions have yet to drop a nickname because they anticipate a dramatic drop). One implication is that the previously estimated treatment effects cannot be generalized to institutions that have yet to drop a nickname. If this were true, then one might expect to find a diminished amount of controversy among the "ever-dropped" institutions in our sample. The anecdotal evidence on this point seems to indicate the opposite. At Eastern Michigan University, for example, there was a "vociferous and persistent opposition" to the elimination of the Huron nickname (Connolly, 2000, p. 528). It is still evident among groups of alumni.[10] Similar patterns are evident at other institutions, including Syracuse University, Springfield College, and St. Johns University.[11]

Robustness Checks

Table 14.4 explores the robustness of the previous results by re-estimating regressions within various subsamples. It applies the semi-log specification that controls for year-specific and school-specific fixed effects, in addition to school-specific time trends. First, we exclude from the sample five schools

Table 14.4.   Additional Estimates

	Dependent Variable (Log)		
	Alumnipercent	*Alumnitotal*	*Alumniavg*
	(−1516.24***)	(≥1214.34)	(<1432.34)
Drop weakly treated schools	−0.11**	0.03	0.13
	(0.05)	(0.08)	(0.08)
N	1516	1635	1532
Drop sporadically observed schools	−0.17***	≥0.01	0.08
	(0.05)	(0.08)	(0.07)
N	1162	1214	1173
Doctoral	0.03	0.02	0.02
	(0.11)	(0.12)	(0.14)
N	410	451	419
Master's	0.03	0.12	0.25*
	(0.13)	(0.15)	(0.13)
N	579	628	582
Bachelor's	−0.24***	<0.01	0.09
	(0.06)	(0.13)	(0.13)
N	666	701	673
Public	−0.05	0.10	0.22
	(0.14)	(0.16)	(0.18)
N	574	632	580
Private	−0.10**	−0.05	<0.01
	(0.04)	(0.08)	(0.08)
N	1081	1148	1094
Religious	−0.16***	−0.05	0.05
	(0.06)	(0.11)	(0.10)
N	773	826	781
Year fixed effects?	Y	Y	Y
School fixed effects?	Y	Y	Y
School time trends?	Y	Y	Y

Note: "Weakly treated" schools are schools that eliminated Native American imagery such as a logo, but preserved its team name (see the Appendix). Sporadically observed schools are those with less than 25 observations.

that are "weakly treated" by virtue of only dropping a logo or other imagery but preserving a Native American nickname (see table 14.5 for details). The coefficient on *Alumnipercent* is now estimated more precisely than in the corresponding full-sample specification. The other coefficients are still statistically insignificant (although the coefficient on *Alumniavg* is slightly larger than its comparable full-sample estimate, and substantial in magnitude).

Second, we limit the subsample to schools that are observed for at least 25 years of the panel, reducing the sample by more than 500 observations. However, the general pattern of results is the same.

Third, we report estimates in subsamples of doctoral, master's, bachelor's, public, private, and religiously affiliated institutions. The most striking outcome of these estimates is that the negative effect on *Alumnipercent* appears to be driven by the subsample of bachelor's institutions. The coefficient implies a decline of approximately 24% in the percentage of alumni who donate. Less pronounced but statistically significant effects are also found among the religious and private subsamples (although these include a majority of bachelor's institutions). There is no effect among doctoral and master's institutions.

There are various explanations. First, it is possible that undergraduate alumni are generally more inclined than graduate alumni to form strong opinions about the merits of a nickname or symbol, perhaps because they attend more athletic events. Thus, they are more likely to respond to its elimination. One would then anticipate stronger effects in institutions that do not grant higher degrees. In such a case, one might further expect to find diminished, but still non-zero effects among master's and doctoral institutions that also have significant undergraduate enrollments. However, this is not the case.

Second, it is possible that the effect is pronounced among undergraduates that happen to study in four-year liberal arts institutions. Prior research with micro data suggests that such students are more likely than university graduates to donate (Clotfelter, 2003; Cunningham & Cochi-Ficano, 2002). If liberal arts graduates feel a greater bond to their institution—and are already more inclined to donate—then they may also respond more vigorously to a disliked policy change.

CONCLUSIONS

This paper has provided empirical evidence on the response of alumni givers to the elimination of Native American team names. The estimates were based upon fixed-effects models estimated in panel data spanning 32 years, in which 34 of 83 colleges and universities were observed to drop a nickname. In the full sample, the results suggest that the percentage of alumni who donate is indeed affected, dropping by around 2 percentage points. However, the

Table 14.5. Schools with Native American Team Names

School	State	Type	Sector	Name or Mascot	Year Dropped
Adams State College	CO	M	Public	Indians	1996
Alcorn State University	MS	M	Public	Braves	—
Arkansas State University	AR	M	Public	Indians	—
Bradley University	IL	M	Private	Braves*	1993
California State University, Stanislaus	CA	M	Public	Warriors	—
Carthage College	WI	M	Private	Redmen	—
Catawba College	NC	B	Private	Indians	—
Central Michigan University	MI	D	Public	Chippewas*	1989
Chowan College	NC	B	Private	Braves	—
Colgate University	NY	B	Private	Red Raiders	2001
College of William and Mary	VA	D	Public	Tribe	—
Cumberland College	KY	M	Private	Indians	2001
Dartmouth College	NH	D	Private	Indians	1969
Dickinson State University	ND	B	Public	Savages	1972
East Stroudsburg University	PA	M	Public	Warriors	—
Eastern Connecticut State University	CT	M	Public	Warriors	—
Eastern Michigan University	MI	M	Public	Huron	1991
Eastern Washington University	WA	M	Public	Savages	1972
Florida State University	FL	D	Public	Seminoles	—
Hartwick College	NY	B	Private	Warriors	1994
Hendrix College	AR	B	Private	Warriors*	2000
Husson College	ME	M	Private	Braves	—
Indiana University of Pennsylvania	PA	D	Public	Indians*	1991
Juniata College	PA	B	Private	Indians	1991
Keuka College	NY	B	Private	Warriors	2001
Knox College	IL	B	Private	Siwash	—
Lewis-Clark State College	ID	B	Public	Warriors	1993
Lycoming College	PA	B	Private	Warriors	—

(continued)

Table 14.5. *(continued)*

School	State	Type	Sector	Name or Mascot[†]	Year Dropped
Marquette University	WI	D	Private	Warriors[†]	1993
Martin Methodist College	TN	B	Private	Indians	2002
Massachusetts College of Liberal Arts	MA	B	Public	Mohawks	2002
McMurry University	TX	B	Private	Indians	—
Merrimack College	MA	B	Private	Warriors	—
Miami University	OH	D	Public	Redskins	1996
Midland Lutheran College	NE	B	Private	Warriors	—
Midwestern State University	TX	M	Public	Indians	—
Minnesota State University, Mankato	MN	M	Public	Indians	1977
Mississippi College	MS	M	Private	Choctaws	—
Montclair State University	NJ	M	Public	Indians	1990
Morningside College	IA	B	Private	Chiefs	1997
Newberry College	SC	B	Private	Indians	—
Northeastern State University	OK	M	Public	Redmen	—
Northwestern College	IA	B	Private	Red Raiders	—
Oklahoma City University	OK	M	Private	Chiefs	1999
Ottawa University	KS	B	Private	Braves	—
Quinnipiac University	CT	M	Private	Braves	2001
Ripon College	WI	B	Private	Red Men	1991
San Diego State University	CA	D	Public	Aztecs	—
Seattle University	WA	M	Private	Chieftans	2000
Shippensburg University	PA	M	Public	Red Raiders*	1993
Siena College	NY	B	Private	Indians	1988
Simpson College	IA	B	Private	Redmen	1992
Southeast Missouri State	MO	M	Public	Indians	—
Southeastern Oklahoma State	OK	M	Public	Savages	—
Southern Nazarene University	OK	M	Private	Redskins	1998
Southern Oregon University	OR	M	Public	Red Raiders	1980
Southern Wesleyan University	SC	M	Private	Warriors	—
Southwestern College	KS	B	Private	Moundbuilders	—

Institution	State		Type	Mascot	Year
Springfield College	MA	M	Private	Chiefs	1995
St. Bonaventure University	NY	M	Private	Brown Indians, Brown Squaws	1992
St. Johns University	NY	D	Private	Redmen	1994
St. Mary's University of Minnesota	MN	M	Private	Red Men	1988
Stanford University	CA	D	Private	Indians, Prince Lightfoot	1972
State University of West Georgia	GA	M	Public	Braves	—
Sterling College	KS	B	Private	Warriors	—
Stonehill College	MA	B	Private	Chieftains	—
Syracuse University	NY	D	Private	Saltine Warrior	1978
Texas Tech University	TX	D	Public	Red Raiders	—
Union College	NE	B	Private	Warriors	—
University of Alaska, Fairbanks	AK	D	Public	Nanooks	—
University of Illinois, Urbana-Champaign	IL	D	Public	Illini	—
University of Louisiana, Monroe	LA	M	Public	Indians	—
University of Massachusetts, Amherst	MA	D	Public	Redmen	1972
University of Massachusetts, Lowell	MA	D	Public	Chiefs	1994
University of North Carolina, Pembroke	NC	M	Public	Braves	—
University of North Dakota	ND	D	Public	Sioux	—
University of Oklahoma	OK	D	Public	Little Red	1970
University of Rio Grande	OH	M	Private	Redmen	—
University of Tennessee at Chattanooga	TN	M	Public	Chief Moccanooga	1996
University of Utah	UT	D	Public	Utes	—
University of Wisconsin, La Crosse	WI	M	Public	Indians	1989
Wayne State University	MN	D	Public	Warriors	—
Western Baptist College	OR	B	Private	Warriors	—
Westmont College	CA	B	Private	Warriors	—
Winona State University	MN	M	Public	Warriors	—

Note: * indicates that a college or university dropped a logo or other Native American imagery, but kept its name. † Marquette University dropped its "Willie Wompum" mascot in 1971 and its "First Warrior" mascot in 1987. For a full list of sources, contact the authors.

effect is driven by the sample of bachelor's institutions. In contrast, there is no strong evidence that total alumni donations are affected, and there is weak evidence that the average donation (among alumni who donate) rises slightly.

One plausible interpretation of these results is that alumni who stopped giving were among the smallest donors, perhaps younger cohorts with relatively smaller incomes. Additional student-level data would be necessary to explore this hypothesis. If it is true, however, it suggests that vocal opposition—especially among currently enrolled students or young alumni—should not be considered the bellwether of overall alumni giving.[12] In the absence of strong revenue concerns, schools are better off focusing debates on the educational effects of using Native American names and symbols.

NOTES

We are grateful to the Council for Aid to Education for providing data. The University of Illinois at Urbana-Champaign provided financial support to the first author. These institutions are not responsible for any errors or conclusions.

1. The role of Chief Illiniwek is assumed by a student who dresses in a buckskin costume and performs dance routines at university athletic events (Spindel, 2000). The results of the university-sponsored dialogue are available at http://www.uiuc.edu/dialogue/

2. For general accounts, see Connolly (2000), King and Springwood (2001), and Spindel (2000).

3. The U.S. Commission on Civil Rights (2001) declared that "the use of stereotypical images of Native Americans by educational institutions has the potential to create a racially hostile educational environment that may be intimidating to Indian students." Other organizations include the National Education Association, the National Association for the Advancement of Colored People, and the NCAA Minorities and Interests Committee.

4. For recent reviews of this literature, see Clotfelter (2003) and Cunningham and Cochi-Ficano (2002).

5. A small literature examines whether schools' athletic success is a determinant of alumni giving, but the results are mixed (e.g., Rhoads & Gerking, 2000; Turner, Meserve, & Bowen, 2001).

6. In particular, see http://www.smargon.net/nicknames/

7. The excluded schools are Southern Wesleyan University and the University of North Carolina, Pembroke.

8. The VSE data are reported in each July–June fiscal year (e.g., 1999–2000, coded as a year 2000 observation). If a school drops its mascot in the 2000 calendar year, we code *Dropname* = 0 for VSE observation in 2000, given the possibility that the

treatment occurred after the end of the fiscal year. In all later years, we code *Drop-name* = 1.

9. The semi-log regressions exclude a small number of observations with zero values for the dependent variable. We re-estimated these regressions using an alternative transformation of $\log(x+1)$, where x is the value of the dependent variable, and it did not alter the pattern of results.

10. See, for example, http://www.huronalumni.org/DesktopDefault.aspx

11. At Syracuse, alumni continued to call for the restoration of the "Saltine Warrior," well after its elimination (Fisher, 2001). At Springfield College, a "Keep-the-Chiefs" committee lobbied for the return to a Native American nickname (Davis & Rau, 2001). The athletic fans of St. John's University still maintain a popular website called http://www.redmen.com/

12. A possible caveat is that disaffected cohorts of younger alumni could begin to restrict larger gifts as they age and their incomes rise.

REFERENCES

Baade, R. A., & Sundberg, J. O. (1996). What determines alumni generosity? *Economics of Education Review, 15,* 75–81.

Brownstein, A. (2001, February 23). A battle over a name in the land of the Sioux. *Chronicle of Higher Education.*

Clotfelter, C. T. (2003). Alumni giving to elite private colleges and universities. *Economics of Education Review, 22,* 109–120.

Connolly, M. R. (2000). What's in a name? A historical look at Native American-related nicknames and symbols at three U.S. universities. *Journal of Higher Education, 71,* 515–548.

Cunningham, B. M., & Cochi-Ficano, C. K. (2002). The determinants of donative revenue flows from alumni of higher education. *Journal of Human Resources, 37,* 540–569.

Davis, L. R., & Rau, M. (2001). Escaping the tyranny of the majority: A case study of mascot change. In C. R. King & C. F. Springwood (Eds.), *Team spirits: The Native American mascots controversy.* Lincoln: University of Nebraska Press.

Fisher, D. M. (2001). Chief Bill Orange and the Saltine Warrior: A cultural history of Indian symbols and imagery at Syracuse University. In C. R. King & C. F. Springwood (Eds.), *Team spirits: The Native American mascots controversy.* Lincoln: University of Nebraska Press.

Harrison, W. B., Mitchell, S. K., & Peterson, S. P. (1995). Alumni donations and college's development expenditures: Does spending matter? *American Journal of Economics and Sociology, 54,* 397–412.

King, C. R., & Springwood, C. F. (Eds.). (2001). *Team spirits: The Native American mascots controversy.* Lincoln: University of Nebraska Press.

Leslie, L. L., & Ramey, G. (1988). Donor behavior and voluntary support for higher education institutions. *Journal of Higher Education, 59,* 115–132.

Okunade, A. A., & Berl, R. L. (1997). Determinants of charitable giving of business school alumni. *Research in Higher Education, 38,* 201–214.

Rhoads, T. A., & Gerking, S. (2000). Educational contributions, academic quality, and athletic success. *Contemporary Economic Policy, 18,* 248–258.

Spindel, C. (2000). *Dancing at half-time: Sports and the controversy over American Indian mascots.* New York: New York University Press.

Turner, S. E., Meserve, L. A., & Bowen, W. G. (2001). Winning and giving: Football results and alumni giving. *Social Science Quarterly, 82,* 812–826.

United States Commission on Civil Rights. (2001). *Statement of U.S. Commission on Civil Rights on the use of Native American images and nicknames as sports symbols.* Retrieved March 17, 2004, from http://www.usccr.gov/press/archives/2001/041601st.htm

Wagner, N. (2001, January 19). UI incurs high cost with Chief dialogue. *Daily Illini.*

Wise, M. (2003, December 16). The squabbling Illini: Rallying cries lead to rift. *New York Times.*

Part III

REFORM AND RESISTANCE

Efforts to change names, logos, and imagery almost invariably foster a backlash: Reform breeds resistance. The reasons for this are many and complex, ranging from tradition, attachment, and a misguided notion that such practices honor American Indians to racism, white privilege, and a lack of empathy. Whatever the origins, students, alumni, and boosters routinely oppose change, finding powerful and perverse ways to endeavor to retain "their" Indian. The essays in this section work through the efforts to change Native American mascots and the push back that frequently emerges in response. C. Richard King details the strategies deployed by institutions to protect their traditions despite criticism of them. Then, Bruce Johansen documents efforts of an intramural basketball team to call attention to the problems posed by American Indian mascots and the centrality of white privilege by naming their team the Fighting Whites. Next, Suzan Shown Harjo critiques attempts to protect imagined Indians while ignoring embodied Native Americans. Against this background, Dave Zirin unpacks the resurrection of Chief Illiniwek after the University of Illinois, in response to changing NCAA policies, retired him. Finally, an editorial from *The Daily Cardinal* challenges the legitimacy of seeking tribal endorsement for imperiled mascots.

15

Defensive Dialogues: Native American Mascots, Anti-Indianism, and Educational Institutions

C. Richard King

Over 30 years after Native Americans began openly challenging the presence of disparaging names, logos, and images in athletics, such uses of Indianness remain central to sports spectacles in the United States. The prevalence of Native American mascots offers clear evidence of the persistence of anti-Indian sentiments in American culture. While activists have worked tirelessly to alert a broader public to this fundamental truth, academics have more recently supported their assertions with solid scholarship into the origins and implications of mascots (Banks, 1993; Churchill, 1994; Connolly, 2000; Coombe, 1999; Davis, 1993; King, 1998; King & Springwood, 2000, 2001a, 2001b; Nuessel, 1994; Pewewardy, 1991; Slowikowski, 1993; Spindel, 2000; Springwood & King, 2000; Staurowsky, 1998; Vanderford, 1996). To date, both political and intellectual accounts have largely focused on the symbols themselves and the arguments advanced in defense of them. That is, much attention has been devoted to unraveling the manner in which mascots depict Native Americans, the ways in which they appropriate aspects of indigenous cultures (e.g., dance and the headdress), the stereotypes embedded in such team names and sports icons, their connections with historic patterns of playing Indian and constructing Indianness, the misguided motivations for preserving them, and the racist ideologies informing both the creation and the defense of mascots.

The tactics employed by supporters and their implications for the place of Native Americans in American society have often been overlooked in these discussions. To fully appreciate the scope and significance of anti-Indianism in contemporary United States, it is necessary to get beyond stereotypes and engage institutional practices and strategies that, at their core, are anti-Indian because of the manner in which they conceive of and affect Native Americans. That is, they disregard the lives and voices of Indians, consciously and callously work against their interests, and by design undermine the possibility of equality, dignity, and humanity for Native Americans.

This article explores the rhetoric and tactics deployed in support of Native American mascots at educational institutions through a reading of official arguments and sanctioned strategies designed to save imaginary Indians, often at the expense of the agency and humanity of embodied Native Americans. It also explores the unofficial ways that boosters and fans have sought to retain control over Indianness and its meaning. In conclusion, the article addresses some of the ways that audiences can critically engage mascots and counter anti-Indianism.

ANTI-INDIANISM

In 1999, residents of Anderson Township, a suburb of Cincinnati, wrestled with the uses of Indian imagery at the local high school, particularly the name given its sports teams, the Redskins. Although the name is disparaging, countless citizens defended the name as honorific, along with associated symbols of Indianness around campus, including a large statue of a warrior. A teacher of history at Anderson High School offered the following disturbing comments:

> Your people came here a few generations before from Asia. You are no more native than I am. You just got here first. . . . Mr. Jones, I saw the videotape from the first meeting, I'd like to just offer this: maybe it's time we both looked at our own houses. But I'll make this deal to most tribes in America [*sic*] live under the same laws I do: no more reservations, no more tribal law and tribal courts, no more gambling on reservations, no more dressing up tall blondes in little Indian suits to be waitress' at those gambling casinos; no smoking dope at your religious ceremonies . . . no more killing whales or pillaging the salmon waters of the Northwest just because an old treaty says so. We both have a lot of things to fix. And I'll tell you what, I guarantee you I'll still teach good things. <http://www.geocities.com/CapitolHill/1364/nmascots.htm>

Uninformed at best, these ramblings underscore the rhetoric and ideologies grounding both the use of Native Americans as mascots and more recent efforts to retain them. They cast Native Americans as wild deviants, shiftless drug users who enjoy special privileges at the expense of European-Americans, and reckless "others" who ravage nature while exploiting white women. Ignoring the history and effects of American imperialism, they question historical covenants between sovereign nations, seeking to terminate rights and obligations guaranteed within them.

Although more involved and overt than most arguments, these comments clearly express the tone and contours of anti-Indianism shaping struggles over Native American mascots. According to Cook-Lynn (2001), anti-Indianism has four key elements:

> [I]t is the sentiment that results in the unnatural death of Indians. Anti-Indianism is that which treats Indians and their tribes as if they do not exist. . . . Second, Anti-Indianism is that which denigrates, demonizes, and insults being Indian in America. The third trait of Anti-Indianism is the use of historical event and experience to place the blame on Indians for an unfortunate and dissatisfying history. And, finally, Anti-Indianism is that which exploits and distorts Indian beliefs and cultures. All of these traits have conspired to isolate, to expunge or expel, to menace, to defame. (p. xx)

Mascots clearly embody all of these elements. So too do the practices and arguments employed by educational institutions to defend such symbols and spectacles of Indianness.

ORIGINS AND INTENTIONS

Native American mascots emerged in the late 19th and early 20th century in conjunction with the rise of intercollegiate and professional athletics, a crisis in white masculinity that was itself associated with the closing of the frontier, urbanization, industrialization, and the subjugation of Native America (Churchill, 1994; Drinnon, 1980). Playing Indian at halftime of football games has become a ubiquitous feature of American culture precisely because of the pleasures, possibilities, and powers it has granted its European-American performers. At the end of the 20th century, more than 2,500 elementary, secondary, and postsecondary schools had Native American mascots (Staurowsky, 1999), including more than 80 colleges and universities (Rodriguez, 1998).

Native American mascots draw on clichéd images of Native Americans that are rooted in the imperial imagination. They play up or play off a set of cultural features that are often wrongly associated with the indigenous peoples of North America: the feathered headdress; face paint; buckskin paints; warfare; dance; and the tomahawk (chop). They make use of these elements to create moving, meaningful, and entertaining icons that many take to be authentic, appropriate, and even reverent. The condensed versions of Indianness rendered through signs and spectacles confine Native Americans within the past and typically within the popular image of the

Plains warrior. Whatever the precise image or reference (real or imagined), mascots trap Native nations within the many overlapping tropes of savagery. At one extreme are romantic renditions of bellicose warriors, including the University of Illinois (Chief Illiniwek and the Fighting Illini), Florida State University (the Seminoles with "their" Chief Osceola), and the University of North Dakota (Fighting Sioux). At the other extreme are perverse burlesque parodies of the physical or cultural features of Indians such as Runnin' Joe at Arkansas State University (Landreth, 2001) or Willie Wampum at Marquette University (King, 2001).

Native American mascots derive from a long tradition of playing Indian (Deloria, 1998; Green 1988; Huhndorf, 1997; Mechling, 1980). European-Americans have always fashioned individual and collective identities by masquerading as Indians. Native American mascots are an extension of a long tradition dating back at least to the Boston Tea Party and continuing today in many manifestations of popular culture: youth groups such as the YMCA Indian princesses and the Boy Scouts; the Grateful Dead; and the ongoing appropriation of indigenous spirituality, dubbed "white shamanism." Native American mascots are meaningful only in the context of American imperialism, where European-Americans not only controlled and remade Native America but also felt nostalgic for that which they had destroyed. Thus, European-Americans banned Indian dance and traditions while also appropriating them as essential elements of their athletic events (Springwood & King, 2000). Moreover, with the rise of public culture, the production of Indianness in spectacles, exhibitions, and other sundry entertainments proliferated, offering templates for elaborations in sporting contexts (Moses, 1996). Because of comments by fans or sportswriters, historic relationships between an institution and indigenous peoples, and regional associations, Native American mascots crystallized as institutionalized icons, encrusted with memories, tradition, boosterism, administrative investment, financial rewards, and collective identity.

Native American mascots have become increasingly embroiled in controversy (King & Springwood, 2001b; Spindel, 2000). Individuals and organizations—from high school students and teachers to the American Indian Movement and the National Congress of American Indians—have passionately and aggressively contested mascots, forcing public debates and policy changes. A handful of institutions (e.g., University of Utah) have revised their use of imagery, while many others, including St. John's University and the University of Miami, have retired their mascots. At the same time, many school boards—for example, the Minnesota Board of Education and the Los Angeles School District—have opted to require that schools change them. Moreover, religious organizations and professional societies—including the Unitarian

Universalist Association of Congregations, the National Education Association, the United Church of Christ, the Modern Language Association, the United Methodist Church, and the American Anthropological Association—have condemned the continued use of Indian icons in education and athletics.

Indeed, the federal government has recently begun to play a more active role in the unfolding struggles over mascots. In April 2001, the United States Commission on Civil Rights issued a strongly worded statement opposing the continued use of Indian names, images, and logos. Two years earlier, the Trademark Trial and Appeal Board invalidated the Washington Redskins' name because it disparaged Native Americans and brought them "into contempt or disrepute." In addition, attorneys with the Department of Justice have sought legal strategies to challenge mascots and remedy their negative effects.

The actions of activists, educators, students, politicians, and administrators concerned with mascots and their effects have made a difference. Over the past 30 years, the total number of mascots has decreased markedly. Suzan Shown Harjo, director of the Morning Star Institute and past president of the National Congress of American Indians, estimates that nearly 1,500 mascots have been changed, retired, or reworked since 1970 (personal communication, December 2, 2001). Moreover, in 1994, the Wisconsin Department of Public Instruction urged all schools in the state to discontinue using "Indian" imagery. As of 1999, 21 of approximately 75 schools had retired such mascots.

COMMON ARGUMENTS

As important as such activism has been, it has often occasioned a virulent defense of antiquated uses of Indians long after parallel imaginings of African-Americans or Latino- and Latina-Americans have all but faded from popular culture. To be sure, the retention of mascots has hinged on the distinct ways in which European-Americans have racialized Native Americans (King & Springwood, 2001b; Springwood & King, 2000). Just as important has been the constellation of arguments offered in support of mascots by fans, alumni, students, pundits, journalists, politicians, and administrators (e.g., Davis, 1993; King, 1998; Prochaska, 2001; Springwood & King 2000, 2001). At root, these overlapping positions emphasize respect, intention, fairness, and common-sense notions of symbols, play, and politics.

Quite simply, these arguments can be summarized as follows: mascots honor Indians; they are not meant to defame, injure, insult, or give offense; they are not racist; mascots are all about fun; there are more important problems to worry about; and critiquing is a form of political correctness. Such arguments, however, refuse to seriously engage living Native Americans in their defense of imagined Indians. Moreover, they often tell Native Americans how to think or how they should feel (namely, respected and honored). At the same time, these arguments question critics, enjoining them to "get real" or "get a life," precisely as they infantalize them through demands that opponents "grow up." Finally, supporters of mascots exhibit an inability and unwillingness to see or talk about race, history, and power. It is in this context that educational institutions endeavor to respond to and retain "their" Indians. In the process, administrators, boosters, students, and alumni implement an array of anti-Indian practices that can be grouped into six categories: myopia and misrecognition; possessiveness; compromising positions; endorsement; incorporating Indians; and invoking terror.

MYOPIA AND MISRECOGNITION

Mascots have always hinged on misrecognition. In fact, most Americans fail to see Native Americans for what they are or have been (Sigelman, 1998), misinterpreting, misusing, and misrepresenting them. Native American mascots tend to be false and clichéd. Chief Illiniwek at the University of Illinois—meant to represent the indigenous inhabitants of what is now Illinois—is a fictional figure, a figment of the European-American imagination, clothed not in Woodland dress, but the more familiar headdress and regalia generically associated with the Plains. Similar images abound throughout the United States, whether at Northeast Louisiana University or countless high schools, including those in Rahway, New Jersey; Martinsdale, Indiana; Marquette, Michigan; and Kingsport, Tennessee (see, for example, http://stutzfamily.com/mrstutz/prejudice/Teams.htm). Moreover, Native American mascots emphasize bellicosity and warfare, often framed in terms of honor and independence. At Florida State University, although Chief Osceola does portray a historic war leader of the Seminoles, he defines Indianness solely in terms of aggressiveness, savagery, and violence. At home football games, a white student in racial drag rides an Appaloosa to midfield and thrusts a lance into the turf. Still others make Indianness a joke, mocking Native Americans as they mimic them. For instance, at Marquette University in the 1960s, a white student donned a huge fiberglass "Indian" head with exaggerated features (e.g., a huge nose), performed crazy antics, and led students and fans in cheers. Elsewhere, Parks Elementary School in Natchitoches, Louisiana, uses an infantilized Indian—reminiscent of one of the ten little Indians—who stalks unseen prey. Whether noble, historic, authentic, humorous, or warlike,

Native American mascots always get it wrong, recycling stereotypes and well-worn imperial clichés.

Not surprisingly, the defense of mascots turns on misrecognition as well. Supporters of mascots argue that mascots do not constitute a problem because they are just names and images that are not meant to harm or offend. Supporters, moreover, argue that critics should "get over it," "get a life," "get real," "grow up," and otherwise worry about more pressing issues. Administrators forced to confront their mascots often rely on a similarly myopic reading. They cannot see Indians and exclude them from their institutional visions. School board members in Manhattan, Kansas, recently voted to retain the Indians as the mascot of the local high school. Some publicly expressed resentment over having to confront the issue, claiming it was "not the biggest problem facing the district." In Des Moines, Iowa, administrators at the predominantly Latino East High School have suggested that their mascot is not a problem because they do not have Indian students, overlooking the fact that a majority of their students from Latin America have Indian ancestry (Jesse Villalobos, personal communication, August 15, 2001). At Wichita North High School—the alma mater of famed professional football player Barry Sanders—alumni, students, and staff have defended their mascot, the Redskins, as a symbol honoring American Indians and reflecting their collective pride for the native nations of North America. In response to charges of racism, Associate Principal Wardell Bell, himself of mixed African-American and Cherokee ancestry, officially legitimates such misreadings: "I've seen the real thing all my life, police stopping me, questioning me and no one else when there's lots of white people around, people staring hard at me. Trust me . . . the Redskins name is not racism" (Wenzl, 1999, p. 12).

In Bell's remarks—no less than in the administrative comments and political decisions in Kansas, Iowa, and countless other places—cultural categories obscure the visibility of Native Americans, undermining the viability of their claims. One should not be surprised to find Native Americans and other oppressed minorities invoking these categories or defending mainstream symbols. Some Native Americans and other peoples of color view mascots as appropriate, positive, and defensible simply because they have accepted and even internalized the values and assumptions central to such uses of Indian imagery (King, 2001). When all is said and done, anti-Indianism often hinges on an unwillingness and/or inability to see. Because educational institutions fail to recognize embodied Indians and choose, instead, to fall back on myopic and false renderings of Indianness, they do not and/or cannot discern why mascots might be problematic, how they might be meaningful to their students or a broader public, or how they could be construed as racist, denigrating, and painful.

POSSESSIVENESS

If the misrepresentations of Indianness animating mascots presuppose mis-recognition, they also demand appropriation and ownership, promoting a possessiveness that often shapes struggles over mascots. Fans, students, and administrators must take from Indian communities—or at least from imagined versions of indigenous cultures—in order to craft their mascots. In the process, the appropriated attributes of Indianness (feathers, dance, headdress, and the like) become their property; the crafted Indian often becomes "their" own as they play at being Indian. Thus, in debates over mascots, when notions of tradition, culture, and Indian surface, more often than not they refer not to the traditions, cultures, and perspectives of actual Indians but rather to white fantasies, institutional practices, and local conventions. In other words, they refer to "their" Indians and their traditions.

Fundamentally, possessing Indians through racial cross-dressing grants European-Americans immense creative power to imagine themselves and their histories. Adamson Middle School in Rex, Georgia—a Georgia School of Excellence—offers a clear example of the possessiveness associated with Indian play at educational institutions. The school's website proudly proclaims that "You have entered Indian Territory" as an animated group of five warriors, against the backdrop of a soft rendition of stereotypical "Indian" music, peeks over an embattlement at the visitor (http://www.clayton.k12.ga.us/schools/019/sitemap.htm). An animated Indian named Chop guides visitors through subsequent pages for chiefs (administrators), Indian guides (teachers), tribe (students), smoke signals (activities), and trading post (community involvement). Such possessiveness has profound transformative implications. At the University of Illinois and at Florida State University, claims of Indianness are not only a means of fashioning identity and community but also of legitimately laying claim to space, to possessing territory and the dispossessed (Springwood & King, 2000).

These entrenched claims and associations, in turn, frame the terms of subsequent debates. For instance, at Anderson High School (Cincinnati), defenders of the Redskins mounted a popular campaign in 1999 to preserve the school symbol. In a campaign dubbed S.O.S., or Save Our Skins, supporters distributed yard signs and actively participated in public forums, asserting the honor and integrity of their tradition and symbols, while denigrating Indians as inferior, deviant, and uncivilized. Clearly, the defense of mascots often has little to do with embodied Indians and their practices and everything to do with European-Americans and their own sense of self-worth. Consequently, efforts to defend the appropriation and reinvention of Indianness in the form of mascots must be interpreted as efforts to preserve white power at the expense of embodied Native Americans.

COMPROMISING POSITIONS

When confronted about "their" Indians, educational institutions often defer and deny. They establish commissions to study the issue; they hold forums and public discussions; they may even meet with critics. Faced with mounting criticism over the name of its mascot, Glen Johnson, president of Southeastern Oklahoma State University, home of the Savages, adopted what can only be described as a typically academic strategy of obfuscation and meaningless loquacity.

> I have asked the strategic planning council to determine if any change would be appropriate based on the school's long-term goal and mission. At this time we are under no deadline to make a decision. We want to proceed slowly to ensure that all points of view are heard. (Southeastern Oklahoma State, 2001)

At the same time, administrators actively deny the charges of critics. They paint themselves and their uses of Indianness as innocent, harmless, respectful, and even educational. They refuse to take symbols or ideologies seriously. They insist that their school symbols are not meant to offend. They reject accountability, arguing that it is not their fault that some fans or students do ugly things or that some members of the public could read racism where respect is meant. For instance, in the early 1990s, then president Dale W. Lick (1993) sought to defend Florida State University's continued use of Seminole imagery through active denial.

> Recent critics have complained that the use of Indian symbolism is derogatory. Any symbol can be misused and become derogatory. This, however, has never been the intention at Florida State. Over the years we have worked closely with the Seminole tribe of Florida ensure the dignity and propriety of the various symbols we use. . . . Some traditions we cannot control. For instance, in the early 1980s, when our band, the Marching Chiefs, began the now famous arm motion while singing the "war chant," who knew that a few years later the gesture would be picked up by other team's fans and named the "tomahawk chop"? It's a term we did not choose and officially do not use.

For Lick and other administrators, the best defense is a good offense. By means of such orchestrated public relations campaigns, institutions hope to convey an image of action while avoiding engagement with the fundamental issues of stereotyping, dignity, and terror.

These tactics of deferral and denial set in motion a subsequent set of strategies centered around resolving the problem (i.e., the controversy over the mascot) without addressing its roots (i.e., reflecting on the illegitimate and inappropriate uses of Indianness and retiring the mascot). In fact, over the past 25 years, institutions have sought to contain critique and retain "their" Indians by seeking a middle ground and/or offering incentives. On the one hand, institutions and booster organizations have sought to bribe critics. They have proposed retaining Indian mascots but, at the same time, have offered to establish or expand Native American Studies programs or, alternately, have offered to create scholarship programs for Native American students. The Chief Illiniwek Educational Foundation (CIEF), an organization dedicated to the retention of said mascot at the University of Illinois, clarifies the anti-Indian core of such proposals and solicitations. In 1999 it planned an essay contest focused around the theme: "How does Chief Illiniwek best exemplify the spirit of the University of Illinois?" Significantly, CIEF sought not only to defend Chief Illiniwek but also to link its defense of an imagined Indian with the struggles of embodied Native Americans insofar as it planned to donate the prize money to a Native American organization that would support its cause.

On the other hand, educational institutions have endeavored to find workable compromises that ensure the retention of Indian symbols. These have ranged from modifying imagery to restricting marketing rights. For instance, at the University of Utah and at Bradley University, the team names (Utes and Braves, respectively) were retained, but team logos were made less offensive—both schools now use a feather in place of antiquated images of Indians—and embodied mascots were retired. At the same time, administrators at the University of Illinois have terminated licensing agreements for products bearing the likeness of Chief Illiniwek that were considered blatantly offensive (e.g., toilet paper and beer). What is noteworthy here is not only that compromise is defined in white terms but also that these proposals would be unimaginable for other ethnic groups in the United States. Can one seriously imagine a proposal that simultaneously encouraged an African-American Studies program but leaves unchanged racist practices toward blacks?

ENDORSEMENT

Educational institutions with besieged mascots frequently seek public endorsements to authorize their uses of Indianness. Often, alumni support plays a crucial role in administrative decisions (e.g., Connolly, 2000). Colleges and universities not only want to cultivate a strong booster culture, but they also want to foster a spirit of giving among their alumni. The promise of donations—or the (real or imagined) threat that gifts will be revoked—shapes how administrators approach mascots. At the University of North Dakota, wealthy donor Roy Englestad threatened to revoke a $100 million gift if the Fighting Sioux team name and logo were discontinued. Not only was the mascot retained, but the state board of regents hastily endorsed it in hopes of ending the ongoing public controversy. If anti-Indian images and practices increase the endowment, many administrators seem more than willing to make use of them.

Embattled institutions and their supporters also seek to protect mascots by engaging in what they believe to be real dialogue and subsequent consensus building, but which, in essence, is nothing more than a democratic masquerade. They stage elaborate public hearings where opponents and proponents speak their minds before a decision is made by the institution. The recent "dialogue" at the University of Illinois exemplifies this "staging" of democracy. A retired judge presided over timed statements from both sides and later issued a voluminous report seeking a middle ground that advocated the retention of Chief Illiniwek. Elsewhere, the governing bodies of colleges and universities and local school boards commonly pass resolutions supporting individual mascots and dismiss criticism as misdirected political correctness. In fact, both the Illinois and Florida legislatures have sought, in the past five years, to legally sanction mascots as the honored and appropriate symbols of their respective state institutions (Legislature, 1999). Sadly, notions of real justice and equality are missing from such sham procedures.

INCORPORATING INDIANS

In addition to strategies of bribery, compromise, and sleight-of-hand, institutions and their supporters often defend mascots by incorporating Indians. It has become almost commonplace for institutions to solicit support from indigenous people. For example, Florida State University authorizes its performances and symbols based on the public statements of a handful of aboriginal leaders, particularly tribal chair James E. Billie. Administrators also point to the fact that a descendent of Osceola publicly champions the reinvented version of his ancestor who opens each home football game of the Seminoles (see also Wheat, 1993). The administration of the University of Illinois relies on televised statements by remnants of the Illini Confederacy—the modern-day Peoria—to endorse the antics of Chief Illiniwek. Miami University of

Ohio relied on the support of the Miami Tribe for its imagined Indian, but when the tribe changed its position, it forced the university to alter its mascot, now called the RedHawk.

Moreover, universities often defend their uses of Indianness through the creative work of indigenous artists and designers. In the late 1970s, Marquette University encouraged Native American students to reimagine its embattled mascot. The result was the First Warrior, an Indian student who would perform traditional and powwow dances during timeouts and at halftime. In the 1990s, the University of North Dakota enlisted Native American artist Bennett Brien to rework the Fighting Sioux icon, hoping that a more romantic rendition created by a Native American would deflect criticism. The defenders of Chief Illiniwek at the University of Illinois have devised an array of schemes to affiliate the mascot with real Indians, from a recent scholarship contest benefiting a social service agency in South Dakota to a long-standing celebration of the fact that indigenous craftspeople fashioned the regalia worn by the Chief.

Of course, some Native Americans do support and even champion mascots. There are a variety of reasons for such support: they find images of braves and warriors to be empowering; they learn that public endorsement brings with it political, economic, and symbolic rewards; they discern an opportunity to challenge more troubling stereotypes about Indians; and they do not or cannot grasp the history and significance of mascots (see King, 2001; Springwood, 2001). The often diametrically opposed views about mascots within the Native American community are a vivid testimony about the complexity of contemporary Indian life. Ideally, these multiple voices and contradictory visions could foster a deeper appreciation of Indianness and lead to a penetrating discussion about the material conditions and sociohistorical foundations animating it within "Indian Country" and mainstream society. Unfortunately, this diverse range of views—as well as the resulting paradoxes—has not encouraged reflection or dialogue, but instead has enabled a divisive and cynical incorporation of Indians by institutions and their boosters for their own purposes. In effect, academic institutions are pleased to think that Native American mascots cannot be problematic because some Native Americans support such mascots, and they are just as ready to label those who complain as troublemakers and malcontents. To say the least, the dichotomy of the "good Indian" and "bad Indian" once again raises its ugly head. Moreover, the practice of affiliation and display—the act of presenting a select few of a group in defense of one's own viewpoint—has a disturbing relationship with treaty making, where European-Americans used segments of indigenous communities to legitimate imperial actions.

INVOKING TERROR

Taken together, the covert anti-Indian expressions and practices discussed above foster—and even nurture—acts of terror whose purpose is to secure, preserve, and defend Native American mascots. Supporters of Indian mascots have commonly harassed critics of the continued misuse of Indianness. At the University of North Dakota and the University of Illinois, they have paired specific threats of violence in anonymous phone calls and letters with more generic and public postings of graffiti and fliers designed to intimidate opponents. At the same time, fans, alumni, and students have frequently taunted and insulted Native American protestors outside sporting events. Defenders of mascots also invoke more subtle forms of terror. Anonymous supporters of mascots at the University of North Dakota have reminded critics that "we won the war" and have promised that Indian rights—not Indian symbols—will be terminated as a result of the ongoing struggles (see http://www.und.nodak.edu/org/bridges/index.html). At the University of Illinois, in the late 1990s, a flyer with a rendering of the cover of the *Orange and Blue Observer*, a local conservative periodical, featured the following image: a white gunslinger knowingly gazes at the viewer while pointing a drawn pistol at an Indian dancer in full regalia. The caption reads: "Manifest Destiny: Go! Fight! Win!" (http://www.csulb.edu/~wwinnesh/orangeandblue.html).

From one perspective, these images and assertions are reiterations of anti-Indian clichés central to the conquest of Native America. In North Dakota, there is a long-standing rivalry between the University of North Dakota Fighting Sioux and North Dakota State University Bison. Supporters of the latter institution typically wear T-shirts with the slogan "Sioux Suck!" Here, then, is a sublime example of how traditional institutional rivalry is encoded as a cross-cultural conflict replaying the conquest of Native America. In the end, even as institutions seek to dissociate themselves from it, terror is simultaneously the most extreme and the most representative tactic employed to defend Native American mascots precisely because it so clearly gives voice to the anti-Indian efforts to retain them.

CONCLUSIONS

The above examples suggest that educational institutions value imaginary Indians above indigenous peoples, their cultures, and their perspectives. Accordingly, they often employ anti-Indian rhetoric and practices to preserve their school spirits. For Native Americans, the strategies discussed above have negative consequences, much like the symbols themselves. They contribute in fundamental ways to the continual construction of public spaces and social institutions as environments hostile to indigenous peoples. On the one hand, they prevent the full recognition of Native Americans, muting their perspectives and marginalizing their value. On the other hand, they discourage Native Americans from participating more fully in American culture. Moreover, they offer uncomfortable analogies between the past and present because they bear an uncanny resemblance to historic patterns of deceit, disrespect, annihilation, appropriation, and distrust. At the same time, efforts to defend mascots contradict the aspirations and values of liberal education. Bribery, deceit, intimidation, and cynicism replace the supposed ideals of dialogue, equality, respect, and reflection. In turn, as educational institutions seek to save "their Indians," they foster inequality and encourage acts of terror. In short, they constantly reinscribe American imperialism and reinforce racial privilege.

The techniques used to defend mascots are as important as the images and imperialism at the heart of playing Indian at halftimes of football games. This is because the institutional defense of mascots reinforces the anti-Indianism of the symbols. Although these arguments and initiatives are meant to give the impression of respect and responsiveness, of sensitivity and support, they work against indigenous peoples, their perspectives, and their presence in public life, revealing the institutional foundations and continuing vitality of anti-Indianism. So long as Indian mascots persist, Native Americans will not only suffer unequal educational opportunities but also will continue to occupy a marginal position in American society.

None of this is inevitable. Mascots are social constructions. Human effort and cultural practices have made Indian images meaningful in schools, sports, and communities. Consequently, Native American mascots and their insidious effects can be undone. They can be reinterpreted, challenged, and changed. Over the past three decades, school boards, professional and political organizations, government agencies, religious groups, and educational institutions have offered impressive rereadings of mascots, calling attention to the histories and ideologies informing such symbols and spectacles. Such reinterpretations have encouraged change and have much to teach about the ways in which students and citizens—no less than educators and administrators—can deconstruct mascots and counter anti-Indianism.

One example of such reinterpretation can serve as a representative case study and point the way toward a broad strategy of resistance. In early 1971, four students petitioned the Marquette University Student Senate to retire Willie Wompum, a caricatured Indian character brought to life at home sporting events by a European-American student wearing a buckskin outfit and a huge fiberglass head (Deady, 1971; Webster, Loudbear, Corn, & Vigue, 1971).

The mascot is definitely offensive to the American Indian. We as Native Americans have pride in our Indian heritage, and a mascot that portrays our forefathers' ancestral mode of dress for a laugh can be nothing but another form of racism. Having a non-Indian play the part is just as degrading to the Indian. From the past to contemporary times there is little the white man has not taken from the Indian. About the only thing left is our pride, and now Marquette University threatens to take that away from us by allowing such a display of racism. . . . We did not give our permission to be portrayed for a laugh, and we are sure no other minority group would condone such flagrant degradation of their heritage and pride. We ask that the mascot be discontinued completely. . . . We are sure the absence of the mascot would not take away any of the effectiveness of the Number 1 basketball team in the nation. (quoted in King, 2001, p. 290)

This petition offers an eloquent and successful model of how to read mascots—a reading that encourages audiences to critically rethink the tradition of playing Indian. In fact, the petition points to three sets of questions that should inform critical interpretations of Native American mascots and all mass-mediated images of race and difference.

First, one must confront the images and, following Pewewardy (1991), "unlearn the stereotypes" embedded within them (p. 19). What imagery is chosen? By whom? Why? Does it confine Indians within the past? Does it flatten the diversity of Native America? Does it exaggerate a cultural or physical feature? Why? How does it correspond to images of Indians in other media? How does it contrast with images of other ethnic groups? Would other ethnic groups be portrayed in that fashion? Why or why not?

Second, because images are meaningful only in context, it is crucial to situate Native American mascots in history. How has playing Indian at halftime been shaped by the conquest of North America? Why did European-Americans play Indian at all? What do mascots have to do with whites and whiteness? How has the appropriation of indigenous cultural elements and Indianness more generally corresponded to the broader pattern of taking land and lives from Native Americans? Beyond European-American imperialism and the sorts of relations it fostered between Native Americans and European-Americans, what were indigenous peoples like? How did they live and dress? What did they believe? What are the differences between Native nations? How do such answers complicate and invalidate mascots? And, finally, on a local level, why was a particular mascot created and under what circumstances? How have administrators, fans, students, and others talked about "their" Indians?

Third, it is not enough to know that mascots are false or to appreciate the broader historical relations between Native Americans and European-Americans. To counter the anti-Indian effects of such images and practices, critics must engage Indians, listen to their perspectives, and affirm their cultures. What are indigenous people saying about such images and about their place in society? How do mascots impact the lives and life chances of Native Americans? What sorts of feelings do they evoke? Why? How does the persistence of mascots fit into the broader context of Native American and European-American relations?

The three-pronged act of questioning images, learning history, and affirming Indianness makes visible the interconnections of culture and power, race and history, and meaning and identity. Together, these reading strategies and critical questions not only challenge us to work through and against anti-Indianism in educational institutions and beyond but also offer the tools necessary to change it.

NOTE

This essay was originally published in 2002 in *Studies in Media and Information Literacy Education, 2*(1), 1–12.

REFERENCES

Banks, D. (1993). Tribal names and mascots in sports. *Journal of Sport and Social Issues, 17*(1), 5–8.

Churchill, W. (1994). *Indians are us? Culture and genocide in Native North America.* Monroe, ME: Common Courage Press.

Connolly, M. R. (2000). What in a name? A historical look at Native American related nicknames and symbols at three U.S. universities. *Journal of Higher Education 71*(5), 515–547.

Cook-Lynn, E. (2001). *Anti-Indianism in North America: A voice from Tatekeya's earth.* Urbana: University of Illinois Press.

Coombe, R. J. (1999). Sports trademarks and somatic politics: Locating the law in critical cultural studies. In R. Martin & T. Miller (Eds.), *SportCult* (pp. 262–288). Minneapolis: University of Minnesota Press.

Davis, L. (1993). Protest against the use of Native American mascots: A challenge to traditional, American identity. *Journal of Sport and Social Issues, 17*(1), 9–22.

Deady, P. (1971, February 10). Indians petition Senate. *Marquette Tribune,* p. 1.

Deloria, P. (1998). *Playing Indian.* New Haven, CT: Yale University Press.

Drinnon, R. (1980). *Facing west: The metaphysics of Indian-hating and empire building.* Minneapolis: University of Minnesota Press.

Green, R. (1988). The tribe called Wannabee: Playing Indian in America and Europe. *Folklore, 99,* 30–55.

Huhndorf, S. (1997). *Going Native.* Ithaca, NY: Cornell University Press.

King, C. R. (1998). *Colonial discourses, collective memories, and the exhibition of Native American cultures and histories in the contemporary United States.* New York: Garland Press.

King, C. R. (2001). Uneasy Indians: Creating and contesting Native American mascots at Marquette University. In C. R. King & C. F. Springwood (Eds.), *Team spirits: Essays on the history and significance of Native American mascots* (pp. 281–303). Lincoln: University of Nebraska Press.

King, C. R., & Springwood, C. F. (2000). Choreographing colonialism: Athletic mascots, (dis)embodied Indians, and Euro-American subjectivities. *Cultural Studies: A Research Annual, 5,* 191–221.

King, C. R., & Springwood, C. F. (2001a). *Beyond the cheers: Race as spectacle in college sports.* Albany: State University of New York Press.

King, C. R., & Springwood, C. F. (Eds.) (2001b). *Team spirits: Essays on the history and significance of Native American mascots.* Lincoln: University of Nebraska.

Landreth, M. (2001). Becoming the Indians: Fashioning Arkansas State University's Indians. In C. R. King & C. F. Springwood (Eds.). *Team spirits: Essays on the history and significance of Native American mascots* (pp. 46–63). Lincoln: University of Nebraska Press.

Legislature: Senate votes to put Seminoles nickname into law. (1999, May 1). *Naples Daily News,* p. 1A.

Lick, D. W. (1993). Seminoles—Heroic symbol at Florida State. Retrieved May 23, 2000, from http://seminoles.fansonly.com/trads/fsu-trads-seminoles.html

Mechling, J. (1980). Playing Indian and the search for authenticity in modern white America. *Prospects, 5,* 7–33.

Moses, L. G. (1996). *Wild West shows and the images of American Indians, 1883–1933.* Albuquerque: University of New Mexico Press.

Nuessel, F. (1994). Objectionable sports team designations. *Names: A Journal of Onomastics, 42,* 101–119.

Pewewardy, C. D. (1991). Native American mascots and imagery: The struggle of unlearning Indian stereotypes. *Journal of Navaho Education, 9*(1), 19–23.

Rodriguez, R. (1998). Plotting the assassination of Little Red Sambo: Psychologists join war against racist campus mascots. *Black Issues in Higher Education, 15*(8), 20–24.

Sigelman, L. (1998). Hail to the Redskins? Public reactions to a racially insensitive team name. *Sociology of Sport Journal, 15,* 317–325.

Slowikowski, S. S. (1993). Cultural performances and sports mascots. *Journal of Sport and Social Issues, 17*(1), 23–33.

Southeastern Oklahoma State has discussed future of mascot. (2001, May 7). *Daily Ardmoreite,* 7. Retrieved June 18, 2001, from http://www.sosu.edu/slife/savages/ardmore.htm

Spindel, C. (2000). *Dancing at halftime: Sports and the controversy over American Indian mascots.* New York: New York University Press.

Springwood, C. F. (2001). Playing Indian and fighting (for) mascots: Reading the complications of Native American and Euro-American alliances. In C. R. King &

C. F. Springwood (Eds.). *Team spirits: Essays on the history and significance of Native American mascots* (pp. 304–327). Lincoln: University of Nebraska Press.

Springwood, C. F., & King, C. R. (2000). Race, power, and representation in contemporary American sport. In P. Kivisto & G. Rundblad (Eds.), *The color line at the dawn of the 21st century* (pp. 161–174). Thousand Oaks, CA: Pine Valley Press.

Springwood, C. F., & King, C. R. (2001, November 9). Playing Indian: Why mascots must end. *Chronicle of Higher Education,* p. B13–B14.

Staurowsky, E. J. (1998). An act of honor or exploitation? The Cleveland Indians' use of the Louis Francis Sockalexis story. *Sociology of Sport Journal, 15*(4), 299–316.

Staurowsky, E. J. (1999). American Indian imagery and the miseducation of America. *Quest, 51*(4), 382–392.

Vanderford, H. (1996). What's in a name? Heritage or hatred: The school mascot controversy. *Journal of Law and Education, 25,* 381–388.

Webster, S., Loudbear, P., Corn, D., & Vigue, B. (1971, February 17). Four MU Indian students describe Willie Wampum as racist symbol. *Marquette Tribune,* p. A9.

Wenzl, R. (1999, September 20). "Redskin" mascot foe wins NAACP as ally. *Wichita Eagle,* p. 12.

Wheat, J. (1993, December 19). Graduate is Seminole by birth . . . and by FSU diploma. *Tallahassee Democrat,* p. 1B.

16

Putting the Moccasin on the Other Foot: A Media History of the "Fighting Whities"

Bruce E. Johansen

Stressing their right to dignity and self-definition of ethnic identity, Native Americans have been bringing increasing pressure on a number of sports teams, from the sandlots to the professionals, to retire stereotypical mascots. "The pace is really picking up," said Cyd Crue, president of the Illinois chapter of the National Coalition on Racism in Sports and the Media. "We're seeing more educators around the country, in middle schools and high schools and at universities, concerned about the racial climate in schools, dropping these symbols" (Johansen, 2001). Since the early 1970s, about 1,250 of the nation's 3,000 elementary schools, high schools, and colleges with American Indian nicknames and mascots have dropped them, said Suzan Shown Harjo, president of Washington, D.C.'s Morningstar Institute (Johansen, 2001). Harjo has successfully sued the Washington Redskins over their use of Indian imagery, and the initial judgment in her favor (*Harjo v. Pro-Football, Inc.*, 1999) has been affirmed in United States Trademark Court.

Native American sports mascots became an active political issue during the late 1960s, with the founding of the American Indian Movement (AIM) in Minneapolis. Because of AIM, some of the first Indian stereotypes fell in the Midwest. At the University of Nebraska at Omaha (UNO), for example, a chapter of AIM spearheaded a change of mascot from "Indians" to "Mavericks," a beef animal with an attitude, in 1971. The change was popular on campus in part because the visual depiction of "Owumpie," the "Omaha Indian," was tacky—tacky enough to make the Cleveland Indians' Chief Wahoo look like a real gentleman. The student body of UNO eventually voted to give "Owumpie" the boot. Stanford University changed its Indian mascot to a cardinal at about the same time. During the late 1960s, the National Congress of American Indians launched a campaign to bring an end to the use of Indian sports mascots and other media stereotypes.

In the meantime, Marquette University has replaced "Warriors" in favor of "Golden Eagles." Dartmouth changed its "Indians" to "Big Green," and Miami of Ohio changed "Redskins" to the "RedHawks." Manufacturers of Crayola Crayons have done away with the color "Indian Red" (Babwin, 2000). In October 1991, when the Atlanta Braves arrived in Minneapolis for the World Series, they found more than 200 protestors surrounding the stadium's gates, with placards reading, among other things, "500 Years of Oppression Is Enough." Minneapolis was AIM's hometown, and even the mayor had made a statement calling on the Braves to sack their Indian imagery. When the Twins management asked the police to move the demonstrators further from the Metrodome, they refused, citing principles of freedom of speech and assembly.

Scholars have also paid attention to the mascot issue, especially King and Springwood (2001) and Spindel (2000). In 1999, the North American Society for the Sociology of Sport initiated annual conferences practically in Chief Wahoo's shadow at the Marriott Hotel in downtown Cleveland, with sessions that included papers with titles such as "Escaping the Tyranny of the Majority: A Case Study of Mascot Change" and "Red, Black, and White: 'Playing Indian' and Racial Hierarchy at Florida State."

THE GENESIS OF THE "FIGHTING WHITES"

A singular moment in the history of the mascot controversy occurred during February 2002, when an intramural basketball team at the University of Northern Colorado (UNC) composed of Native American, Latino, and European-American students collectively decided to change its name from "Native Pride" to the "Fighting Whites." The new name was a parody of North America's many Native American mascots, most notably nearby Eaton High School's "Fighting Reds." It was the first time in popular memory that a multi-ethnic sports team had decided to adopt a European-American stereotype as a mascot. The team printed a few T-shirts (their uniform of choice) on which were printed the team's new name, a be-suited, clean-cut white man with a bland smile on his face, and the slogan "Everythang's Gonna be All White." A wave of nearly instant, continent-wide publicity ensued—a wave that stood the long-standing debate over the decency of Native sports-team mascots on its head. The Fighting Whites set thousands of virtual tongues wagging. Everyone had an opinion, from AIM to affiliates of the Ku Klux

Klan (KKK). The reactions provide a flash-frozen ideoscape of racial humor in an age of political correctness.

Within weeks, the Fighting Whites (or, as they soon became known in many circles, the Fighting Whities) had become nearly as well known as established professional monikers such as the Washington Redskins and the Cleveland Indians. A Google search in March 2002 for the phrase "Fighting Whities" turned up 4,700 hits. The publicity helped to sell thousands of T-shirts and other items for a hastily endowed scholarship fund to aid Native American students. By the end of 2002, the team had raised $100,000 in merchandise sales for Native American students.

As Ryan White, John Messner, and Charles Cuny explained on the official home page of the Fighting Whites:

> We came up with the "Fighting Whites" logo and slogan to have a little satirical fun and to deliver a simple, sincere, message about ethnic stereotyping. Since March 6, when our campus newspaper first reported on the Fighting Whites, we have been launched into the national spotlight, propelled by a national debate over stereotyping American Indians in sports symbolism. (White, Messner, & Cuny, 2002)

The Fighting Whites' parody quickly sprang from the sports pages to the front pages. From the student newspaper, the story spread to the *Greeley Tribune*, then over the state, regional, and national Associated Press wire services. Some of the stories popped up as far away as the *Guardian* in the United Kingdom. The "Whities" also were contacted by Fox Sports Net and NBC News, among many other electronic media. Soon, the Fighting Whites had developed at least nine T-shirt designs for sale on an Internet site, with receipts fueled by publicity in many major daily newspapers, electronic news outlets, and such other large-audience venues as the *Jay Leno Show*. The effect on sales was downright salubrious. Soon the merchandise was available not only on T-shirts but also on sweatshirts, tank tops, baseball jerseys, several styles of caps, a coffee mug, boxer shorts, and mouse pads.

On the court, the Whities confessed that they were hardly championship caliber, but soon their prowess at basketball didn't matter. Their reputation soon had very little to do with dribbling, jumping, or shooting, and more to do with the incendiary nature of the ongoing debate regarding Native American names for sports teams. Brooks Wade, a member of the Fighting Whites who is a Choctaw and an employee at UNC Native American Student Services, told the *Rocky Mountain News*: "It's a huge media rush. It kind of snowballed out of control, really. We started it as more of a protest so we could change things in our little world, and suddenly it's worldwide" (BeDan, 2002, p. 12A).

The original protest had been aimed at Eaton (Colorado) High School's Indian mascot, the "Fightin' Reds," after the wife of one of the "Fighting Whites" resigned a job there in anger over the issue. The protest parody quickly cut a much wider swath. Solomon Little Owl, a Crow, whose wife resigned at Eaton, was director of Native American Student Services at UNC when he joined the team. Little Owl's wife, Kacy Little Owl (who is European-American), taught special education at the high school seven miles north of Greeley for two years before leaving at the end of the previous school year (Garner, 2002).

"The message is, let's do something that will let people see the other side of what it's like to be a mascot," said Little Owl (Fighting Whities, 2002). The Whities had reason to agree with a comment on the Wampum Chronicles message board, a Native American website: "They'll swamp the country with publicity which has everyone laughing at their opponents, all the while our boys will be laughing all the way to the bank. Way to go, Fighting Whities. Give 'em hell" (Wampum Chronicles, n.d.). Little Owl said that the couple, as parents of a son who is half-European American and half-Native, felt uncomfortable mingling with townspeople at school events, especially at ball games where Eaton High School's large-nosed Indian caricature was the prominent team symbol. "It was offensive in its own way," said Little Owl (Garner, 2002).

WHO WAS INSULTING WHOM?

The Eaton Fighting Reds found themselves unwillingly sucked into the tornado of publicity created by the Fighting Whites' parody. The defenders of the Fighting Reds did not take kindly to the notion of basking unwillingly in the reflected glory of the Fighting Whites. According to a report in the *New York Daily News*:

> School officials have been unresponsive to the protests of local Native American activists. John Nuspl, the school district superintendent, has said the Indian logo is not offensive but that the Fighting Whities are insulting. Yesterday, a school official would only offer, "The Eaton school district has no comment, but thank you for your call." The inquiring sportswriter was then disconnected. (Bondy, 2002)

A reporter for the Associated Press was told by Nuspl that Eaton's logo is not derogatory. "There's no mockery of Native Americans with this," Nuspl said. As for the Fighting Whites, he said, "Their interpretations are an insult to our patrons and blatantly inaccurate" (Team Chooses, 2002).

The reaction of Eaton's school superintendent brought to light an unintended irony that dogged the Fighting Whites wherever their newly minted name went. Many people who had no problem with naming a sports team after a Native American image became profoundly offended when the same thing was done, tongue in cheek, with a European-American mascot. GOPUSA, a Colorado web page of "Republican resources," declared the naming of the "Whities" a case of "Political correctness gone mad!" (GOPUSA, 2002).

Aside from a small number of people in Eaton and one editorial writer in Omaha (described below), most "white" people harvested a belly laugh or two from the parody. Some commentators went out of their way to show that, as European-Americans, they could take a joke. The "Portal of Evil" website declared the Fighting Whities to be a "mascot for the rest of us." Another virtual commentator had a suggestion for Fighting Whities team colors: "Off-white and Velveeta Cheese yellow!" (Mr. Cranky, 2002). Rush Limbaugh, the popular radio commentator, used the controversy to demonstrate his appreciation of all stereotypes: "Now, I think that's great! The team chose a white man as its mascot to raise awareness of stereotypes that some cultures endure. I love this, and it doesn't offend me at all! I'd be proud to be on the team—which is the difference here. There isn't a white person around that's going to be offended by this" (Limbaugh, 2002).

Limbaugh, who called Native Americans "Injuns" in this commentary, aimed perhaps to show that he is as good at taking ethnic stereotypes as he has been at dishing them out. "That's great!" he said. "I had to laugh and laugh on the air" (Limbaugh, 2002). Limbaugh disagreed with Eaton's offended school superintendent: "Now, come on. This is not insulting, Whitie; it's funny" (Limbaugh, 2002). "If these Native Americans had wanted to offend," Limbaugh continued,

> They could have come up with something a lot worse than the Fighting Whities. . . . What's going to happen is you're going to have a bunch of civil-rights groups led by Jesse Jackson saying, "You can't do that!" Still, it's just too good. The Fighting Whities? It just rolls off the tongue. Who wouldn't want to be on that team? (Limbaugh, 2002)

The Fighting Whities nearly sent Limbaugh into rhapsody:

> In fact, let's rename the 101st Airborne Division the "Fighting Whities." I mean, can't you see that painted on some Air Force squadron, on the tail of a bunch of F-16s: the Fighting Whities—and paint the airplanes all white. Oh-ho! I'll guarantee you that this is not going to fly well with the NAACP crowd, folks, because it's good, the Fighting Whities. I really do wish that I had authored this. (Limbaugh, 2002)

Barry Benintende, executive editor of the *La Jolla Light* in California, loved the idea almost as much as Limbaugh. "In this day and age it's tough to come up with a nickname for an athletic department [or] team that won't offend at least some portion of the population," he wrote in the publication's March 2002 edition.

> Short of naming every school or pro-sports team "the Vanillas," someone is go-ing to have their knickers in a twist over a nickname. Well, speaking of vanilla, let me bring up the name of my favorite sports team of all time, edging out the Banana Slugs of UCSC [University of California at Santa Cruz]—"Fighting Whities." The slogan they adopted—"Everythang's gonna be all white!"—is pure genius. (Benintende, 2002)

Sadly, lamented Benintende, only the most self-conscious "whites" were offended by the turnabout. "What was intended to turn the tables on insensi-tivity and support for teams like the Redskins, et al., the reaction shocked the team founders: Caucasians not only loved the name but sent them congratu-latory e-mails and requests to buy Fighting Whities jerseys" (Benintende, 2002). Benintende continued: "I'm a fan of the San Diego Padres, who could be seen as offensive to Catholics. Instead, many of us find the Swinging Friar a lovable guy with whom to identify, much like we would a briefcase-toting Middle-America dad type" (Benintende, 2002). Like many other com-mentators, Benintende used the Fighting Whities parody to take issue with an April 2001 United States Commission on Civil Rights opinion that said Indian-themed sports teams may violate antidiscrimination laws, and should be dropped. "Does this commission finding also apply to the Fighting Irish at Notre Dame? The Celtics of Boston? And why limit it to sports teams? Does the name Rabbinical School Dropouts offend Jewish people who do not listen to the Klezmer band?" (Benintende, 2002).

One virtual tongue wagged at "The Geekery: Biased and Unbalanced News":

> See, this is what I'm talking about. Racial stereotypes got you down? Now you can reverse the stereotypes back on your oppressors and not receive ANY backlash whatsoever. God, I love this country. This is probably the best idea any minority has ever had. Next we just need a baseball team, maybe "the Atlanta Trailer Park Trash" or "the Nebraska Rednecks." Hell, let's not stop there. Let's branch off into rugby too and have "the Preppy White Boys From Upper-class Neighborhoods That Look Down Upon Every Color They Have Only Seen on TV." The possibilities are endless. (Geekery, 2002)

Clarence Page, an African-American syndicated columnist based at the *Chicago Tribune*, opined, tongue in cheek, that "Sometimes offense is the best defense" (Page, 2002). Page remarked that network television, major news-papers, and radio talk shows had made the Fighting Whites the best-covered intramural squad in the nation. The *Greeley Tribune*'s website crashed when demand for the story soared to 29,000 from the usual 200 hits a day for a high-interest local story (Page, 2002). Yet, quipped Page, "Caucasians have proved to be remarkably resistant to offense. Many agreed with an e-mailer who saw the new name as an 'honor' to white Americans, who apparently don't get enough credit for their many contributions to history" (Page, 2002). "Help me out here," asked one e-mail to the *Greeley Tribune*. "Why am I sup-posed to be offended?" (Page, 2002). In Page's opinion,

> Whether their experiment turned out the way they expected to or not, the Fight-ing Whites deserve to go to the head of the class for giving us all at least one important lesson in cross-cultural differences: It's not what you slur that counts, it is who is slurring it—and how. . . . As an African-American who has heard more than my share of slurs, I can tell you: to be truly offensive, it helps for a slur to carry at least a hint of a threat. . . . Most Redskins fans undoubtedly mean no harm by their passivity about their team's name. If it reminds some Indians of the days when there were bounties on Indian scalps, that's just tough tomahawks, pal. (Page, 2002)

Page concluded, "I give the Fighting Whites credit for keeping their wit about them. Humor often opens doors that battering rams fail to budge. If nothing else, they've stumbled across an unusual way to raise scholarship money. It's like the old saying: If you can't beat 'em, make a few bucks off 'em" (Page, 2002).

The texture and potency of assumed insult soon became the main point of debate for many European-Americans. "Some people online were saying that the mascot should be . . . a fat guy with buckteeth kissing his sister," said Tom Crebbs of Oakland, Calif., who heard about the idea and started his own website selling spin-off shirts, hats, and mugs (Fighting Whities, n.d.). Mi-chael Gonsalves wondered whether, "If you are fighting against a perceived injustice, is the proper recourse to go out and do the very same thing?" (Fight-ing Whities, n.d.). Dimitri Vassilaros, a columnist for the Pittsburgh *Tribune Review*, asserted that no one would give a mascot name to a "business or pet" that carried negative connotations. George Junne, a professor in the Univer-sity of Northern Colorado's Africana Studies Department, said that a mascot "is like a pet. People don't want to be pets" (Good, 2002).

Vassilaros, who is a Greek-American, wrote that is "just my luck" that "drunken college frat brothers [are called] 'Greeks.'" He asked: "Are there any white men who feel violated whenever they see fighting whities mas-cots such as the Schenley Spartans, Peabody Highlanders, Central Catholic

Vikings, North Catholic Trojans, Duquesne Dukes, or even the Quaker Valley Quakers?" In his court of public opinion, Vassilaros finds that "The perpetually offended are intellectually bankrupt" (Vassilaros, 2002). A radio station in Grand Rapids, Michigan, WOOD Newsradio 1300, conducted an on-air poll, asking: "Do you think a basketball team named the 'Fighting Whites' is racially insensitive?" The results: 84.19% "no," 15.81% "yes" (Newsradio, n,d.).

A number of commentators assumed that the members of the Fighting Whites had set out to offend non-Indians, even after a number of newspaper pieces quoted them as saying this was not the case. Usually, such allegations were aired as the commentator strove to display his or her open-mindedness. An example was provided by John Ledbetter:

> Offended? I want one of his team's T-shirts. They feature a white dude with a coat and tie and slicked-back hair. He looks like an IRS agent on crack, which isn't a bad name for a team either. But really, if offending us honkies was Owl's criteria for success, he may want a job with the visa department in the INS [Immigration and Naturalization Service]. It's just not that often that an angle on the Anglos is spun toward something fierce or feisty. Unless you're Scandinavians—Vikings—or from Ireland—Fightin' Irish—there's not a lot of scrappy Caucasians that end up on banners in an auditorium. Of course, if you're Irish you're fighting because you're drunk—and a happy St. Patrick's Day to you too. I'm also part Irish, allegedly, so kiss my blarney if you're offended. And I'm even a lawyer. Now, talk about a maligned group. The San Jose Sharks today rejected a plan to name their team the San Jose Barristers. Ha! (Ledbetter, 2002)

In the interests of parody, Ledbetter then raised the intellectual stakes of the argument in a way that the Fighting Whites never had intended: "Earth to [Spotted] Owl: Don't count on Osama bin Laden to give you the Plains States back, or let you worship the way you want" (Ledbetter, 2002).

An editorial in the Omaha *World-Herald* called the "Whities" parody an ineffective insult. In an editorial titled "'Whities' on the Court; Insult Doesn't Work if Name Doesn't Hurt," the newspaper said that "The lack of deep, personal insult in the term 'white' may reflect the inequality of racial relationships. Because the majority typically has more power—political, economic, social—than minorities, its members are not so likely to feel diminished by words of contempt" (Whities, 2002). The *World-Herald* argued that "The white population is in the majority and lacks the depth of race consciousness needed to make a group sensitive to name-calling. Break whites down into smaller ethnic groups, however—everyone is familiar with the disrespectful names for Jews, Irish, Italians, French-Canadians and so on—and the anger can surface quickly" (Whities, 2002). By the *World-Herald*'s reasoning, perhaps "The Fighting Knee-Knocking Norwegians" might have been more effective. The editorial continued: "'The Reds' is a generic-enough name that the Greeley high school could easily move from an Indian logo to something less potentially offensive. Neither the Cincinnati Reds nor Nebraska's Big Red refers to ethnicity" (Whities, 2002).

The *World-Herald*'s editorial writer composed this piece without checking how the mascot was being depicted at Eaton High School. While "Big Red" is characterized visually by Herbie Husker, definitely a down-home farm boy, the Eaton mascot is a no-bones-about-it American Indian, which was described by Owen S. Good of the *Rocky Mountain News* as "a cross-armed, shovel-nosed, belligerent caricature" (Good, 2002). The *World-Herald* was too polite to let loose with the names it might use to address the "Fighting Whites." Another commentator was not as shy, providing a number of very specific team names meant to insult "white" people, including: "[The] White Slaveowners; Light-Skinned Nigger-Killers; Fighting Crackers; Blue-Eyed Devils; The Rhythm Lackers; The Small Penises; The Non-Dancers; The Big House Massas" (T. Rex Essay, 2002). The author commented: "I suggest that, if they really want to get their point across, and they really want to do the equivalent of names like 'Redskins.' I think names like these more accurately represent the negative stereotyping of names like "Redskins" and the use of images of the 'savage' American Indian" (T. Rex Essay, 2002).

Some European-Americans were severely offended at the use of a "white" mascot, and became very eager to pay back the perceived insult. One militant "white" nationalist web page characterized the "Fighting Whities" parody this way:

> Some redskins on an intramural basketball team up at the University of Northern Colorado got their feathers all in a bunch recently and decided to show white folks, and especially those at nearby Eaton High School, whose motto is "Fightin' Reds," and whose logo is a caricature of an Indian—how insulting it is to have their identity pre-empted this way. "Damn, didn't the Sambo's Restaurant chain get into heap big trouble with blackskins and have to change their name because black folks found it offensive to be portrayed as anything less than nuclear physicists? If the blackskins can back whiteskins down so easily, then certainly redskins can do the same thing." (Millard, 2002)

The same site offered links to another seeking orders for its own European-American icon: a T-shirt portraying knights of the Ku Klux Klan in white sheets burning a cross, above lettering reading "The Knight Time's the White Time" (Klan T-shirts, n.d.).

SERIOUS DEBATES NATIONALLY

Aside from a debate over who was offending whom, the "Fighting Whities" parody provoked a great deal of serious debate on the mascot issue nationally. Student editorialists at the University of Illinois *Daily Illini*, where a controversy has long raged regarding the school's Chief Illini mascot, suggested that the Fighting Whities take its place.

> When University Board of Trustees member Roger Plummer addressed the board about Chief Illiniwek, he said the board has two decisions. Alas, at this prestigious University, we must strive for excellence. That's why Scout was disappointed to see Plummer did not suggest the University adopt The Fighting Whities, the symbol a group of students in Colorado used to make a point. The school could keep "Fighting" on all its merchandise. Just scratch out "Illini." People couldn't call it offensive because it's actually just taking the idea of the Fighting Irish to the next level." (Campus Scout, 2002)

"In sports," the *Daily Illini* editorial concluded, "There's nothing better than taking it to the next level. In life, there's nothing better than poking a little fun at yourself. The students like 'The Fighting Whities,' too. Scout's received numerous e-mails supporting the suggestion" (Campus Scout, 2002). Tanya Barrientos, a *Philadelphia Inquirer* columnist, took issue with a survey conducted by Harris Research in the March 4, 2002, edition of *Sports Illustrated*, which asserted that only 32% of Indians living on reservations believed Indian names and mascots used by professional sports teams contributed to discrimination against them. The same survey stated that the proportion of Native Americans not living on reservations who perceived no discrimination in Indian team names or mascots was 83%. Barrientos wrote: "Perhaps I should lighten up. But my gut tells me that Chief Wahoo is wrong. He smacks of a Sambo, a lawn jockey, or one of those Mexicans sleeping under a broad-brimmed sombrero. There has to be a good reason why 600 schools, minor-league teams, and other pro-sports franchises have dropped or changed their Indian names and mascots since 1969" (Barrientos, 2002). Bob DiBiasio, vice president for public relations for the Cleveland Indians, had told Barrientos that Chief Wahoo was never meant to be a racist logo and that "if there is no intent to demean, how can something demean?" "Tell that," she concluded, "to the Fighting Whities" (Barrientos, 2002).

A DEMONSTRATION IN EATON

Eaton High School's 450 students found themselves neighbors of a rally against its Fighting Reds mascot. The demonstration coincided with Eaton

High School's graduation ceremony, which was held during the afternoon, after the rally had dispersed. The Eaton police rehearsed for weeks in anticipation of the event, and called in reinforcements from nearby Ault, as well as the Weld County Sheriff's Office. "We are prepared to handle this event," said Sgt. Arthur Mueller of the Eaton Police Department. "We don't anticipate problems, but we do have several contingency plans in place" (Ochoa, 2002). The plans included mounted horse patrols, a K-9 unit, police teams patrolling the perimeter of the demonstration, and officers mingling through the crowd, as well as officers posted on nearby rooftop. "We will have zero tolerance when there is an issue of safety for the officers, participants or residents. . . . And we will have zero tolerance for the destruction of private property or public property" (Ochoa, 2002). Unarmed security guards trained by AIM also planned to provide added security to the rallying group. Dozens of local and county police, on foot and horseback, as well as private security guards, awaited the protesters. As the rally concluded, roughly 300 marchers promised to return next year and the year after that, until the mascot image was retired. Coloradans Against Ethnic Stereotyping in Colorado Schools wants nearly 40 public schools statewide to change American Indian mascots that it believes are hurtful and racist.

"This is our introduction to Eaton on how to live respectfully," said Russell Means, a founder of AIM and a longtime national activist for Native American rights. "If Eaton wants to put up with this every year for their graduation, then so be it" (Nigoya, 2002). According to a report in the *Denver Post*, "Protesters marched through town—drums beating, chants rising—on their way to Eaton City Park. There were speeches of heritage and strife, racism and tolerance" (Nigoya, 2002). "They're upset, saying we ruined their graduation," Means said. "With this [mascot], they ruin every single day of our lives" (Nigoya, 2002).

Fred Gibbs, a 26-year-old fifth-generation Eaton High graduate, said he couldn't understand why some people chose to be offended by a symbol that most in town considered a respectful honor to American Indians. The mascot was called "a tough little warrior that we're very proud of" by Gibbs, who was watching from his front lawn. "None of us feels like it's a negative portrayal" (Good, 2002). But Means, who is well known in Denver for demonstrating against the city's Columbus Day parade, said there was nothing even remotely honorable about using American Indian images as sports mascots: "It [comes from] the day when only the fiercest animals were used as team mascots—Lions, Tigers. . . . That's what Indians are to these teams, the fiercest of beasts" (Good, 2002). Means suggested that next year's demonstration might confront the school's graduation ceremony directly (Good, 2002).

EVALUATING THE "WHITIES" IN IDEOLOGICAL CONTEXT

On an Internet page devoted to anarchist causes, Bob Maxim wrote that "Acceptance of racial stereotypes of 'Indians' as they're commonly called is not only more widespread than any other race, but actually ingrained so steadfastly into the American culture that most people don't see what all the fuss is about" (Maxim, 2002). The proponents of Native American mascots often profess no malice—indeed, they loudly broadcast an admiration of their own stereotyped creations. Sometimes this sense of "respect" can be taken to absurd lengths, as when some European-Americans defend the use of the word "squaw" as a place name with full knowledge that it originated as a reference to Native women's vaginas. However, wrote Maxim, "The fact is . . . [that] disrespect . . . is disrespect in the eyes of the offended, not the offender."

The use of a prototypical European-American figure as a mascot for a sports team (even a minor, intramural one) ignited an explosion of debate illustrative of a touchstone issue that has inflamed tempers for years. Maxim proposed that the offensiveness of Native stereotypes be tested by using other ethnic caricatures in their places.

> Take any name and caricature and change the stereotype and tell me if it seems offensive to your own sensibilities. For example, ask yourself if you would feel offended if they announced they were changing the Washington Redskins to the Washington "Blackskins," and put a flared-nostrilled caricature of Kunta Kinte on the helmets, or a crazed-eyed Zulu Warrior with a bone in his nose wielding a spear. Do you think folks would argue that they were honoring black people, and their noble fighting spirit? (Maxim, 2002)

The defense of Native American mascots by non-natives can be seen as enforcement of sense of conquest, of a reminder that European-Americans now set the perceptual rules. Maxim continued: "How about the Fighting Kikes, or Wops . . . or a Boston favorite, the Washington Micks? Imagine the Washington 'Whiteskins,' with a caricature of George W. [Bush] on the helmet" (Maxim, 2002). With a sense of gentle sarcasm, that was the message that the Fighting Whities chose to send. The noise with which the message was received is illustrative of the perceptual power of images.

CONCLUSION

It's been years since Step-n-Fetchit was sent packing to the racial-stereotype graveyard; it has likewise been a couple of decades since Frito-Lay discarded its Frito Bandito. Yet, at the beginning of the 21st century, we find ourselves arguing over whether professional athletes should wear the likeness of Chief Wahoo, and whether fans who believe themselves to be decent people should regret doing the tomahawk chop. Tim Giago, editor of the *Lakota Journal*, comments: "Would you paint your face black, wear an afro wig, and prance around a football field trying to imitate your perceptions of black people? Of course not! That would be insulting to Blacks. So why is it OK to do it to Indians?" (Nevard, n.d.).

Why are sponsors of Native American mascots so possessive of their fantasy images? The struggle over sports mascots can evoke anger and even violence. In the otherwise peaceful Catskills town of West Hurley, New York, a mascot struggle sparked a struggle for control of a local school board. A ban on use of racial images was enacted in April 2000 by the board governing the 2,300-student Onteora school board. The mascot then became the lead issue in a campaign for control of the school board. During May, supporters of the Indian image won a majority of board seats. In June, the school district's Indian imagery was reinstated. During the fall of 2000, opponents of the Indian mascot found their cars vandalized, with nails and screws driven into tires and paint splattered on windshields, usually while the cars were parked at school board meetings.

Supporters of Onteora's Indian imagery (which included a tomahawk chop, totem poles in the school cafeteria, and various pseudo-Indian songs and dances) have been known to bristle at any suggestion that their images degrade Native Americans in any way. Joseph Doan, a member of the school board that voted to reinstate the Indian imagery, said that many white citizens see the Indian image as a symbol of honor and environmental protection. "Our Indian has nothing to do with degrading Indians. It's our symbol and we're proud of it," said Doan (Gormley, 2000).

More than two decades ago, Choctaw filmmaker Phil Lucas addressed the question on the pages of *Four Winds*, a short-lived glossy magazine devoted to Native American art, history, and culture, by asking how whites would react if a sports team was named the "Cleveland Caucasians." What would European-Americans think, Lucas asked, if Indians adopted racial names (such as the "Window Rock Negroes" or the "Tahlequah White Boys") for their sports teams (Lucas, 1980, p. 69). Native Americans have come to make this point with increasingly intense emphasis, asking sponsors of such mascots who insist they are "honoring" Native Americans to put the moccasin on the other foot.

The "Fighting Whites" (or "Whities") spawned intense controversy by doing just that, igniting controversy on a profoundly sensitive issue. Why is the issue so sensitive? In his foreword to *Team Spirits*, Vine Deloria Jr. identifies several reasons: residues of racism, a sense of the Indian as "other," and the fact that "Indians represent the American past, and Europeans and Americans have been fleeing from their own past since the days of discovery and settlement" (King & Springwood, 2001, pp. ix–x). These images are ideological artifacts reflecting attitudes toward "race, power, and culture" (King & Springwood, 2001, p. 1). For all of these reasons, a parody created by an intramural basketball team in a small Colorado college town set off a firestorm of debate.

NOTE

This essay was originally published in 2003 in *Studies in Media and Information Literacy Education*, 3(1), 1–11.

REFERENCES

Babwin, D. (2000, November 6). Opposition to Indian mascots mounts. *Associated Press*. Retrieved from www.copleynewspapers.com/couriernews/top/e06mascots.htm

Barrientos, T. (2002, March 16). A chief beef: Some teams still seem insensitive to Indians. *Philadelphia Inquirer*. Retrieved from www.philly.com/mld/philly/living/columnists/tanya_barrientos/2872629.htm

BeDan, M. (2002, March 15). International eye drawn to "Fightin' Whities;" Protest of mascot for Eaton High School "has kind of snowballed." *Rocky Mountain News*, p. 12-A.

Benintende, B. (2002, March). At least they didn't call themselves the "Ragin' Caucasians." *La Jolla [California] Light*. Retrieved from www.lajollanews.com/News/2002/March/Opinion1514.shtml

Bondy, F. (2002, March 14). Intramural name pales by comparison. *New York Daily News*, p. 76.

Campus Scout: The Fighting Whities. (2002, April 2). *Daily Illiini* [University of Illinois]. Retrieved from www.dailyillini.com/apr02/apr02/news/stories/scout.shtml

"Fighting Whities" make a statement; American Indian students try to raise awareness of stereotypes. (2002, March 12). *Philadelphia Daily News*. Retrieved from www.philly.com/mld/dailynews/sports/2841746.htm

Garner, J. (2002, March 12). Whities' mascot about education, not retaliation; intramural basketball team takes shot at Indian caricature used by Eaton High School. *Rocky Mountain News*. Retrieved from www.rockymountainnews.com/drmn/state/article/0,1299,DRMN_2 1_1026337,OO.html

Geekery: Biased and unbalanced news. (2002, March 11). Retrieved from www.gotthegeek.com/newspro/arc-20020311.shtml

Good, O. S. (2002, May 20). School's nickname fuels fury; American Indians march against "Reds" moniker. *Rocky Mountain News*. Retrieved from www.rocky mountainnews.com/drmn/state/article/0,1299,DRMN_21_1156968,OO.html

GOPUSA. (2002). Bringing the conservative voice to America. Retrieved from http://gopusa.com/colorado

Gormley, M. (2000, October 28). State commissioner to take a stand on Indian mascots, names. *Boston Globe* On-line. Retrieved from www.boston.com/dailynews/302/region/state_commissioner_to_ take a_s:.html

Harjo v. Pro-Football, Inc. (1999, April 2). Citation: 1999 WL329721. The Trademark Trial and Appeals Board, U.S. Patent and Trademark Office. Retrieved from www.kentlaw.edu/student_orgs/jip/trade/skins.htm

Johansen, B. E. (2001, Spring). Mascots: Honor be thy name. *Native Americas, 18*(1), 58–61.

King, C. R., & Springwood, C. F. (Eds.). (2001). *Team spirits: The Native American mascots controversy*. Lincoln: University of Nebraska Press.

Klan T-Shirts. (No date). Retrieved between September 15, 2002 and November 30, 2002, from www.americanknights.com/tees.htm

Ledbetter, J. (2002, March 8). Cantankerous Caucasian fights back. *Destin (Florida) Log*. Retrieved from www.destin.com/archives/columnists/ledbetter/020315a.shtml

Limbaugh, R. (2002, March 12). The cutting edge: Go Whities!!! Retrieved from www.rushlimbaugh.com/home/daily/site_031202/content/cut.gue st.html

Lucas, P. (1980, Autumn). Images of Indians. *Four Winds: The International Forum for Native American Art, Literature, and History*, 69–77.

Maxim, B. (2002, March 17). Stereotyping of Native Americans: Links and commentary from my crypto-anarcho-libertarian perspective. Retrieved from www.bill stclair.com/blog/020317.html

Millard, H. (2002). Fightin' Whities—Pale faces want 'um Tshirts, not blankets. Retrieved between September 15, 2002 and November 30, 2002, from www.newnation.org/Millard/millard_Fightin_Whities.htmll

Mr. Cranky rates the movies: Iris. (2002, March 12). Posted by off@white.com (mister_mucus). Retrieved from www.mrcranky.com/movies/iris/16/3.htmll

Nevard, D. (No date). Wahooism in the USA; A red socks journal. Retrieved between September 15, 2002 and November 30, 2002, from www.ultranet.com/kuras/bhxi3d.htm

Newsradio WOOD 1300: Daily Buzz results. (No date). Retrieved between September 15, 2002 and November 30, 2002, from www.woodradio.com/polls/viewlatest.html?pollD=4111

Nigoya, D. (2002, May 20). Mascot foes march into Eaton; Fightin' Reds protest given quiet response. *Denver Post*. Retrieved from www.denverpost.com/framework/0,1918,36%7E53%7E622747%7E,00.html

Ochoa, J. (2002, May 18). Eaton calls in security for mascot rally. *Greeley Tribune*. Retrieved from www.greeleytrib.com/article.php?sid=8641&mode=thread&order =0

Page, C. (2002, March 19). The "Fighting Whites" offer lesson in cultural diversity. *Newsday*, A32.

Spindel, C. (2000). *Dancing at Halftime: Sports and the Controversy Over American Indian Mascots*. New York: New York University Press.

T. Rex Essay: The Fighting Whities. (2002, March 25). Retrieved from www.geocities.com/Hollywood/Theater/4619/sports/essay/whities.html

Team chooses a white man as its mascot. (2002, March 11). *Daily Camera* (Boulder, Colorado). Retrieved from www.thedailycamera.com/news/statewest/lllwhit.htmll

Vassilaros, D. (2002, March 17). Political correctness off-base on mascots. *Pittsburgh Tribune-Review*. Retrieved from pittsburghlive.com/x/tribune review/columnists/vassilaros/s_61645.htm1

Wampum Chronicles message board. (No date). Retrieved between September 15, 2002 and November 30, 2002, from publl.ezboard.com/fwampumchroniclescurrent events.showMessage?topicID=265.topic

White, R., Messner, J., & Cuny, C. (2002, May). Fighting Whites: Everthang's gonna be all white. Official Home Page. Retrieved from www.fightingwhites.org

"Whities" on the court; insult doesn't work if name doesn't hurt. (2002, March 13). Omaha *World-Herald,* 6B.

17

Note to Congress: Stop Shielding "Indian" Mascots and Start Defending Indian People

Suzan Shown Harjo

It seems that you have to be an "Indian" mascot or an Abramoff-like high roller in a skybox to get the attention of some members of Congress.

At the same time that Native Americans are still denied full access to the justice system, some legislators want to throw open the courthouse doors to those who stereotype Native peoples.

Usually, it doesn't matter when a few congressmen drop a private interest bill. But when one of the sponsors is Speaker of the House Dennis Hastert, it matters.

The Hastert bill would hand a few schools a lawsuit against the National Collegiate Athletic Association, which has ruled that its members' "hostile" and "abusive" sports signifiers are not permitted in championship games. The bill is an admission that the schools don't have a legal leg to stand on.

Hastert's May 4 bill was introduced in reaction to the NCAA's April 28 decision to retain three universities on the list of those "subject to restrictions on the use of Native American mascots, names and imagery at NCAA championships."

Among the objectionable "Indian" references is one in Hastert's home state, "Chief Illiniwek," mascot of the University of Illinois at Urbana-Champaign.

The other schools are the University of North Dakota's "Fighting Sioux" and the Indiana University of Pennsylvania's "Indians." Illinois and Pennsylvania cleared their states of Indian people long ago. North Dakota shares borders with Native nations and none of them supports the "Fighting Sioux."

In denying the universities' appeals of earlier decisions, the NCAA concluded that their "Native" references "create hostile or abusive environments inconsistent with the NCAA constitution and inconsistent with the NCAA commitment to diversity, respect and sportsmanship."

The NCAA's decision means the schools "will only be invited to participate in NCAA championships if they elect to do so without Native American references on their uniforms and associated athletic program activities. It also means these institutions will not be allowed to host NCAA championship events."

Hastert's bill would allow institutions of higher education to reach back to August of 2005, before the NCAA rendered any decisions, to sue the NCAA and collect attorney fees and damages. The bill specifies that lawsuits would be "against entities that improperly regulate intercollegiate sports activities."

It is virtually unheard of for Congress to provide retroactive causes of action because courts usually toss them out as unconstitutional.

Two other Illinois members co-sponsored the bill, Rep. Timothy Johnson, a Republican who represents the district home of "Chief Illiniwek," and Rep. Jerry F. Costello, a Democrat.

The other original sponsor is Rep. F. Allen Boyd Jr., who represents Tallahassee, Fla., home of the Florida State University "Seminoles." The NCAA let FSU off the hook after Gov. Jeb Bush and state legislators professed undying admiration for the Seminole Tribe, which gave its blessing to FSU.

Johnson says House Bill 5289 is "in the interest of preserving the sovereignty of member institutions." That statement envisions creating an academic sovereignty that is on a par with tribal sovereignty, and it's a slam at the NCAA for recognizing tribal sovereignty in matters regarding usage of tribal names and images.

The NCAA "has assumed the mantle of social arbiters," says Johnson. "They need to go back to scheduling ballgames and leave the social engineering to others."

Stephen J. Kaufman, a UIUC professor of cell and structural biology, says the bill is "hypocrisy" on Johnson's part. "Johnson was a co-sponsor of a bill in the Illinois State Legislature to make Chief Illiniwek the symbol of the [school]," says Kaufman, "thus taking away the decision-making power from the university."

Kaufman also points out that the "elected Student/Faculty Senate of the University of Illinois voted overwhelmingly, 97 to 29, to remove [the mascot]. It was political interference by people like Mr. Johnson that subverted the autonomy of the university and quashed that vote."

Johnson paints a dire picture of economic chaos: "Local economies across the country would be impacted if the NCAA's recent decisions are allowed to prevail unchecked."

It is difficult to imagine the negative economic impact Johnson predicts.

NCAA rulings only affect NCAA-member schools and only those with "Indian" names and symbols that are "hostile" or "abusive."

The schools are voluntary members of the NCAA and aren't forced to change anything. They just have to leave their racial stereotypes behind when they compete for championships.

Even if the schools do change their "Indian" references, they have only a one-time cost, but a double sales opportunity in both memorabilia and new paraphernalia.

When the Washington "Wizards" changed from the "Bullets" in 1997, the merchandise sales offset the costs of converting to the new name.

There are fans and there are fanatics. The UIUC diehards will likely wear their orange "Chief Illiniwek" shirts to the nursing homes.

It's an odd spectacle to see the occasional septuagenarian fans in tattered "Indians" paraphernalia at Stanford University and Dartmouth College games, where their "Indian" references were jettisoned in 1973 and 1974, respectively.

Most people don't recall that the University of Oklahoma once had a mascot called "Little Red." That was the first "Indian" reference to be eliminated from the American sports scene. Then, in 1970, there were over 3,000 "Indian" sports references. Now, there are fewer than 1,000.

In the past 36 years, as over two thirds of the schools have eliminated their "Indian" sports references, the economic impact has been negligible. Native people measure the difference in terms of a more civil society.

Most of the remaining "Indian" references remaining are in athletic programs of elementary, middle, and high schools.

Of the institutions of higher education on the NCAA list, the NCAA reports that four were removed because of approvals by "namesake" tribes; five changed or are changing their references; six remain on the list, with one appeal pending; three are pending NCAA staff review; and one is on a watch list.

The Hastert bill is the "Protection of University Governance Act of 2006." Its name is so innocuous that Rep. Dan Boren, D-Okla., mistakenly added his name to the bill because he thought it "would help schools such as Southeastern Oklahoma State University [formerly, 'Savages'] recoup costs associated with eliminating offensive mascots."

Boren withdrew support for the bill on May 9, saying, "Upon further inspection it is clear to me that this bill does not achieve that goal. Rather, this bill helps those schools that refuse to change and I cannot support that effort."

Every major national Native organization since the 1960s has advocated for the elimination of all "Indian" names, images, symbols, logos, mascots, and behaviors.

At the same time, Native peoples have pleaded with Congress, to no avail, for a right of action to defend sacred places. Without that, irreplaceable treasures are being desecrated and destroyed.

It is disgraceful that any member of Congress would open the door to frivolous lawsuits to shield offensive sports signifiers while keeping the courthouses barricaded against living Native Americans who are trying to gain religious freedom.

NOTE

This essay was originally published in 2006 on the Woodland Indians Forum, http://www.woodlandindians.org

18

The Resurrection of the Chief

Dave Zirin

This past weekend, an unfortunate figure returned to the University of Illinois, and it wasn't Jeff George. The devil in question was Chief Illiniwek. The former school mascot returned to adorn floats and assorted regalia at Homecoming to the cheers of some and the bitter horror of those who thought the feathered one had been resigned to history's trash heap.

You may have thought that the Chief was banned last year after the NCAA called Illiniwek a "hostile or abusive" mascot and prevented the school from hosting postseason games as long as it paraded him about. You may have thought Illinois had joined dozens of other schools from Stanford to St. John's in putting Native American caricatures to bed. You thought wrong. A victory 20 years in the making was overturned when Chancellor Richard Herman declared that the Homecoming ban violated the U.S. Constitution, saying, "The University values free speech and free expression and considers Homecoming floats, decorations, costumes and related signage all representations of such personal expression." Yes, our forefathers fought and died to protect the right to display caricatures of the conquered at public institutions of higher learning. The word *Illiniwek* means "tribe of superior men." In their decision, Herman acted in a manner of the inferior, following instead of leading.

Those whose heart is with the dancing chief were thrilled, calling Homecoming "a victory parade." The organization Students for Chief Illini had issued a statement that the original policy was a "slap in the face to people in the community to say you can't support your symbol." In an irony that could only be found in the bizarre lexicon of university political correctness, the group uses the world "symbol" instead of "mascot" because the

term "mascot" is offensive to Chief Illiniwek. Keep in mind that there never
was a Chief Illiniwek. No one with that name ever existed. His costume is not
in keeping with anything the Illini tribe ever wore and the dance at halftime
was created in 1926 by the Boy Scouts. But by all means support such a noble
symbol. Students for Stepin Fetchit are meeting down the hall.

The Chief was certainly celebrated at Homecoming. No counter protestors
were reported and thousands of attendees wore Chief regalia. Although no
Native American organizations support the Chief, he was celebrated lustily.
The same students and alumni that clamor for the Chief as a symbol of Native
American nobility put far more time and energy into a fictional chief than aid-
ing actual Native Americans. Students of Native American descent are a mere
0.2% of the overall student population, and 0.1% of the faculty. "Honoring"
Native Americans is confined to a white guy in buckskin pants and feathers
(only whites have portrayed the Chief throughout its 81-year history).

There was little said about the fact that while Chief Illiniwek never existed,
the Illini tribe did. They were torn apart, forcibly removed, and exterminated
so schools like UIUC could take root. Chief Ron Froman of the Peoria tribe—
the descendents of the Illiniwek—once said of the Chief, "I don't think it was
to honor us, because, hell, they ran our [butts] out of Illinois."

Since there is nothing honorable about resurrecting the Chief, is it then an
issue of freedom of speech? In a letter to Chancellor Herman, Prof. Antonia
Darder wrote, "If a float maker wants to use KKK imagery or a noose hang-
ing from a tree on a homecoming float, is this now also acceptable under
the auspices of 'free expression'? Or if a float maker wants to use images of
people copulating or nude participants on a float, would this also be accepted
as the freedom of personal expression? And if not, why not? Certainly if
public nudity is considered immoral or at least inappropriate, why not public
racism?"

The noose example was not used by Darder idly. Recent weeks have seen
the prevalence of noose hangings on college campuses to inflame and intimidate. This is the climate in which Herman resurrects the Chief.

The latest in this marathon battle of memory, history, and the role of sports
in this process goes down two weeks after the death of Native American
activist and longtime leader of the American Indian Movement Vernon Bellecourt. Bellecourt spent years as a thorn in the side of organizations like the
Redskins and Cleveland Indians, demanding that they put the Minstrelsy to
rest. He once said, "Our detractors always say, 'We are honoring you.' It's
not an honor. In whose honor, we have to ask. Beginning with the pilgrims
at Plymouth Rock, about 16 million of us were wiped out, including whole
villages in Washington, where native girls were sold on the auction block as
sex slaves in mining towns, and young boys were made slaves on ranches."

To other teams with Indian nicknames and to their fans, he said, "No more chicken feathers. . . . No more paint on faces. The chop stops here."

NOTE

This essay was originally published in *Sports Illustrated* (October 30, 2007).

19

Tribe Approval of Mascots Not Enough

Daily Cardinal *Editorial Board, University of Wisconsin*

All claims of deference and honor to indigenous populations aside, there are few things in sports more offensive than the caricatures of American Indians that populate a surprising number of college and professional logos.

There is of course a spectrum of disrespect, ranging from the extreme—such as the Cleveland Indians' giant-toothed, red-faced cartoon character or the University of Illinois' former dancing Illini chief—to the relatively restrained. But regardless of just how culturally insensitive each individual mascot happens to be, the fundamental idea of co-opting Native identity and slapping pictures on football helmets, baseball hats, and hockey jerseys remains indicative of race-based oppression, and, in some cases, a refusal to view American Indians fully as people.

It is then commendable that the University of Wisconsin refuses to schedule athletic events with schools that do not have the prior approval of specific tribes and the NCAA to caricaturize Native peoples or use their names in competition. In fact, until last week, UW refused to play any "Indian" teams at all unless forced by conference scheduling or traditional rivalry. A recent decision will allow the Badgers to play schools such as Florida State, who have the approval of the local Seminole tribe, and Utah, whose Ute tribe has also given the go-ahead, but not teams who do not meet official standards.

Picking on such obvious villains, however, does little to address other persisting issues regarding American Indian mascots. For example, Florida State still features a screaming white man painting his face, riding a horse to the 50-yard line, and throwing a burning spear in the ground at home football games. Will UW refuse to play a team that exhibits such insensitivity, even if it does so within the rules? It certainly should if the goal is to respect Native populations and not simply to avoid bad publicity.

Teams such as the Brewers and Packers—whose mascots were and in a sense still are fat, sausage-eating Germans—and the Vikings, who feature a bearded barbarian with horns on his head, have also used negative stereotypes in sports.

But there is a difference, namely that hundreds of thousands of Germans and Scandinavians were not chased, murdered, and scalped across the country for hundreds of years before then being used as logos in a spirit akin to naming a team after an extinct animal. UW should address that problem before it pats itself on the back for not letting Chief Illiniwek into the Kohl Center.

Part IV

DOCUMENTS: POLICIES, RESOLUTIONS, AND LEGISLATION

The most comprehensive understanding of the controversy over Native American mascots emerges from a reading of primary sources. A reading of institutional policy statements, organizational resolutions, and legislation proposed at the state and federal levels provides keen insight into the evolving public debate over team names, logos, and practices incorporating Indianness and foregrounding the central issues of concern. Once largely a concern of tribal governments and interest groups, now mainstream organizations and societal gatekeepers, from the NCAA to the U.S. Civil Rights Commission, are increasingly taking part. Moreover, the perspectives articulated have become increasingly nuanced, informed by a growing literature and cognizant of a complex array of issues. Finally, while a number of documents center on condemnation and critique, more often than not policy statements and legislation work to change attitudes and practices. The documents selected for this section seek to illustrate this history and detail the range of institutions and groups who have spoken out against and worked to remedy the impacts associated with Native American mascots.

20

Statement on the Use of Native American Images and Nicknames as Sports Symbols (2001)

United States Commission on Civil Rights

The U.S. Commission on Civil Rights calls for an end to the use of Native American images and team names by non-Native schools. The Commission deeply respects the rights of all Americans to freedom of expression under the First Amendment and in no way would attempt to prescribe how people can express themselves. However, the Commission believes that the use of Native American images and nicknames in school is insensitive and should be avoided. In addition, some Native American and civil rights advocates maintain that these mascots may violate anti-discrimination laws. These references, whether mascots and their performances, logos, or names, are disrespectful and offensive to American Indians and others who are offended by such stereotyping. They are particularly inappropriate and insensitive in light of the long history of forced assimilation that American Indian people have endured in this country.

Since the civil rights movement of the 1960s many overtly derogatory symbols and images offensive to African-Americans have been eliminated. However, many secondary schools, post-secondary institutions, and a number of professional sports teams continue to use Native American nicknames and imagery. Since the 1970s, American Indian leaders and organizations have vigorously voiced their opposition to these mascots and team names because they mock and trivialize Native American religion and culture.

It is particularly disturbing that Native American references are still to be found in educational institutions, whether elementary, secondary or post-secondary. Schools are places where diverse groups of people come together to learn not only the "Three Rs," but also how to interact respectfully with people from different cultures. The use of stereotypical images of Native

Americans by educational institutions has the potential to create a racially hostile educational environment that may be intimidating to Indian students. American Indians have the lowest high school graduation rates in the nation and even lower college attendance and graduation rates. The perpetuation of harmful stereotypes may exacerbate these problems.

The stereotyping of any racial, ethnic, religious or other groups when promoted by our public educational institutions, teach all students that stereotyping of minority groups is acceptable, a dangerous lesson in a diverse society. Schools have a responsibility to educate their students; they should not use their influence to perpetuate misrepresentations of any culture or people. Children at the elementary and secondary level usually have no choice about which school they attend. Further, the assumption that a college student may freely choose another educational institution if she feels uncomfortable around Indian-based imagery is a false one. Many factors, from educational programs to financial aid to proximity to home, limit a college student's choices. It is particularly onerous if the student must also consider whether or not the institution is maintaining a racially hostile environment for Indian students.

Schools that continue to use Indian imagery and references claim that their use stimulates interest in Native American culture and honors Native Americans. These institutions have simply failed to listen to the Native groups, religious leaders, and civil rights organizations that oppose these symbols. These Indian-based symbols and team names are not accurate representations of Native Americans. Even those that purport to be positive are romantic stereotypes that give a distorted view of the past. These false portrayals prevent non-Native Americans from understanding the true historical and cultural experiences of American Indians. Sadly, they also encourage biases and prejudices that have a negative effect on contemporary Indian people. These references may encourage interest in mythical "Indians" created by the dominant culture, but they block genuine understanding of contemporary Native people as fellow Americans.

The Commission assumes that when Indian imagery was first adopted for sports mascots it was not to offend Native Americans. However, the use of the imagery and traditions, no matter how popular, should end when they are offensive. We applaud those who have been leading the fight to educate the public and the institutions that have voluntarily discontinued the use of insulting mascots. Dialogue and education are the roads to understanding. The use of American Indian mascots is not a trivial matter. The Commission has a firm understanding of the problems of poverty, education, housing, and health care that face many Native Americans. The fight to eliminate Indian nicknames and images in sports is only one front of the larger battle to eliminate obstacles that confront American Indians. The elimination of Native American nicknames and images as sports mascots will benefit not only Native Americans, but all Americans. The elimination of stereotypes will make room for education about real Indian people, current Native American issues, and the rich variety of American Indian cultures in our country.

21

The Five Civilized Tribes Intertribal Council Mascot Resolution (July 14, 2001)

Five Civilized Tribes Intertribal Council

Whereas, the Intertribal Council of the Five Civilized Tribes is an organization that united the tribal governments of the Chickasaw, Choctaw, Cherokee, Muscogee (Creek), and Seminole Nations, representing over 400,000 Indian people throughout the United States; and

Whereas, the Intertribal Council of the Five Civilized Tribes Education Committee is dedicated to promoting quality education for American Indian students that includes cultural awareness and a sense of diversity among America's student population; and,

Whereas, the Five Civilized Tribes believe the use of derogatory American Indian images such as mascots by public schools perpetuate a stereotypical image of American Indians that is likely to have a negative impact on the self-esteem of American Indian children; and

Whereas, negative images and stereotypes about American Indians as mascots contribute to a hostile learning environment that affirms the negative images and stereotypes that persist in America about American Indians; and

Whereas, American Indians as mascots is a negative means of appropriating and denigrating our cultural identity that involves the display and depiction of ceremonial symbols and practices that may have religious significance to American Indians; and

Whereas, to continue the negative use of American Indians' tribal names and images is an offensive and disgusting practice that would be considered intolerable were other ethnic groups or minorities depicted in a similar manner; and

Whereas, on April 13, 2001, the United States Commission on Civil Rights issued a Statement on the Use of Native American Images and Nicknames as

Sports Symbols that called for an end to the use of American Indian images and team names by non-Indian schools; that stereotyping of any racial, ethnic, religious or other groups when promoted by public education institutions, teach all students that stereotyping of minority groups is acceptable, a dangerous lesson in a diverse society; that schools have a responsibility to educate their students; they should not use influence to perpetuate misrepresentations of any culture or people; and

Now therefore be it resolved, that the Intertribal Council of the Five Civilized Tribes joins the United States Commission on Civil Rights call to eliminate the stereotypical use of American Indian names and images as mascots in sports and other events and to provide meaningful education about real American Indian people, current American Indian issues, and, the rich variety of American Indian cultures in the U.S.

Chadwick Smith, Principal Chief, Cherokee Nation (Signed)
Bill Anoatubby, Governor, Chickasaw Nation (Signed)
R. Perry Beaver, Principal Chief, Creek Nation (Signed)
Jerry Haney, Principal Chief, Seminole Nation (Signed)
Gregory E. Pyle, Principal Chief, Choctaw Nation (Signed)

22

Opposition to the University of North Dakota's Use of the Fighting Sioux Name and Logo (2002)

Governing Body of the Three Affiliated Tribes of the Fort Berthold Indian Reservation

Whereas, This Nation having accepted the Indian Reorganization Act of June 18, 1934, and the authority under said Act; and

Whereas, the Three Affiliated Tribes Constitution authorizes and empowers the Mandan, Hidatsa & Arikara Tribal Business Council to engage in activity on behalf of and in the interest of the welfare and benefit of the Tribes and of the enrolled members thereof; and

Whereas, the use of an American Indian stereotype demeaning by its very nature, whether intended as such or not; and

Whereas, these stereotypical symbols create an environment in which degrading acts become more acceptable and promote practices that trivialize and demean Native American culture, traditions and spirituality; and

Whereas, this is an issue of human rights because the use of such a name and symbol at the University of North Dakota limits the ability of all Native Students to learn and take part in campus and community activities; and

Now, therefore be it resolved, that the Mandan Hidatsa & Arikara Nation does hereby support the ending of the use of outdated and politically incorrect American Indian stereotypes at the University of North Dakota and all across America that demean the history and culture of Indian nations; and

Be it further resolved, that Mandan Hidatsa & Arikara Nation supports the aforementioned request to end the University of North Dakota's use of the "Fighting Sioux" name and its accompanying "Indian-head" symbol; and

Finally, be it resolved, that Mandan Hidatsa & Arikara nation does hereby support this resolution in response to end the national use of stereotypical images that demean, rather than honor American Indian Nations.

23

Denouncement of the Use of Any American Indian Name or Artifice Associated with Team Mascots by Any Professional/Nonprofessional Sport Teams (1993)

National Congress of American Indians

Whereas, the American Indian and Alaska Tribal Government and people have gathered in Green Bay, Wisconsin, for the Mid-Year Meeting of the National Congress of American Indians (NCAI) in order to promote the common interests and welfare of American Indians and Alaskan Native peoples; and

Whereas, NCAI is the oldest and largest intertribal organization representative of and advocate for national, regional, and local tribal concerns; and,

Whereas, the NCAI condemns the racist and condescending attitude of team owners, colleges and high schools, which continue to demean the members of our Nations; and,

Now therefore be it resolved that the NCAI denounces the use of any American Indian name or Artifice associated with Indian mascots; and,

Be it further resolved that the NCAI calls upon all reasonable individuals in decision making positions to voluntarily change racist and dehumanizing mascots

Adopted by the Executive Council at the Mid-Year Meeting of the National Congress of American Indians, June 28–30, 1993.

24

Resolution in Opposition to Native American Mascots (1999)

National Association for the
Advancement of Colored People

Whereas, the National NAACP is committed to caring for and affirming the gifts of all people, with special regard to oppressed or disenfranchised on the basis of race, national origin, and cultural origin; and

Whereas, the use of Native American people, images, symbols, and cultural and religious traditions as sports names and mascots perpetuates racist stereotypes and undermines the self-determination and dignity of Indian people; and

Whereas, the National NAACP, as a nationally and internationally recognized protector of civil and human rights, is in the unique position to impact public and corporate policies and practices,

Therefore, Be It Resolved, that the National NAACP calls upon all members and friends to refrain from purchasing items with Native American sports team logos, and to cross out such logos on merchandise already in their possession.

Be It Further Resolved, that the National NAACP call upon member branches and State Conferences of Branches to inform themselves of and support local efforts to eliminate the use of Native American people, images, symbols, and cultural and religious traditions as sports names, logos, and mascots.

Be It Finally Resolved, that the National NAACP call upon all professional sports teams, and public and private schools and universities currently using such names and images to reject the use of Native Americans, and all historically oppressed people and their cultural traditions, as sports mascots and symbols, and affirm their commitment to respectful racial and cultural inclusion in all aspects of their institutions.

25

Statement on Team Names (1993)

American Jewish Committee

Whereas it is the mission of the American Jewish Committee to combat bigotry and promote intergroup relations, and;

Whereas the use of racial or ethnic stereotypes in the names, nicknames, or titles of business, professional, sport, or other public entities is frequently demeaning, whether intended as such or not;

Whereas demeaning symbols create an environment in which degrading acts become more acceptable;

Whereas many teams still sport names such as "Indians," "Braves," "Redskins," "Chiefs," "Redmen," etc.;

Whereas such names are degrading and promote practices that trivialize and demean people and religious beliefs and symbols;

Therefore, the American Jewish Committee deplores and opposes the use of racial or ethnic stereotypes in the names or titles of business, professional, sport, or their public entities when the affected group has not chosen the name itself. The AJC resolves to encourage such entities to end their use of offending stereotypes.

26

Statement on the Use of American Indian Sports Mascots (January 27, 1999)

Society of Indian Psychologists

We, the undersigned members of the Society of Indian Psychologists of the Americas, write this letter in support of "retiring" all Indian personalities as the official symbols and mascots of universities, colleges, or schools (and athletic teams). We support doing so because of a variety of concerns related to the ethical practice of psychology. As a professional society of psychologists we operate under these professional ethical guidelines.

We are concerned that the continued use of Indian symbols and mascots seriously compromises our ability to engage in ethical professional practice and service to the campus (delete campus if addressing all mascots) community. We believe that it establishes an unwelcome academic environment for Indian (students, staff, and faculty) and contributes to the miseducation of all members of the (campus) community regarding the cultural practices and traditions of an entire ethnic group. In our view, the use of a historically and culturally inaccurate, stereotypic image undermines the educational experience of all members of the (university) community. It seems especially problematic for those who have had little or no contact with Indian people and their cultures.

Stereotypical and historically inaccurate images of Indians in general interfere with learning about them by creating, supporting, and maintaining oversimplified and inaccurate views of indigenous peoples and their cultures. When stereotypical representations are taken as factual information, they contribute to the development of cultural biases and prejudices (clearly a contradiction to the educational mission of the university). In the same vein, we believe that continuation of the use of Indians as symbols and mascots is incongruous with the philosophy espoused by many Americans as promoting inclusivity and diversity.

We understand that some affiliated with the institutions having a long history of use of these symbols may have a special attachment to them. We also understand and believe that this attachment may not have been formed out of maliciousness or negative intentions. To the extent, however, that tradition and/or economic issues are major obstacles to change, they should not usurp the principles of a society struggling to put an end to racism. What once may have been a unifying symbol for the various bodies using these symbols has become a source of cross-cultural conflict. In light of all of these factors, we strongly support and encourage all such entities to develop a new symbol consistent with and contributing to the positive realization of national principles (our educational mission.)

In support of our concern about the ethically problematic nature of this issue for the professional practice of psychology, we cite relevant portions of the "Ethical Principles of Psychologists and Code of Conduct" (American Psychological Association [APA, 1992]) and the "Guidelines for Providers of Psychological Services to Ethnic, Linguistic and Culturally Diverse Populations" (APA, 1992).

Principle D (Respect for People's Rights and Dignity) states:

Psychologists accord appropriate respect to the fundamental rights, dignity, and worth of all people. They respect the rights of individuals to privacy, confidentiality, self-determination, and autonomy, mindful that legal and other obligations may lead to inconsistency and conflict with the exercise of these rights. Psychologists are aware of cultural, individual, and role differences, including those due to age, gender, race, ethnicity, national origin, religion, sexual orientation, disability, language, and socioeconomic status. Psychologists try to eliminate the effect on their work of biases based on those factors, and they do not knowingly participate in or condone unfair discriminatory practices.

Principle E (Concern for Others' Welfare) states:

Psychologists seek to contribute to the welfare of those with whom they interact professionally. In their professional actions, psychologists weigh the welfare and rights of their patients or clients, students, supervisees, human research participants, and other affected persons. . . .

When conflicts occur among psychologists' obligations or concerns, they attempt to resolve these conflicts and to perform their roles in a responsible fashion that avoids or minimizes harm. Psychologists are sensitive to real and ascribed differences in power between themselves and others, and they do not exploit or mislead other people during or after professional relationships.

Principle F (Social Responsibility) states:

Psychologists are aware of their professional and scientific responsibilities to the community and the society in which they work and live. They apply and make public their knowledge of psychology in order to contribute to human welfare. Psychologists are concerned about and work to mitigate the causes of human suffering. When undertaking research, they strive to advance human welfare and the science of psychology. Psychologists try to avoid misuse of their work. Psychologists comply with the law and encourage the development of law and social policy that serve the interests of their patients and clients and the public.

In addition, several of the "Guidelines for Providers of Psychological Services to Ethnic, Linguistic and Culturally Diverse Populations" also address our concerns on this issue.

#5. Psychologists respect client's religious and/or spiritual beliefs and values, including attributions and taboos, since they affect worldview, psychosocial functioning, and expressions of distress.
   a. Part of working in minority communities is to become familiar with indigenous beliefs and practices and respect them. . . .
#7. Psychologists consider the impact of adverse social, environmental, and political factors in assessing problems and designing interventions. . . .
   b. Psychologists work within the cultural setting to improve the welfare of all persons concerned, if there is a conflict between cultural values and human rights.
#8. Psychologists attend to as well as work to eliminate biases, prejudices, and discriminatory practices.
   a. Psychologists acknowledge relevant discriminatory practices at the social and community level that may be affecting the psychological welfare of the population being served.

We applaud the current efforts across the nation to have this crucial issue raised and addressed in a responsible and productive way. It is our hope this letter contributes to that effort.

27

Resolution Recommending the Immediate Retirement of American Indian Mascots, Symbols, Images, and Personalities by Schools, Colleges, Universities, Athletic Teams, and Organizations

American Psychological Association

Whereas, the American Psychological Association has recognized that racism and racial discrimination are attitudes and behavior that are learned and that threaten human development (American Psychological Association, 2001);

Whereas, the American Psychological Association has resolved to denounce racism in all its forms and to call upon all psychologists to speak out against racism, and take proactive steps to prevent the occurrence of intolerant or racist acts (American Psychological Association, 2001);

Whereas, the continued use of American Indian mascots, symbols, images, and personalities undermines the educational experiences of members of all communities—especially those who have had little or no contact with Indigenous peoples (Connolly, 2000; U.S. Commission on Civil Rights, 2001; Society of Indian Psychologists, 1999; Webster, Loudbear, Corn, & Vigue, 1971);

Whereas, the continued use of American Indian mascots, symbols, images, and personalities establishes an unwelcome and often times hostile learning environment for American Indian students that affirms negative images/stereotypes that are promoted in mainstream society (Clark & Witko, in press; Fryberg, 2003; Fryberg & Markus, 2003; Fryberg, 2004a; Munson, 2001; Society of Indian Psychologists, 1999; Staurowsky, 1999);

Whereas, the continued use of American Indian mascots, symbols, images, and personalities by school systems appears to have a negative impact on the self-esteem of American Indian children (Chamberlin, 1999; Eagle and Condor Indigenous People's Alliance, 2003; Fryberg, 2004b; Fryberg & Markus, 2003; Maryland Commission on Indian Affairs, 2001; Society of Indian Psychologists, 1999; The Inter-Tribal Council of the Five Civilized Tribes, 2001; Vanderford, 1996);

Whereas, the continued use of American Indian mascots, symbols, images, and personalities undermines the ability of American Indian Nations to portray accurate and respectful images of their culture, spirituality, and traditions (Clark & Witko, in press; Davis, 1993; Gone, 2002; Rodriquez, 1998; Witko, 2005);

Whereas, the continued use of American Indian mascots, symbols, images, and personalities presents stereotypical images of American Indian communities, that may be a violation of the civil rights of American Indian people (Dolley, 2003; King, 2001; King & Springwood, 2001; Pewewardy, 1991; Springwood & King, 2000; U.S. Commission on Civil Rights, 2001);

Whereas, the continued use of American Indian mascots, symbols, images, and personalities is a form of discrimination against Indigenous Nations that can lead to negative relations between groups (Cook-Lynn, 2001; Coombe, 1999; U.S. Commission on Civil Rights, 2001; Witko, 2005);

Whereas, the continued use of American Indian symbols, mascots, images, and personalities is a detrimental manner of illustrating the cultural identity of American Indian people through negative displays and/or interpretations of spiritual and traditional practices (Adams, 1995; Banks, 1993; Nuessel, 1994; Staurowsky, 1999; Witko, 2005);

Whereas, the continued use of American Indian mascots, symbols, images, and personalities is disrespectful of the spiritual beliefs and values of American Indian nations (Churchill, 1994; Gone, 2002; Sheppard, 2004; Staurowsky, 1998);

Whereas, the continued use of American Indian mascots, symbols, images, and personalities is an offensive and intolerable practice to American Indian Nations that must be eradicated (U.S. Commission on Civil Rights, 2001; Society of Indian Psychologists, 1999);

Whereas, the continued use of American Indian mascots, symbols, images, and personalities has a negative impact on other communities by allowing for the perpetuation of stereotypes and stigmatization of another cultural group (Fryberg, 2004b; Gone, 2002; Staurowsky, 1999; U.S. Commission on Civil Rights, 2001);

Therefore be it resolved that the American Psychological Association recognizes the potential negative impact the use of American Indian mascots, symbols, images, and personalities have on the mental health and psychological behavior of American Indian people;

Therefore be it resolved that the American Psychological Association encourages continued research on the psychological effects American Indian mascots, symbols, images, and personalities have on American Indian communities and others;

Therefore be it resolved that the American Psychological Association encourages the development of programs for the public, psychologists, and students in psychology to increase awareness of the psychological effects that American Indian mascots, symbols, images, and personalities have on American Indian communities and others;

And, therefore be it resolved that the American Psychological Association supports and recommends the immediate retirement of American Indian mascots, symbols, images, and personalities by schools, colleges, universities, athletic teams, and organizations.

—Adopted by the APA Council of Representatives on August 21, 2005

JUSTIFICATION STATEMENT FOR THE RESOLUTION RECOMMENDING THE IMMEDIATE RETIREMENT OF AMERICAN INDIAN MASCOTS, SYMBOLS, IMAGES, AND PERSONALITIES BY SCHOOLS, COLLEGES, UNIVERSITIES, ATHLETIC TEAMS, AND ORGANIZATIONS (AMERICAN PSYCHOLOGICAL ASSOCIATION)

1. Historical Perspective On This Issue.

Through historical processes of colonization, boarding schools, disempowerment, and relocation, the U.S. government has sought to devalue, dehumanize, and assimilate American Indian nations, cultures, and contributions (Witko, 2005). The legacy of the detrimental effects of these historical processes continues today through the devaluing and dehumanization inherent in the public use of American Indian symbols, mascots, images, and personalities (King, 2002; Springwood & King, 2000; Rodriguez, 1998; Davis, 1993).

This history has led to a legacy of internalized oppression that comes from centuries of dehumanizing practices intended to promote American Indian self-hatred and encourage non-American Indians to believe that they are heroic conquerors (Munson, 2001; King & Springwood, 2000; Staurowsky, 1998; Adams, 1995; Drinnon, 1980). Oddly enough, even though most American Indian leaders and organizations have been voicing their discontent with the mockery and trivialization of their religion and culture, no one seems to be listening (Sheppard, 2004; U.S. Commission on Civil Rights, 2001; Pewewardy, 1991). In fact many people, including some American Indians, continue to believe that American Indian mascots and symbols serve to honor American Indian people, even though less than ten percent of American Indians surveyed in a 2001 Indian Country Today poll felt that mascots and symbols generally honored American Indian communities.

Today there have been several groups and tribes that have advocated for the retiring of American Indian mascots, symbols, images, and personalities used by athletic teams and education systems, primarily citing the damage such images/symbols have on an American Indian individual's self-esteem, self-worth, and identity (Society of Indian Psychologists, 1999; The Intertribal Council of the Five Civilized Tribes, 2001; Maryland Commission on Indian Affairs, 2001; Eagle and Condor Indigenous People's Alliance, 2003).

2. Relevance To Psychology And Psychologists And Importance To Psychology Or To Society As A Whole.

There are many negative psychological consequences of the use of American Indian mascots, symbols, images, and personalities by schools, colleges, universities, athletic teams, and others. The damage to self-esteem and identity are the aspects that appear to be the most severely compromised (Witko, 2005; Springwood & King, 2000; Vanderford, 1996; Webster, Loudbear, Corn, & Vigue, 1971).

Issues Related To Self-Esteem:

When schools promote the use of American Indian mascots, it leads to a devaluing of self and a decrease in self-esteem for American Indian peoples (Chamberlin, 1999; Society of Indian Psychologists, 1999). Self-esteem is an important ingredient in resiliency and positive mental health adjustment. It is important that a group does not feel compromised in this important area of psychological functioning, as impairment of self-esteem can contribute to negative behaviors such as substance use and abuse, self-harming, and interpersonal violence (Witko, 2005; Cook-Lynn, 2001; Coombe, 1999).

Issues Related To Identity:

It is especially difficult when American Indian peoples are trying to present their tribal identity as accurately as possible, to have the dominant culture employ symbols, mascots, images and personalities that depict American Indians in an inaccurate and offensive manner (Staurowsky, 1999; Pewewardy, 1991). This can be especially challenging for American Indian children and adolescents whose identities are still in the formative stage of development (Clark & Witko, in press). Such challenges to American Indian children's identity can be equally challenging for their parents who are attempting to transfer cultural history in a positive way (Staurowsky, 1999). For a group that already occupies an ethnic minority status in this country and is not often depicted in a positive manner within mainstream media, literature, books, and education, the display of denigrating symbols, images, and mascots can be very damaging.

Infringement of Civil Rights:

The stereotyping of any racial, ethnic, or religious group by other groups and social institutions—especially public educational institutions and educators—has the potential to teach children and youth that stereotyping of ethnic minority groups is acceptable (U.S. Commission on Civil Rights, 2001). This is a dangerous lesson that can have harmful effects on communities of color and others. The use of American Indian mascots, symbols, images, and personalities is a form of discrimination against American Indian people because they are an inaccurate portrayal of a cultural group (Dolley, 2003; King & Springwood, 2001a; Springwood & King, 2001b).

All people of this nation have a right to self-determination. The use of American Indian mascots, symbols, images, and personalities infringes on American Indian peoples' pride and right to self-determination (King, 1998, 2001; Staurowsky, 1998). If not attended to immediately, the continued use of such symbols stands the risk of causing serious harm to future generations of American Indian people.

Cultural Misinformation:

Depicting cultures in an inaccurate and inappropriate manner promotes a negative perception of those cultures by other groups and creates an environment in which one group may be perceived as less than another group. For American Indian people, whose history is not often portrayed accurately in public education systems, the stereotypes that mascots, symbols, images, and personalities portray become the norm and miseducate American Indians and non–American Indians about American Indian culture, society, and spirituality (Gone, 2002; Connolly, 2000; Moses, 1996; Churchill, 1994; Nuessel, 1994; Banks, 1993).

3. Likely Degree of Consensus Among APA Constituents.

As psychologists we are bound by ethical standards that require us to: (1) Respect Peoples Rights and Dignities (Principle D), and (2) Have Concern for Others' Welfare (Principle E) (American Psychological Association, 2002).

Adherence to such standards would suggest unanimous consensus among APA constituents on the need to retire American Indian mascots, symbols, images, and personalities

4. Likelihood That The Proposed Resolution Will Have A Constructive Impact On Public Opinion/Policy, Assessment, Consultation, and Training.

In view of knowledge that psychologists have on the negative impact of stereotyping on communities of color and others, APA could serve as a major resource for those wanting to end the dehumanization and racial stereotyping of American Indian communities. In addition it is likely that APA's bold step in this matter will encourage other national professional and scientific associations to take similar steps, therefore leading to an end of racial stereotyping of American Indian people through use of American Indian mascots, symbols, images, and personalities.

REFERENCES

Adams, D. W. (1995). *Education for extinction: American Indians and the boarding school experience*. Lawrence: University Press of Kansas.

American Psychological Association. (2001, June). *An emergency action of the Board of Directors: Resolution against racism and in support of the goals of the 2001 United Nations World Conference*. Washington, DC: Author.

American Psychological Association. (n.d.). *Against racism, racial discrimination, xenophobia, and related intolerance*. Washington, DC: Author. Retrieved from http://www.apa.org/pi/racismresolution.html

Banks, D. (1993). Tribal names and mascots in sports. *Journal of Sport and Social Issues, 17*(1), 5–8.

Chamberlin, J. (1999). Indian psychologists support retiring of offensive team mascots. *APA Monitor, 30*(4).

Churchill, W. (1994). *Indians are us? Culture and genocide in Native North America*. Monroe, ME: Common Courage Press.

Clark, R., & Witko, T. (in press). Growing up Indian: Understanding urban Indian adolescents. In American Psychological Association, *No longer forgotten: Addressing the mental health needs of urban Indians*. Washington, DC: Author.

Connolly, M. R. (2000). What's in a name? A historical look at Native American related nicknames and symbols at three U.S. universities. *Journal of Higher Education, 71*(5), 515–547.

Cook-Lynn, E. (2001). *Anti-Indianism in North America: A voice from Tatekeya's earth*. Urbana: University of Illinois Press.

Coombe, R. J. (1999). Sports trademarks and somatic politics: Locating the law in critical cultural studies. In R. Martin & T. Miller (Eds.), *SportCult* (pp. 262–288). Minneapolis: University of Minnesota Press.

Davis, L. (1993). Protest against the use of Native American mascots: A challenge to traditional, American identity. *Journal of Sport and Social Issues, 17*(1), 9–22.

Dolley, J. (2003). The four r's: Use of Indian mascots in educational facilities. *Journal of Law and Education, 32*(1), pp. 21–35.

Eagle and Condor Indigenous People's Alliance (2003). *Resolution by the Eagle and Condor Indigenous Peoples' Alliance on eliminating Native American Indian descriptions naming mascots, logos, and sports team nicknames in Oklahoma public schools.* Retrieved from http://www.aistm.org/2003ecipa.htm

Fryberg, S. A. (2003, June). *Free to be me? The impact of using American Indians as mascots.* Invited address at the 16th annual convention of American Indian Psychologists and Psychology Graduate Students, Utah State University, Logan, Utah.

Fryberg, S. A. (2004a, November). *"Dude, I'm honoring you": The impact of using American Indian mascots.* Invited address at the North American Society for Sociology of Sports, Tucson, Arizona.

Fryberg, S. A. (2004b, June). *American Indian social representations: Do they honor or constrain identities?* Invited address at the Mellon Humanities Center Workshop/ Research Institute for Comparative Studies in Race and Ethnicity network, "How do identities matter?" Stanford University, Stanford, California.

Fryberg, S. A., & Markus, H. R. (2003). On being American Indian: Current and possible selves. *Journal of Self and Identity, 2*, 325–344.

Gone, J. P. (2002). Chief Illiniwek: Dignified or damaging? In T. Straus (Ed.), *Native Chicago* (2nd ed., pp. 274–286). Chicago: Albatross.

Inter-Tribal Council of the Five Civilized Tribes (2001). *The Five Civilized Tribes Intertribal Council Mascot Resolution.* Retrieved from http://aistm.org/2001.civilized.tribes.htm

King, C. R. (2001). Uneasy Indians: Creating and contesting Native American mascots at Marquette University. In C.R. King & C. F. Springwood (Eds.), *Team spirits: Essays on the history and significance of Native American mascots* (pp. 281–303). Lincoln: University of Nebraska Press.

King, C. R. (1998). Colonial discourses, collective memories, and the exhibition of Native American cultures and histories in the contemporary United States. New York: Garland.

King, C. R., & Springwood, C. F. (2000). *Beyond the cheers: Race as spectacle in college sports.* Albany: State University of New York Press.

Maryland Commission on Indian Affairs (2001). *Resolution of the Maryland Commission on Indian Affairs.* Retrieved from http://aistm.org/maryland.resolution.2001.htm

Moses, L. G. (1996). Wild West shows and the images of American Indians, 1883–1933. Albuquerque: University of New Mexico Press.

Munson, B. (2001). *Tolerance in the news.* Retrieved from http://www.tolerance.org/news/article_tol.jsp?id=169.]

Nuessel, F. (1994). Objectionable sports team designations. *Names: A Journal of Onomastics, 42*, 101–119.

Pewewardy, C. D. (1991). Native American mascots and imagery: The struggle of unlearning Indian stereotypes. *Journal of Navaho Education, 9*(1), 19–23.

Rodriguez, R. (1998). Plotting the assassination of Little Red Sambo: Psychologists join war against racist campus mascots. *Black Issues in Higher Education, 15*(8), 20–24.

Sheppard, H. (2004). Assembly: No redskins—Ban on name advances to Senate. *Los Angeles Daily*. Retrieved from http://www.dailynews.com/Stories/0,1413,200~20954~1923795,00

Society of Indian Psychologists. (1999). *Position statement in support of "retiring" all Indian personalities as the official symbols and mascots of universities, colleges, or schools (and athletic teams)*. Retrieved from http://www.aics.org/mascot/society.html

Springwood, C. F., & King, C. R. (2000). Race, power, and representation in contemporary American sport. In P. Kivisto & G. Rundblad (Eds.), *The color line at the dawn of the 21st century* (pp. 61–174). Thousand Oaks, CA: Pine Valley Press.

Staurowsky, E. (1998). An act of honor or exploitation? The Cleveland Indian's use of the Louis Francis Socalexis Story. *Sociology of Sports Journal, 15*, 299–316.

Staurowsky, E. (1999). American Indian imagery and the miseducation of America. *Quest, 51*(4), 382–392. Retrieved from http://www.aistm.org/staurowsky.miseducation.htm

U.S. Commission on Civil Rights (2001, April 13). *Statement of U.S. Commission on Civil Rights on the use of Native American images and nicknames as sports mascots*. Retrieved from http://www.aics.org/mascot/civilrights.html

Vanderford, H. (1996). What's in a name? Heritage or hatred: The school mascot controversy. *Journal of Law and Education, 25*, 381–388.

Webster, S., Loudbear, P., Corn, D., & Vigue, B. (1971, February 17). Four MU Indian students describe Willie Wampum as racist symbol. *Marquette Tribune*, p. A9.

Witko, T. (2005, January). In whose honor: Understanding the psychological implications of American Indian mascots. *California Psychologist*.

28

Native American Imagery Resolution (2005)

North American Society for the Sociology of Sport

Whereas, the continued use of Aboriginal/Native American symbols, names, imagery, culture, and personas in sport offer up stereotypical, misleading, monolithic, and flat images that demean Aboriginal Peoples/Native Americans;[1]

Whereas, the continued use of Aboriginal/Native American symbols, names, imagery, culture, and personas in sport reflects a history of stereotyping, prejudice, and discrimination directed against indigenous peoples in North America;

Whereas, the continued use of Aboriginal/Native American symbols, names, imagery, culture, and personas in sport by educational institutions, corporations, and sport franchises allows them to profit from racially exploitative practices;

Whereas, the continued use of Aboriginal/Native American symbols, names, imagery, culture, and personas in sport has been perpetuated by many media outlets through biased coverage, reliance on shoddy research, and general acceptance of widely held but flawed ideas about race;

Whereas, the continued use of Aboriginal/Native American symbols, names, imagery, culture, and personas in sport inhibits teaching and learning about the realities of Aboriginal Peoples/Native Americans for individuals who have had little or no interaction with them;

Whereas, the continued use of Aboriginal/Native American symbols, names, imagery, culture, and personas in sport often transforms stadiums and classrooms into hostile environments for many Aboriginal Peoples/Native Americans and their allies;

Whereas, the continued use of Aboriginal/Native American symbols, names, imagery, culture, and personas in sport negatively impacts self-concept and self-worth among Aboriginal/Native American youth;

Whereas, the continued use of Aboriginal/Native American symbols, names, imagery, culture, and personas in sport undermines the sovereignty of indigenous nations, including their ability to represent themselves to a broader public;

Whereas, the continued use of Aboriginal/Native American symbols, names, imagery, culture, and personas in sport denigrates Aboriginal/Native American spirituality;

Whereas, the continued use of Aboriginal/Native American symbols, names, imagery, culture, and personas in sport has been condemned by numerous civil rights groups, educational associations, health organization, and the vast majority of Aboriginal/Native American advocacy groups;

And, whereas NASSS [North American Society for the Sociology of Sport] is committed to the communication and application of accurate knowledge about sport and society through teaching, research, and social action;

Now therefore, be it resolved that NASSS joins the United States Commission on Civil Rights, the American Anthropological Association, the American Psychological Association, the National Congress of American Indians, Native American Journalists Association, National Coalition for Racism in Sport and the Media, and numerous other professional, advocacy, and civil rights organizations to call for the discontinuation of Aboriginal/Native American symbols, names, imagery, culture, and personas in sport and upon sports teams and educational institutions to provide meaningful teaching and research about living Aboriginal/Native American Peoples, current Aboriginal/Native American issues, and the rich variety of Aboriginal/Native American cultures in North America.

NOTE

1. "Aboriginal Peoples" is the inclusive term commonly used in Canada to identify First Nations, Metis, and Inuit individuals. "Native Americans" is a term commonly used in the United States to identify individuals of Native heritage. Together, these terms are meant to refer to all individuals who share a heritage as the indigenous peoples (i.e., the first residents) of North America.

29

Policy on Native American Logos and Names (1993)

University of Wisconsin Athletic Department

The attached five-point policy on Native American Logos and Names was passed by the Athletic Board this past spring. Since it represents a new campus policy, it was presented to the University Committee, which provisionally approved it and has now placed it on the Faculty Senate agenda. Discussion of this policy began shortly after Wisconsin played a home basketball game on December 29, 1992, against the Alcorn State "Scalping Braves." Several UW-Madison American Indian students, staff, and faculty were concerned about the Alcorn State nickname and asked the Athletic Board to establish a policy which would ban athletic competition against any team that used an American Indian mascot or team name. Later, the Great Lakes Intertribal Council, which represents most of the major Indian groups in Wisconsin, also asked for such a ban. A subcommittee of the Athletic Board, chaired by Professor Barbara Wolfe, thoroughly examined the issue, invited a number of American Indians to speak, and consulted with the office of the Vice Chancellor for Legal and Executive Affairs. This subcommittee then proposed the new policy to the full Athletic Board. The entire Board also carefully considered the issue, asked a representative of the Legal Affairs office to make a presentation, and invited several members of the University Indian community to be heard. The Board then adopted a policy, which it then forwarded to the University Committee. Associate Vice Chancellor Gary Sandefur, who participated in a number of the meetings, has written the following summary of the process and policy:

> I think that the process worked very well, and the policy is a sound one. We discourage the use of Indian images and mascots on our campus, and we refuse to schedule games with teams, other than those to which we have long-standing

commitments, that use Indian mascots, images, or team names. The university has taken a clear stand in opposition to the use of American Indian mascots, images, or team names, but in a way that does not infringe on the freedom of speech or expression. The University of Wisconsin Athletic Department adds its name to those who desire to stop the use of American Indian symbols and names by athletic teams. We are concerned that the use of war chants, American Indian–related mascots and logos by teams both perpetuates a stereotype and causes insult to many Native Americans. We therefore adopt the following policy:

1. We will discourage all teams from bringing their American Indian mascots to UW Athletic facilities. Furthermore, we will request that any band not play war chants and that the cheerleaders/pompom squads also not use American Indian gestures, chants, and so forth.
2. For all users of UW Athletic facilities, we will discourage planned events using an American Indian mascot, symbol, names, and activities if that use is disrespectful.
3. The sale of athletic wear or other souvenirs with American Indian mascots or logos will be discouraged on the grounds of the University's athletic facilities.
4. UW representatives to our conferences (Big Ten and WCHA) will present our policy to other members of the conference and the Board of Regents. They will convey to the conference the sensitivity of the use of such names and logos and ask the conference to consider appropriate policies. The intent of this presentation is to exert a leadership in our conferences and in the UW system which will lead institutions with such mascots and names to review the nature and uses of Native American names and symbols.
5. Scheduling. During the regular season, UW Athletic Department will not schedule any team with a Native American mascot or nickname unless the team is a traditional rival or a conference member.

30

Competition and Anti-Discrimination Policy (2002)

Advisory Committee on Athletics, University of Minnesota

The University of Minnesota Athletics Department strongly endorses the NCAA Principle of Nondiscrimination:

> The Association shall promote an atmosphere of respect for and sensitivity to the dignity of every person. It is the policy of the Association to refrain from discrimination with respect to its governance policies, educational programs, activities and employment policies.

To promote an atmosphere of respect the University of Minnesota Athletics Department shall make every effort to avoid scheduling home events with schools that use Native American mascots. The use of Native American mascots by athletic teams is perceived by many in our community as portraying Native American culture in demeaning and stereotypical ways. Consequently, the department will strongly discourage the scheduling of athletic events on campus when the team(s) involved use Native American mascots. When teams using Native American mascots participate in athletic events on this campus, the Native American mascots, nicknames, and symbols will not be permitted to be displayed (except as they pre-exist on teams uniforms, equipment, and apparel). Teams will be described and announced using the institution's name only.

In addition, the University of Minnesota's Athletics Department shall make every effort not to host any preseason, regular season, or postseason competition at sites, venues, or facilities which have membership requirements or practices which result in discrimination on the basis of race, gender, national origin, religion, or sexual orientation.

31

Guideline for Use of Native American Mascots (2005)

National Collegiate Athletic Association

1. Universities may adopt any mascot they wish.

2. Mascots, nicknames, or images deemed hostile or abusive in terms of race, ethnicity, or national origin should not be visible at championship events controlled by NCAA.

3. Universities with hostile or abusive mascots, nicknames, or imagery are prohibited from hosting any NCAA championship events after February 1, 2006.

4. Institutions with hostile or abusive references must take reasonable steps to cover up those references at any predetermined NCAA championship site that has been previously awarded effective February 1, 2006.

5. Institutions displaying or promoting hostile or abusive references on the mascots, cheerleaders, dance teams, and band uniforms are prohibited from wearing the material at NCAA championships, effective August 1, 2008.

6. Institutions with student-athletes wearing uniforms or having paraphernalia with hostile or abusive references must ensure that those uniforms or paraphernalia not be worn or displayed at NCAA championship competitions.

7. Institutions affects by the new policy can seek further review of the matter through the NCAA governing structure.

8. NCAA suggest that institutions follow the best practices of institutions that do not support the use of Native American mascots or imagery; i.e., not scheduling athletic competitions with schools that use Native American nicknames, imagery, of mascots.

9. Institutions should review their publications and written material for hostile or abusive references and remove those depictions.

10. Institutions are encouraged to educate their internal and external constituents on the understanding and awareness of the negative impact of hostile or abusive symbols, nicknames, and imagery, and to create a greater level of knowledge of Native American culture through outreach efforts and other means of communications.

32

Resolution on the Elimination of American Indian Mascots (1997)

Los Angeles City Board of Education

Whereas, the Los Angeles Unified School District has a policy, "The Respectful Treatment of All Persons;"

Whereas, the American Indian Education Commission, an arm of the Board of Education, unanimously supports the abolishment of the use of American Indian names and images as mascots in schools;

Whereas, it is district policy, as stated in "Educating for Diversity: A Framework for Multicultural and Human Relations Education," that institutional forms of racism be identified and challenged, that schools promote a positive image of the students' identity groups and incorporate accurate history, role, and achievements of traditionally omitted groups;

Whereas, the use of American Indian mascot names and images in schools evokes negative images that become deeply imbedded in the minds of students, depicting American Indians in inaccurate, stereotypic, and often violent manners;

Whereas, the cause and effect in the inappropriate and insensitive use of American Indian names and images violates the culture and traditions of American Indians and may prevent American Indian children from developing a strong positive self-image; therefore be it

Resolved, that the use of American Indian mascots and names such as Apaches, Mohicans, Warriors, and Braves will not be used by any Los Angeles Unified School District School.

Resolved, that the Superintendent direct the Office of Intergroup Relations to work with the affected school communities and the appropriate District offices to effect this change during the 1997–98 school year; and

Resolved, that the Superintendent identify resources to cover the expenses of change within reasonable limits.

33

Resolution Condemning Use of Derogatory Sports Team Names, Mascots, and Symbols (1999)

Hutchinson Human Relations Commission

1. Whereas the Hutchinson Human Relations Commission has responsibility of administering and enforcing the provisions stated in Chapter 3 of the Hutchinson City Code, which prohibits discrimination with regard to *race, religion, color, sex, disability, national origin, ancestry, or age* in employment, housing and public accommodation; and,

2. Whereas HHRC's mission is founded upon "eliminating prejudice among various groups and creating harmonious relationships among persons within this city"; and,

3. Whereas there exits ethnic, cultural, and various minority groups who suffer oppression that is created by the use of stereotypical names, mascots, and symbols which perpetuate the dehumanization of those ethnic, cultural, and minority groups who live and work in this nation; and,

4. Whereas said usage also presents a false distinctiveness and encourages racism and abuses of various ethnic, cultural, racial, and religious symbols; and,

5. Whereas such terms as "redskins" have been and still are being used as team names and usage of such mascots have been legally defined as racially bigoted and offensive to and against Native American people; and,

6. Whereas many public and private businesses, places of public accommodation and entertainment establishments, employers, and individuals living and working within the City of Hutchinson are encouraged to discontinue use, acceptance, and promotion of derogatory team names, mascots, and like symbols in relation to ethnic, cultural, racial, or minority groups;

7. Be it therefore resolved that the HHRC denounces the use of derogatory names, mascots, and/or symbols that depict false and offensive characteristics of any ethnic, cultural, racial, or minority group; and,

8. Be it also resolved that the HHRC will diligently work toward the elimination of such false and offensive uses of names, mascots, or symbols with or without collaboration of individuals, groups, or public and private organizations; and,

9. Be it further resolved that it is the desire of the commission that public and private businesses, places of amusement and entertainment, and individuals residing and working within the City of Hutchinson do not tolerate or promote the use of derogatory names, mascots, or symbols which depict ethnic, cultural, racial, or minority groups in any offensive manner; and, finally,

10. Be it resolved that the HHRC encourages public and private entities, including the Kansas Human Relations Association, the Hutchinson City Council, the USD 308 Board of education, the Hutchinson/Reno County Branch NAACP, and Hutchinson Community College to support and adopt policies and legislative action in opposition of the use of names, mascots and symbols depicting ethnic, cultural, and minority groups of peoples in such manner.

Now, therefore, the following members of the City of Hutchinson's Human Relations Commission do hereby proclaim our endorsement and commitment to resolution.

34

Resolution on Native American Mascots (1998)

Governors' Interstate Indian Council

Whereas, the Governors' Interstate Indian Council (GIIC) is a national organization established in 1949 by what is now the National Governors' Association to promote and enhance government relations between Tribal Nations and the states, to respect and recognize the individual sovereignty of the Tribal Nations and the states, to support the preservation of traditional Indian culture, language, and values, and to encourage socioeconomic development aimed at tribal self-sufficiency, and;

Whereas, as demonstrated by Resolution number 4–91, previously accepted by this organization, GIIC recognition of this issue has been established, and;

Whereas, the use of Native American slogans and symbols as mascots are often viewed as derogatory, demeaning, and disrespectful to American Indian/ Alaska Native people, and;

Whereas, the numerous public schools, sports teams, and businesses use American Indian/Alaskan Native Mascots in their slogans and/or symbols, and;

Whereas, there is a tremendous need for American Indians/Alaskan Natives to address this issue on a national basis;

Now, therefore, be it resolved that the Governors' Interstate Indian Council at its 49th Annual Conference in Raleigh, North Carolina, August 23 through 27, 1998, reaffirms its previously established view and encourages all public schools, sports teams, and private businesses to discontinue using Native American mascots in their slogans and/or symbols.

35

Resolution on Native American Mascots (2002)

New Hampshire State Board of Education

Whereas, the New Hampshire State Board of Education is aware that various Native American organizations, state and local officials, and private citizens find the use of Native American mascots and symbols within our public schools to be offensive; and

Whereas, the use of Native American symbols as mascots, logos, and sport team nicknames have, in the opinion of the Board, a detrimental affect on the achievement, education, self-concept, and self-esteem of American Indian students and sends an improper message to everyone of the true meaning and spirit of being of American Indian heritage; and

Whereas, several schools in New Hampshire continue to have Indian sports mascots; and

Whereas, all heritages, cultures, races, and religion have the right to be treated with dignity and respect; and

Whereas, it is important to be culturally sensitive and to educate everyone working within the New Hampshire School Education System that no matter how well meaning their intentions, that their actions may be offensive and harmful to some and therefore, need to be eliminated; and

Whereas, the National Indian Education Association, the Society of Indian Psychologists, and the U.S. Commission of Civil Rights have all endorsed the elimination of the use of Indian sports mascots; and

Whereas, the State Board of Education recognizes this is a matter that is, and rightfully so, should be addressed at the local level of each separate school district.

Now, therefore, be it resolved that the New Hampshire Board of Education endorses the elimination of the use of Indian sports mascots and encourages all districts to examine this issue and to eliminate the use of sports mascots.

36

Resolution of the Nebraska Commission on Indian Affairs (1999)

Nebraska Commission on Indian Affairs

Whereas, the Nebraska Commission on Indian Affairs was formed pursuant to LB 904, 1971, and section 81–1215 which sets out the purpose of the Commission, which shall be to join representatives of all Indians in Nebraska to do all things which it may determine to enhance the cause of Indian rights and to develop solutions to problems common to all Nebraska Indians, including assisting Native peoples preserve their traditions, values, spirituality, religions, and cultures; and

Whereas, many elementary, junior, and senior high school, college, and national sports teams, including a significant number of Nebraska schools, continue to have symbols, logos, and names that depict American Indian people in a negative light, categorizing their proud cultures and heritage along with mascots of animals and inanimate objects; and

Whereas, such prestigious entities as the National Congress of American Indians, the National Education Association, the Governors' Interstate Indian Council, along with Nations, Tribes and Bands (and numerous respected Indian organizations) have spoken out against the use and misuse of American Indian imagery; and

Whereas, exposure to displays of cultural stereotypes serve to perpetuate ignorance and racism against diverse cultures, and such teams and mascots have never been honorary or respectful, but instead perpetuates a pejorative, derogatory, denigrating, offensive and racist designation of Native Americans; and

Whereas, Indian children deserve an education that exposes them to positive role models which enhance their self-image, fosters and atmosphere wherein self-esteem and cultural identity are nurtured, and where an attitude of safe, respectful learning is equitably provided regardless of race or cultural affiliation; and

Whereas,, schools that use names, logos, or mascots, or other cultural abuses and stereotypes, separate, marginalize, confuse, intimidate, and harm Indian children and create barriers to their learning throughout their school experience; and

Whereas, allowing logos which denigrate Native peoples' cultures, sacred objects, ceremonial traditions, and components of traditional dress to remain unchallenged within our educational institutions teaches both Indian and non-Indian children to tolerate and accept racism in our schools; and

Whereas, other cultures and religious groups are not used as mascots for the purposes of school or professional sports leagues and their fans, nor would such mascots or negative imagery be tolerated within any public or private school or business without an outcry from the citizens of the great State of Nebraska as an affront to basic human rights and dignity; and

Whereas, the dictates of moral principles that protect other United States citizens need to be expanded to include this country and state's first citizens, American Indians; and

Whereas, the Nebraska Commission on Indian Affairs' mission statement encourages the education of both Indian and non-Indian peoples with regards to racism, cultural diversity, and civil/human rights issues that impact the lives of Nebraska's Indian citizens and their children; and

Whereas, the Nebraska Commission on Indian Affairs is committed to banishing racism and stereotyping, including negative imagery, by educating Nebraska's citizenry with regards to cultural sensitivity and the rich diversity Nebraska's Tribes and Indian people bring to our lives; and

Whereas, the Nebraska Commission on Indian Affairs believes that advocating for the removal of names, logos, and/or other mascots depicting Indian people or their cultures strengthens and promotes a spirit of tolerance and social justice within Nebraska, modeling for all our children the traits of thoughtfulness, courage, and respect for all Nebraska citizens; and

Now therefore, be it resolved, that the Nebraska Commission on Indian Affairs, in its continuing efforts to extinguish racism and cultural exploitation in society's institutions, especially Nebraska educational institutions, where Indian citizens are not always treated with the same respect and equity as non-Indian citizens, calls upon all Nebraska schools and institutions of higher learning, their students, teachers, administrators, families, and supporters to call for a halt to the use of tribal symbols, religious objects, and depictions of tribal peoples by other than schools whose student body is made up of predominately Indian students, to ensure that the language, cultures, and religions of Indian Tribes are not demeaned, and that Indian students are provided with appropriate representations of themselves in texts and the media; and

Be it finally resolved, the Nebraska Commission on Indian Affairs authorizes its officers and staff to support this resolution by seeking the support of Governor Johanns, the Commissioner of Education, the Nebraska Legislature, and all interested individuals and organizations to end the use of Native American logos, symbols, and names as mascots in Nebraska schools by December 31, 1999.

37

Report on Use of Nicknames, Logos, and Mascots Depicting Native American People in Michigan Education Institutions (1988)

Michigan Civil Rights Commission

VIII. RECOMMENDATIONS AND ACTION STEPS

1. Any use of Indian names, logos, and mascots should be discontinued because racial stereotyping of Native Americans is prevalent and destructive.
2. Since much of the stereotypic use of Indian names and logos appears to arise from lack of information about Indian culture and the impact of stereotyping on Indian and non-Indian students, a program for public information and discussion should be engaged, including several steps.

   - Mailing of this report to all institutions and Indians organizations
   - Local review and discussion of the report in communities which have Indian team names and symbols
   - Discussion among civil rights organizations
   - Staff discussion with the Michigan Department of Education regarding a possible State Board policy on use of Indian names
   - Mailing to mail order houses

3. Local districts or individual schools within districts which have Indian athletic team names or logos should establish study committees to discuss this report. These committees should involve significant numbers of Indian organizations such as Title IV parent groups, Indian centers, individual Indians, and local community groups which have an interest in Indian rights issues. Curriculum materials which relate to Indians are available and should be used.

4. Following the 1989–90 school year this Commission will again survey Michigan education institutions to determine the level of stereotyping level of presence of Indian stereotypes in use. If stereotyping continues as a problem, the Commission will consider at least following options:

   • Receipt and investigation of formal complaints from Indian students or groups alleging that use of names or logos violate the Elliott-Larsen Civil Rights Act
   • Public hearings on continued use of Indian names and logos

5. Department staff should support and cooperate with research efforts to establish the impact Indian and non-Indian students.
6. We encourage all school districts to closely examine all instructional materials to determine the extent to which stereotyping of Indians occurs in the institution.
7. Those schools which use Indian names and logos should incorporate course work into the significance of the name and symbol in Indian culture and in the history of this state.

38

California Racial Mascots Act, AB 858 (2004)

State of California

The people of the State of California do enact as follows:

221.2. The Legislature finds and declares all of the following:

    (a) The use of racially derogatory or discriminatory school or athletic team names, mascots, or nicknames in California public schools is antithetical to the California school mission of providing an equal education to all.

    (b) Certain athletic team names, mascots, and nicknames that have been and remain in use by other teams, including school teams, in other parts of the nation are discriminatory in singling out the Native American/American Indian community for the derision to which mascots or nicknames are often subjected.

    (c) Many individuals and organizations interested and experienced in human relations, including the United States Commission on Civil Rights, have concluded that the use of Native American images and names in school sports is a barrier to equality and understanding, and that all residents of the United States would benefit from the discontinuance of their use.

    (d) No individual or school has a cognizable interest in retaining a racially derogatory or discriminatory school or athletic team name, mascot, or nickname.

221.3

    (a) Commencing on January 1, 2006, all public schools are prohibited from using the term Redskins for school or athletic team names, mascots, or nicknames.

    (b) This section does not apply to a school located within, or with enrollment boundaries that include a portion of, "Indian country," as defined in Section 1151 of Title 18 of the United States Code, provided that the tribe having regulatory jurisdiction over the territory within that boundary has authorized the use of the school or athletic team name, mascot, or nickname through an appropriate enactment or resolution.

(c) Notwithstanding this section, a school may continue to use uniforms or other materials bearing the term Redskins as a school or athletic team name, mascot, or nickname that were purchased before January 1, 2006, if all of the following requirements are met:

    (1) The school selects a new school or athletic team name, mascot, or nickname.

    (2) (A) Except as provided in subparagraph (B), the school refrains from purchasing or acquiring, for the purpose of distribution or sale to pupils or school employees, any uniform that includes or bears the term Redskins.

    (B) Notwithstanding subparagraph (A), prior to January 1, 2008, a school using uniforms that bear the term Redskins may purchase or acquire a number of uniforms equal to up to 20 percent of the total number of uniforms used by a team or band at that school during the 2005–06 school year for the purposes of replacing damaged or lost uniforms.

    (3) Refrains from purchasing or acquiring, for the purpose of distribution or sale to pupils or school employees, any yearbook, newspaper, program, or other similar material that includes or bears the prohibited school or athletic team name, mascot, or nickname in its logo or cover title.

    (4) Refrains from purchasing or constructing a marquee, sign, or other new or replacement fixture that includes or bears the prohibited school or athletic team name, mascot, or nickname.

(d) This section is not subject to waiver by the State Board of Education pursuant to Section 33050, except as specified in this section.

39

Oklahoma Racial Mascots Act, Senate Bill 567, 1st Session of the 50th Legislature (2005)

Bill Introduced in the Oklahoma State Senate

*A*s Introduced

An Act relating to schools; creating the Oklahoma Racial Mascots Act; providing short title; stating legislative findings; prohibiting the use of racially derogatory or discriminatory Native American school or athletic team names, nicknames, and mascots; specifying certain requirements; providing penalty and enforcement; providing for codification; and providing an effective date.

Be It Enacted by the People of the State of Oklahoma:
Section: New Law A new section of law to be codified in the Oklahoma Statutes as Section 24–154 of Title 70, unless there is created a duplication in numbering, reads as follows:

A. This act shall be known and may be cited as the "Oklahoma Racial Mascots Act."

B. The Legislature finds and declares the following:

1. The use of racially derogatory or discriminatory school or athletic team names, mascots, or nicknames in Oklahoma public schools is antithetical to the Oklahoma school mission of providing an equal education to all;

2. Certain athletic team names, mascots, and nicknames that have been and remain in use by athletic teams, including school teams, in other parts of the nation are discriminatory in singling out the Native American/American Indian community for the derision to which mascots or nicknames are often subjected;

3. Many individuals and organizations interested and experienced in human relations have concluded that the use of Native American

images and names in school sports is a barrier to equality and understanding, and that all residents of the United States would benefit from the discontinuance of their use; and

4. No individual or school has a cognizable interest in retaining a racially derogatory or discriminatory school or athletic team name, mascot or nickname.

B. All public schools in Oklahoma, including institutions of elementary, secondary and higher education, are prohibited from using any of the following school or athletic team names, mascots, or nicknames:

1. Savages;
2. Redskins;
3. Indians;
4. Braves;
5. Chiefs;
6. Apaches;
7. Comanches;
8. Papooses;
9. Warriors;
10. Sentinels;
11. Any other Native American tribal name; and
12. Any other racially derogatory or discriminatory school or athletic team name, mascot or nickname.

C. Notwithstanding the provisions of this section, a school may continue to use uniforms or other materials bearing a school or athletic team name, mascot, or nickname specified in subsection B of this section that were purchased before the effective date of this act, if the school does all of the following:

1. Selects a new school or athletic team name, mascot, or nickname;
2. Refrains from purchasing or acquiring, after the effective date of this act, for the purpose of distribution or sale to pupils or school employees, any uniform that includes or bears the prohibited school or athletic team name, mascot, or nickname;
3. Refrains from purchasing or acquiring, for the purpose of distribution or sale to pupils or school employees, any yearbook, newspaper, program, or other similar material that includes or bears the prohibited school or athletic team name, mascot, or nickname in its logo or cover title; and

4. Refrains from purchasing or constructing, a marquee, sign, or other new or replacement fixture that includes or bears the prohibited school or athletic team name, mascot, or nickname.

D. Except for a school that meets the requirements of subsection C of this section, any school that uses a racially derogatory or discriminatory Native American school or athletic team name, nickname, logo or mascot in violation of this section shall be subject to a penalty of not less than Five Hundred Dollars ($500.00) to be enforced as follows:

1. The State Board of Education shall enforce the penalty prescribed in this subsection for offending elementary and secondary public schools by reducing the offending school district's State Aid during the next school year;

2. The Attorney General shall enforce the penalty prescribed in this subsection for offending public institutions of higher education; and

3. Each day of use of the racially derogatory or discriminatory Native American name, nickname, logo or mascot in violation of this section constitutes a separate violation.

Section. This act shall become effective November 1, 2005.

40

Tennessee Mascot Act: House Bill no. 133 (2007) by Representatives Bell, Matlock, Hill; Substituted for: Senate Bill no. 162 by Senator Bunch

State of Tennessee

An Act to amend Tennessee Code Annotated, Title 1, Chapter 4 and Title 49, relative to use of American Indian symbols, images, and names.

Be It Enacted by the General Assembly of the State of Tennessee:
Section 1.
- (a) The general assembly recognizes that many Tennessee institutions, both public and private, have elected to select symbols, mascots, and names to represent such institutions. Such symbols, mascots, and names are often chosen in recognition of the area's heritage and to honor and respect certain persons or cultures and their contributions to our citizens and our state.
- (b) No state agency has the authority to require or to prohibit or impair in any way the right of any public or private institution to continue to honor certain persons or cultures through the use of symbols, names, and mascots.

Section 2. This act shall take effect upon becoming a law, the public welfare requiring it.

41

U.S. House Resolution 1933 (2005)

109th Congress, U.S. House of Representatives

To authorize the Secretary of Education to make grants to eligible schools to assist such schools to discontinue use of a derogatory or discriminatory name or depiction as a team name, mascot, or nickname, and for other purposes.
In the House of Representatives
April 27, 2005
Mr. Pallone (for himself, Mr. Towns, Mr. Rangel, and Ms. Lee) introduced the following bill; which was referred to the Committee on Education and the Workforce

A BILL

To authorize the Secretary of Education to make grants to eligible schools to assist such schools to discontinue use of a derogatory or discriminatory name or depiction as a team name, mascot, or nickname, and for other purposes.
Be it enacted by the Senate and House of Representatives of the United States of America in Congress assembled

Sec. 2. Findings.

The Congress finds the following:

(1) Based on article I, section 8 of the United States Constitution, treaties, Federal statutes, and court decisions, the United States has a unique historical and legal relationship with American Indian and Alaska Native people, which serves as the basis for the Federal Government's trust responsibility and obligations.

(2) There are 558 federally recognized Indian tribes in the United States, with some 40 percent of Indian tribes located in the State of Alaska.

(3) Indian tribes have principal responsibility for lands and people within their jurisdiction.

(4) This responsibility extends to educating their students and providing adequate educational facilities in which their students can learn.

(5) Because of this responsibility, Indian schools should be eligible for the funding available under this Act.

(6) Elementary and secondary schools all over the Nation use words and symbols representing their schools that are offensive to Native Americans.

(7) Nationally, more than 1,200 schools inappropriately use such offensive names or nicknames. Often, these names or symbols become mascots and are used at athletic games for mascot characters, chants, and other antics.

(8) Although these school communities do not intend disrespect toward Native Americans, that is the end result of allowing these offensive terms to continue in these educational institutions. Therefore, Federal funding should be available to schools to assist them to discontinue use of offensive names and symbols on equipment and apparel, including team jerseys, signs, stationery, walls, fields, and gymnasium floors.

Sec. 3. Grants.

(a) *Grants to Discontinue Use of a Derogatory or Discriminatory Name or Depiction.*

(1) *In General.*—During the 1-year period beginning at the end of the period described in section 4(b)(2), the Secretary of Education, acting through the Committee on Indian Relations, may make grants to eligible schools to assist such schools to discontinue use of a name or depiction that is derogatory or discriminatory (as provided under section 5) as a team name, mascot, or nickname of the school or any entity sponsored by the school.

(2) *Use of Funds.*—The Secretary may not make a grant to an applicant under this subsection unless the applicant agrees to use the grant for the following:

(a) Replacement of uniforms or other materials that bear a discontinued derogatory or discriminatory name or depiction.

(b) Alteration of facilities, including walls, floors, and signs, to the extent necessary to remove a discontinued derogatory or discriminatory name or depiction.

(3) *Eligible Schools.*—(a) For purposes of this subsection, the term "eligible school" means a school that has made a formal decision to discontinue use of a name or depiction that is derogatory or discriminatory.

    (a) Construction Grants.—Not sooner than the end of the 1-year period during which grants may be made under subsection (a)(1), the Secretary may make grants to Indian schools and to schools that received grants under subsection (a)(1) for school construction or renovation.

    (b) Consultation.—Before making any grant under this section, the Secretary shall consult with Indian tribes concerning the grant.

    (c) Ap*plication.*—To seek a grant under this section, an applicant shall submit an application at such time, in such manner, and containing such information as the Secretary reasonably requires.

Sec. 4. Committee on Indian Relations.

(a) *Establishment.*—Not later than 6 months after the date of the enactment of this Act, the Secretary shall establish within the Department of Education a committee to be known as the Committee on Indian Relations.

(b) *Duties.*—The Committee shall—

    (1) in accordance with section 5(c), determine names and depictions that are derogatory or discriminatory;

    (2) not later than 1 year after the date of the enactment of this Act—(A) identify schools that use a name or depiction that is derogatory or discriminatory as a team name, mascot, or nickname of the school or any entity sponsored by the school; and (B) inform any school so identified of the assistance available under this Act to discontinue use of such name or depiction;

    (3) assist the Secretary to make grants under section 3; and

    (4) provide cultural proficiency training at schools receiving assistance under section 3 to effect positive and long-term change regarding any derogatory or discriminatory name or depiction.

(c) *Director.*—The Committee shall have a Director, who shall be appointed by the Secretary in consultation with tribal governments involved in Indian education program activities. The Director shall be paid at the rate of basic pay for level V of the Executive Schedule.

(d) *Staff.*—The Director may appoint such personnel as the Director considers appropriate to carry out the purposes of the Committee.

(e) *Termination.*—The Committee shall terminate at the end of fiscal year 2010.

Sec. 5. Derogatory or Discriminatory Names and Depictions.

(a) *In General.*—For purposes of this Act, a name or depiction is derogatory or discriminatory if listed in 16 subsection (b) or designated under subsection (c).

(b) *Listed Names.*—The names listed in this subsection are the following:
  (1) *Indians.*
  (2) *Redskins.*
  (3) *Braves.*
  (4) *Chiefs.*

(c) *Designated Names and Depictions.*—A name or depiction is designated under this subsection if the Committee determines, after notice and comment, that the name or depiction is derogatory or discriminatory on the basis of race, ethnicity, nationality, or Indian or Native Alaskan tribal affiliation.

Sec. 6. Reports.

(a) *In General.*—Not later than 1 year after the date of the enactment of this Act, and annually for each of the 4 succeeding fiscal years, the Secretary, in consultation with the Committee, shall submit a report to the Committee on Resources of the House of Representatives and the Committee on Indian Affairs of the Senate.

(b) *Contents.*—Each report submitted under this section shall include the following:
  (1) A summary of the activities conducted by the Secretary, including those conducted by the 15 Committee, to carry out this Act.
  (2) Any recommendations for legislation that the Secretary, in consultation with the Committee, determines to be necessary to carry out this Act.

Sec. 8. Authorization of Appropriations.

There are authorized to be appropriated such sums as may be necessary to carry out this Act, to remain available until expended, for each of fiscal years 2006 through 2010. Such authorization of appropriations shall be in addition to any other authorization of appropriations for Indian education.

42

Protection of University Governance Act of 2006, H. R. 5289 (May 4, 2006)

Bill Introduced in the U.S. House of Representatives

SEC. 2. FINDINGS.

The Congress finds the following:

(1) Voluntary collegiate self-regulation of intercollegiate sports activities is a traditional and desirable undertaking.

(2) The regulation of intercollegiate sports activities significantly affects interstate commerce.

(3) Any attempt by an entity that regulates intercollegiate sports activities to impose its view of correct social policy on institutions of higher education participating in such activities is inimical to the traditions of higher education in America and is inconsistent with university governance and academic freedom. Attempts to regulate institutions in this manner detract from the diversity of America and the independence of thought and spirit that are the essence of higher education in this Nation.

SEC. 3. IMPROPER ACTIONS BY ENTITIES THAT REGULATE INTERCOLLEGIATE SPORTS ACTIVITIES.

(a) In General—An entity that regulates intercollegiate sports activities shall not impose any penalty or sanction on, or deny any benefit to, an institution of higher education by reason of the team name, symbol, emblem, or mascot of any intercollegiate sports activity of such institution.

(b) Liability—An entity that regulates intercollegiate sports activities shall be liable to an institution of higher education that is aggrieved by such entity as a result of any violation of subsection (a). In any action brought under this subsection, the entity that regulates intercollegiate sports activities may be subject to injunction and shall be liable to the aggrieved institution of higher education for any damages caused thereby, including reasonable attorneys' fees and costs.

(c) Jurisdiction—Any action brought under subsection (b) may be filed in an appropriate district court of the United States.

SEC. 4. DEFINITIONS.

In this Act:

(1) *Entity That Regulates Intercollegiate Sports Activities*—The term "entity that regulates intercollegiate sports activities" means any entity that regulates intercollegiate sports activities and that is not a Federal, State, Tribal, territorial, or local government entity.

(2) *Institution of Higher Education*—The term "institution of higher education" means an institution defined in section 102 of the Higher Education Act of 1965 (20 U.S.C. 1002), except that such term does not include an institution described in subsection (a)(1)(C) of that section.

SEC. 5. SEVERABILITY AND EFFECTIVE DATE.

(a) Severability—The provisions of this Act are severable. If any provision of this Act, or any application thereof, is found unconstitutional, that finding shall not affect any provision or application of the Act not so adjudicated.

(b) Effective Date—This Act shall apply to any violation of section 3(a) by an entity that regulates intercollegiate sports activities which occurs on or after August 4, 2005.

Part V

ADDITIONAL RESOURCES

43

Organizations Advocating Change

Advocates for American Indian Children (California)
The Affiliated Tribes of Northwest Indians
American Counseling Association
American Indian Language and Culture Education Board
American Indian Mental Health Association (Minnesota)
American Indian Movement
American Indian Opportunities Industrialization Center of San Bernardino
    County
American Indian Student Services at the Ohio State University
American Jewish Committee
American Psychological Association
American Sociological Society
Asian American Journalists Association
Associated Students Council of San Diego State University
Association on American Indian Affairs
BRIDGES—Building Roads Into Diverse Groups Empowering Students
Buncombe County Native American Intertribal Association (North Caro-
    lina)
Calvert Investment Group
Center for Artistic Revolution (North Little Rock, AR)
Center for the Study of Sports in Society
Cincinnati Zapatista Coalition
COLOR—Community One Love One Race
Committee to End Cultural Genocide (St. Cloud State University)
Concerned American Indian Parents (Minnesota)
Council for Indigenous North Americans (University of Southern Maine)

Eagle and Condor Indigenous Peoples' Alliance
Fontana Native American Indian Center, Inc.
Governor's Interstate Indian Council
Georgia House of Representatives (Resolution drafted but not passed)
Grand Traverse Band of Ottawa and Chippewa Indians (Michigan)
Greater Tulsa Area Indian Affairs Commission
Great Lakes Inter-Tribal Council
Gun Lake Band of Potawatomi Indians (Michigan)
HONOR—Honor Our Neighbors Origins and Rights
Hutchinson Human Relations Commission
Illinois State University Student Government Association
Inter-Ethnic Children's Council (Los Angeles)
Inter-Faith Council on Corporate Responsibility
Inter-Tribal Council of the Five Civilized Tribes
Juaneño Band of Mission Indians
Kansas Association for Native American Education
Latino Children's Action Council (Los Angeles)
League of United Latin American Citizens
Little River Band of Ottawa Indians (Michigan)
Maryland Commission on Indian Affairs
Mascot Abuse San Francisco Bay Area
Medicine Wheel Intertribal Association (Louisiana)
Menominee Tribe of Indians (Wisconsin)
Michigan Civil Rights Commission
Michigan Education Association
State of Michigan, State Board of Education
Minnesota Indian Education Association
Minnesota State Colleges and Universities Board
Minnesota State Board of Education
Modern Language Association
Morning Star Institute
NAACP
National Association of Black Journalists
National Association of Hispanic Journalists
National Coalition on Racism in Sports and the Media
National Conference of Christians and Jews
National Conference for Community and Justice
National Congress of American Indians
National Education Association
National Indian Education Association
Native American Caucus of the California Democratic Party

Native American Indian Center of Central Ohio
Native American Journalists Association
Nebraska Commission on Indian Affairs
New Hampshire State Board of Education
New York State Education Department
Nottawaseppi Huron Band of Potawatomi
North American Society for the Sociology of Sport
North Carolina Commission of Indian Affairs
North Dakota Indian Education Association
North Dakota State University Student Senate
Office of Native American Ministry, Diocese of Grand Rapids
Ohio Center for Native American Affairs
Oneida Tribe of Indians of Wisconsin
Presbyterian Church, U.S.A.
Progressive Resource/Action Cooperative
Rainbow Coalition
San Bernardino/Riverside Counties Native American Community Council
Students Making All Races Tolerant
Society for the Study of Social Problems
Society of Indian Psychologists of the Americas
Southern California Indian Center
Southern Christian Leadership Conference
St. Cloud State University—American Indian Center
Sault Ste. Marie Tribe of Chippewa Indians
Tennessee Chapter of the National Coalition for the Preservation of Indig-
  enous Cultures
Tennessee Commission of Indian Affairs
Tennessee Native Veterans Society
Unified Coalition for American Indian Concerns, Virginia
Unitarian Universalist Association of Congregations
United Church of Christ
The United Indian Nations of Oklahoma
United Methodist Church
United States Commission on Civil Rights
Virginia American Indian Cultural Resource Center
Western North Carolina Citizens for an End to Institutionalized Bigotry
Wisconsin Indian Education Association
Wisconsin State Human Relations Association
Woodland Indian Community Center—Lansing
Youth "Indian" Mascot and Logo Taskforce (Wisconsin)

44

American Indian Mascot and Nickname Changes: A Chronology

Compiled by Jay Rosenstein

1969, October 12—Dartmouth College, originally founded to educate American Indians, changes from the Indians to Big Green.

1971—Marquette University (WI) abolishes Willie Wampum mascot.

1971—Mankato State College (MN) drops Indian caricature mascot.

1972, March 2—Stanford University changes from Indians to Cardinal and drops Prince Lightfoot mascot.

1972—Dickinson State University (ND) changes from Savages to Blue Hawks.

1973—University of Oklahoma drops Little Red mascot.

1973—Eastern Washington University changes from Savages to the Eagles.

1978—Syracuse University (NY) drops Saltine Warrior mascot.

1980—Southern Oregon State University drops Red Raiders motif.

1987–88—St. John's University (NY) drops caricature logo and mascot.

1988—Siena College (NY) changes from Indians to Saints.

1988—Saint Mary's College (MN) changes from Red Men to Cardinals.

1989—Montclair State College (NJ) drops nickname and mascot.

1989, October 13—Bradley University (IL) drops mascot and replaces Indian caricature logo.

1991, February—Eastern Michigan University changes from Hurons to Eagles on recommendation of a state civil rights commission.

1992—Naperville Central High School (IL) drops nickname Redskins.

1992—Simpson College (IA) changes from Redmen to Storm.

1993—Arkansas State University drops Runnin' Joe mascot.

1993—Arvada High School (CO) changes from Redskins to Reds.

1993, April 9—University of Wisconsin passes a resolution refusing to play nonconference games against teams with Indian nicknames.

1993, November 2—Bradley University (IL) adopts Bobcats mascot and drops all Indian references in its logo, but keeps nickname Braves.

1994, April—University of Iowa bans the University of Illinois mascot, Chief Illiniwek, and announces it won't schedule games with teams with Indian mascots.

1994, May 2—Juanita College (PA) changes from Indians to Eagles. According to committee chair Charles C. Brown Jr., "the utilization of a cultural stereotype as a mascot is inconsistent with the educational mission of the college."

1994, May 3—Marquette University (WI) changes from Warriors to Golden Eagles.

1994, June 6—St. John's University (NY) changes from Redmen to Red Storm.

1994, December 8—University of Southern Colorado drops Indian mascot after 57 years.

1994 (?)—Montclair State College (NJ) changes from Indians to Red Hawks,

1996, March 31—Newton High School (CT) announces they will drop their Indian mascot.

1996, July 3—University of Tennessee–Chattanooga drops mascot, Chief Moccanooga.

1996, September 26—Miami of Ohio University votes 7–1 to drop nickname Redskins after being used for 68 years.

1997—Marist High School (IL) changed from Redskins to Redhawks.

1998, March 20—Yakima Valley Community College (WA) drops Indian nickname.

1998, April 7—Federal judge in Los Angeles upholds district policy banning Indian mascots at all of its schools.

1998, April 22—Southern Nazarene University (OK) changes from Redskins to Crimson Storm. According to the school's president "with the increased attention in the country to do it, we just did not want to be the last to make a change, and I feel eventually most schools with that kind of mascot or nickname will do."

1999, March 5—Indiana University of Pennsylvania announces it will retain nickname Indians, but change mascot to a black bear.

1999, March 5—Erwin High School, Asheville (NC) discontinues calling girl's teams Squaws, but retains Warriors nickname.

1999—Since 1991, 25 Wisconsin schools have eliminated Indian mascots or nicknames; 43 remain.

1999, June—Seattle University (WA) changes from Chieftains to Redhawks and drops its Indian head logo.

2000, September 22—Scarborough (Maine) High School drops nickname Redskins.

2000, October 17—Niles West High School (IL) drops nickname Indians.

2001, May 10—Southwestern College (CA) changes mascot from Apache to Jaguar.

2001, May 21—Woonsocket High School (SD) votes to drop Redmen nickname and mascot by 3–2 board vote.

2001, May 25—San Diego State University (CA) drops Montey Montezuma mascot.

2001, May 27—Parsippany High School (NJ) changes from Redskins to Redhawks.

2001, June 10—Saranac Lake High School (NY) changes from Redskins to Red Storm by 6–1 school board vote.

2001, June 13—Canastota High School (NY) drops Indian mascot by 6–0 board vote.

2001, June 20—Ball-Chatham school board (IL) votes 5–2 to get rid of Indian mascots and nicknames in district schools. Chatham Glenwood High School changes to Titans from Redskins, and Glenwood Junior High no longer Braves.

2001, July 11—West Seattle High School (WA) drops nickname Indians.

2001, July 19—Georgetown High School (SC) drops Waccamaw Warriors symbol.

2001, July 25—Maryland State School Board passes resolution opposing Indian mascots by 10–2 vote.

2001, August—Bloomington High School (IL) drops Red Raiders nickname.

2001, August 15—Colgate University drops word "Red" from "Red Raiders" nickname.

2001, August 29—Montgomery School Board (MD), largest school system in the state, bans Indian mascots, logos, and nicknames by 7–1 vote. Included is Poolesville High School, which was the Indians. Montgomery Village Middle School had voluntarily stopped using the nickname Warriors.

2002, February 25—Milford High School (MI) drops Redskins.

2004, July 6—Ottawa Hills High School (MI) drops Indian mascot.

2004, July 12—Rice Memorial High School (VT) retires "Little Indian" mascot.

2004, November 8—Southeast Missouri State changes from Indians to Redhawks.

2005, September 23—Old Town High School (ME) drops Indian nickname.

2005, October 10—Carthage College changes from Redmen to Red Men. NCAA removes them from list.

2005, October 10—Midwestern State University drops Indians. NCAA removes them from list.

2006, January 8—West Georgia University changes from Braves to Wolves.

2006, January 20—Southeastern Oklahoma State University changes from Savages to Savage Storm.

2006, January 26—Chowan College (NC) drops Braves nickname and mascot.

2006. January 30—Muscatine Community College (IA) drops Indians nickname and mascot.

2006, March 23—Kelseyville High School (CA) drops "Indians" nickname, and Mountain Vista Middle School (CA) drops "Braves" nickname.

2006, April 8—University of Louisiana–Monroe changes from Indians to Warhawks after being one of 18 schools on the NCAA list. References to the campus as "the Reservation" also stopped.

2006, October—McMurry University (TX) declared it would no longer uses Native American imagery or the name "Indians" for its sport teams, but would retain school traditions that revolved around Indianness.

2006, October 10—College of William and Mary (VA) announces it will remove two feathers from its logo to comply with NCAA rule.

2006, October 20—Tomah (WI) School Board drops Indian mascot and logo by 4–1 board vote.

2006, November 12—Newberry College (SC) drops Indian nickname. NCAA removes them from banned list.

2006, December 14—Ypsilanti High School (MI) drops nickname Braves on a 4–3 board vote.

2007, January 19—Salesian High School (CA) changes from Chieftains to Pride.

2007, February 17—The University of Illinois Board of Trustees announces it will remove Chief Illiniwek from performing at athletic events after February 21, 2007. This final performance is popularly dubbed "The Last Dance."

2007, February 17—The NCAA exempt five colleges and universities from its mascot policy because they had received the support of tribes: Catawba College, Central Michigan University, Florida State University, Mississippi College, and the University of Utah.

2007, March 13—the University of Illinois Board of Trustees passes a resolution officially eliminating Chief Illiniwek, discontinuing the use of its Chief head logo, regalia, and the names "Chief Illiniwek" and "Chief." It passes by a 9–1 vote.

2007, June 18—Arkansas State University Mascot Review Committee voted to retire "The Indians" nickname and all Native American mascots. They later changed the name of their sports teams to the Red Wolves.

2007, October 28—University of Illinois grants permission for students to use the image of Chief Illiniwek in the Homecoming Parade.

2008, November 15—Students for Chief Illiniwek organize "The Next Dance" at the University of Illinois in an effort to revive the mascot.

2009, October 1—Poynette High School drops its Indians nickname in favor of the Pumas.

2010, January—An anti-mascot bill is introduced to the Colorado State Legislature. It is later withdrawn.

2010, April 9—The North Dakota State Board of Higher Education voted to retire the Fighting Sioux nickname, logos, and mascots after an effort to find tribal support, a protracted legal battle with the NCAA, and an unfavorable Supreme Court ruling.

2010, April 13—The Wisconsin Legislature passes a ban on race-based mascots.

References

American Indian opinion leaders. (2001). American Indian mascots; Respectful gesture or negative stereotype? *Indian Country Today, 21*(8), A5.

Baca, L. (2004). Native images in schools and the racially hostile environment. *Journal of Sport and Social Issues, 28*, 71–78.

Berkhofer, R. F. (1978). *The white man's Indian: Images of the American Indian from Columbus to present.* New York: Vintage/Random House.

Bird, S. E. (Ed.) (1996). *Dressing in feathers: The construction of the Indian in American popular culture.* Boulder: Westview.

Churchill, W. (1994). Let's spread the fun around. In *Indians are us? Culture and genocide in Native North America* (pp. 65–72). Monroe, ME: Common Courage Press.

Clark, A.T. (2005). "Wa a o, wa ba ski na me ska ta! 'Indian' mascots and the pathology of anti-indigenous racism." In Amy Bass (Ed.), *In the game: Race, identity, and sports in the twentieth century* (pp. 137–166). New York: Palgrave Macmillan.

Clarkson, G. (2003). Racial imagery and Native Americans: A first look at empirical evidence behind the Indian mascot controversy. *Cardozo Journal of International and Comparative Law, 11*, 393–407.

Claussen, C. L. (1996). Ethnic team names and logos: Is there a legal solution? *Marquette Sports Law Journal, 16*, 409–421.

Clegg, R. (2002). American Indian nicknames and mascots for team sports: Law, policy, and attitude. *Virginia Sports and Entertainment Law Journal, 1*, 274–282.

Condit, C. M. (1989). The rhetorical limits of polysemy. *Critical Studies in Mass Communication, 6*, 103–122.

Connolly, M. R. (2000). What in a name? A historical look at Native American related nicknames and symbols at three U.S. universities. *Journal of Higher Education 71*, 515–547.

Coombe, R. J. (1999). Sports trademarks and somatic politics: Locating the law in critical cultural studies. In R. Martin & T. Miller (Eds.), *SportCult* (pp. 262–288). Minneapolis: University of Minnesota Press.

Davis, L. R. (1993). Protest against the use of Native American mascots: A challenge to traditional, American identity. *Journal of Sport and Social Issues, 17,* 9–22.

Davis, L. R. (2002). The problems with Native American mascots. *Multicultural Education, 9,* 11–14.

Davis, L. R. (2007). "Eliminating Native American mascots ingredients for success." *Journal of Sport and Social Issues, 31*(4), 340–373.

Davis, L. R. & M. Rau. (2001). Escaping the tyranny of the majority. In C. R. King & C. F. Springwood (Eds.), *Team spirits: Essays on the history and significance of Native American mascots* (pp. 304–327). Lincoln: University of Nebraska Press.

Deloria, P. (1998). *Playing Indian.* New Haven: Yale University Press.

Eckert, R. C. (2001). Wennebojo meets the Mascot: A trickster's view of the Central Michigan University mascot/logo. In C. R. King & C. F. Springwood (Eds.), *Team spirits: Essays on the history and significance of Native American mascots* (pp. 64–81). Lincoln: University of Nebraska Press.

Eitzen, D. S., & Zinn, M. B. (1989). The de-athleticization of women: The naming and gender marking of college sport teams. *Sociology of Sport Journal, 7,* 362–369.

Eitzen, D. S., & Zinn, M. B. (1993). The sexist naming of collegiate athletic teams and resistance to change. *Journal of Sport and Social Issues, 17,* 34–41.

Fisher, D. M. (2001). Chief Bill Orange and the Saltine Warrior: A cultural history of Indian symbols and imagery at Syracuse University. In C. R. King & C. F. Springwood (Eds.), *Team spirits: Essays on the history and significance of Native American mascots* (pp. 25–45). Lincoln: University of Nebraska Press.

Fryberg, S. (2002). *Representations of American Indians in the media: Do they influence how American Indian students negotiate their identities in mainstream contexts?* Unpublished dissertation, Department of Psychology, Stanford University.

Fryberg, S. (2004, November 4). *"We're honoring you, dude": The impact of using American Indian mascots.* Paper presented at the annual meeting of the North American Society for the Sociology of Sport, Tucson, Arizona.

Gawiser, S. R., & Witt, G. E. (1994). *A journalist's guide to public opinion polls.* Westport, CT: Praeger Press.

Green, R. (1988). The tribe called Wannabee: Playing Indian in America and Europe. *American Journal of Folklore, 99,* 30–55.

Hall, S. (1984). Encoding/decoding. In S. Hall, D. Hobson, A. Lowe, & P. Willis (Eds.), *Culture, media, language: Working papers in cultural studies, 1972–79* (pp. 128–138). London: Hutchinson and the Centre for Contemporary Cultural Studies, University of Birmingham.

Harjo, S. S. (2001). Fighting name calling: Challenging "Redskins" in court. In C. R. King & C. F. Springwood (Eds.), *Team spirits: Essays on the history and significance of Native American mascots* (pp. 189–207). Lincoln: University of Nebraska Press.

Heck, M. C. (1984). The ideological dimension of media messages. In S. Hall, D. Hobson, A. Lowe, & P. Willis (Eds.), *Culture, media, language: Working papers in cultural studies, 1972–79* (pp. 122–127). London: Hutchinson and the Centre for Contemporary Cultural Studies, University of Birmingham.

Kelber, B. C. (1994). "Scalping the Redskins": Can trademark law start athletic teams bearing Native American nicknames and images on the road to reform? *Hamline Law Review, 17,* 533–588.

King, C. R. (1998). Spectacles, sports, and stereotypes: Dis/playing Chief Illiniwek. In *Colonial discourse, collective memories, and the exhibition of Native American cultures and histories in the contemporary United States* (pp. 41–58). New York: Garland Press.

King, C. R. (2001). Uneasy Indians: Creating and contesting Native American mascots at Marquette University. In C. R. King & C. F. Springwood (Eds.), *Team spirits: Essays on the history and significance of Native American mascots* (pp. 281–303). Lincoln: University of Nebraska Press.

King, C. R. (2002). Defensive dialogues: Native American mascots, anti-Indianism, and educational institutions. *Studies in Media & Information Literacy Education, 2*(1). Retrieved from http://www.utpress.utoronto.ca/journal/ejournals/simile

King, C. R. (2003). Arguing over images: Native American mascots and race. In R. A. Lind (Ed)., *Race/gender/media: Considering diversity across audiences, content, and producers.* Boston: AB-Longman.

King, C. R. (2004). Borrowing power: Racial metaphors and pseudo-Indian mascots. *CR: The New Centennial Review, 4,* 189–209.

King, C. R. (forthcoming). Being a warrior: Race, gender, and Native American mascots. *Men and Masculinities.*

King, C. R., & Springwood, C. F. (2000). Choreographing colonialism: Athletic mascots, (dis)embodied Indians, and Euro-American subjectivities. *Cultural Studies: A Research Annual, 5,* 191–221.

King, C. R., & Springwood, C. F. (2001a). *Beyond the cheers: Race as spectacle in college sports.* Albany: State University of New York Press.

King, C. R., & Springwood, C. F. (Eds.). (2001b). *Team spirits: Essays on the history and significance of Native American mascots.* Lincoln: University of Nebraska.

King, C. R., Staurowsky, E. J., Baca, L., Davis, L. R., & Pewewardy, C. (2002). Of polls and race prejudice: *Sports Illustrated*'s errant "Indian Wars." *Journal of Sport and Social Issues, 26,* 382–403.

Landreth, M. (2001). Becoming the Indians: Fashioning Arkansas State University Indians. In C. R. King & C. F. Springwood (Eds.), *Team spirits: Essays on the history and significance of Native American mascots* (pp. 46–63). Lincoln: University of Nebraska Press.

LeBeau, P. R. (2001). The fighting braves of Michigamua: Adapting vestiges of American Indian warriors in the halls of Academia. In C. R. King & C. F. Springwood (Eds.), *Team spirits: Essays on the history and significance of Native American mascots.* Lincoln: University of Nebraska Press.

Likourezos, G. (1996). A case of first impression: American Indians seek cancellation of the trademarked term 'Redskins.'" *Journal of the Patent and Trademark Office Society, 78,* 275–290.

McEwan, P. J., & Belfield, C. (2004). *What happens when schools stop playing Indian?* Retrieved May 5, 2004, from http://www.wellesley.edu/Economics/mcewan/Papers/playing.pdf

National Spectator Association. (1999). Fan Poll. Retrieved from http://www.nsa
.com/Po111.cfm?Poll_ID=260

Native American Journalists Association. (2003). *Reading Red Report 2003: A call
for the news media to recognize racism in sport team nicknames and mascots.* Retrieved from: http://www.naja.com/docs/2003ReadingRed.pdf

Nuessel, F. (1994). Objectionable sports team designations. *Names: A Journal of
Onomastics, 42,* 101–119.

Pace, K. A. (1994). The Washington Redskins and the doctrine of disparagement.
Pepperdine Law Review, 22, 7–57.

Peter Harris Research Group. (2002). Methodology for *Sports Illustrated* survey on
the use of Indian nicknames, mascots, etc. Document produced by the Peter Harris
Research Group and shared with Ellen Staurowsky in January 2003.

Pewewardy, C. D. (1991). Native American mascots and imagery: The struggle of
unlearning Indian stereotypes. *Journal of Navaho Education, 9,* 19–23.

Pewewardy, C. D. (1998). Fluff and feathers: Treatment of American Indians in the
literature and the classroom. *Equity and Excellence in Education, 31,* 69–76.

Pewewardy, C. D. (2001). Educators and mascots: Challenging contradictions. In
C. R. King & C. F. Springwood (Eds.), *Team spirits: Essays on the history and
significance of Native American mascots* (pp. 257–279). Lincoln: University of
Nebraska Press.

Pickle, D. (2002). Members to be queried on Indian mascot issue. *The NCAA News,*
n.p. Retrieved November 4, 2002, from http://www.ncaa.org/news/2002/20020401/
active/3907n02.html

Price, S. L. (2002, March 4). The Indian wars. *Sports Illustrated, 96*(10), 66–72.

Prochaska, David. (2001). At home in Illinois: Presence of Chief Illinwek, absence
of Native Americans. In C. R. King & C. F. Springwood (Eds.), *Team spirits: Essays on the history and significance of Native American mascots* (pp. 157–188).
Lincoln: University of Nebraska Press.

Rodriquez, R. (1998). Plotting the assassination of Little Red Sambo: Psychologists
join war against racist campus mascots. *Black Issues in Higher Education, 15*(8),
20–24.

Rosenstein, J. (2001). "In whose honor?" Mascots, and the media. In C. R. King &
C. F. Springwood (Eds.), *Team spirits: Essays on the history and significance of
Native American mascots* (pp. 241–256). Lincoln: University of Nebraska Press.

Sigelman, L. (1998). Hail to the Redskins? Public reactions to a racially insensitive
team name. *Sociology of Sport Journal, 15,* 317–325.

Simms, R. (2002, June 13). Do you favor or oppose keeping Native American mascots
for high school, college, or professional sport teams. *King County Weekly Poll.* Retrieved from http://www.metrokc.gov/exec/survey/feedback mascots.html

Spindel, C. (2000). *Dancing at halftime: Sports and the controversy over American
Indian mascots.* New York: New York University Press.

Splichal, S. (1999). *Public opinion: Developments and controversies in the twentieth
century.* Lanham, MD: Rowman & Littlefield.

Springwood, C. F. (2001). Playing Indian and fighting (for) mascots: Reading the
complications of Native American and Euro-American alliances. In C. R. King &

C. F. Springwood (Eds.), *Team spirits: Essays on the history and significance of Native American mascots.* Lincoln: University of Nebraska Press.

Springwood, C. F., & King, C. R. (2000). Race, power, and representation in contemporary American sport. In P. Kivisto & G. Rundblad, (Eds.), *The color line at the dawn of the 21st century* (pp. 161–174). Thousand Oaks, CA: Pine Valley Press.

Stapleton, B. (2001). *Redskins: Racial slur or symbol of success?* San Jose, CA: Writers Club Press.

Staurowsky, E. J. (1998). An act of honor or exploitation? The Cleveland Indians' use of the Louis Francis Sockalexis story. *Sociology of Sport Journal, 15,* 299–316.

Staurowsky, E. J. (1999). American Indian imagery and the miseducation of America. *Quest, 51,* 382–392.

Staurowsky, E. J. (2000). The Cleveland Indians: A case study in cultural dispossession. *Sociology of Sport Journal, 17,* 307–330.

Staurowsky, E. J. (2001). Sockalexis and the making of the myth at the core of the Cleveland "Indians" imagery. In C. R. King & C. F. Springwood (Eds.), *Team spirits: Essays on the history and significance of Native American mascots* (pp. 82–107). Lincoln: University of Nebraska Press.

Trainor, D. J. (1995). Native American mascots, schools and the Title VI hostile environment analysis. *University of Illinois Law Review, 5,* 971–997.

University of North Dakota. (2000). *Name Commission Poll.* Retrieved from http://www.und.edu/namecommission/index.html

USA Weekend. (1997). Chief Wahoo Poll. Retrieved from http://www.usaweekend.com/quick/results/chief_wahoo_qp_results.html

Vanderford, H. (1996). What's in a name? Heritage or hatred: The school mascot controversy. *Journal of Law and Education, 25,* 381–388.

Williams, D. M. (2006)."Patriarchy and 'The Fighting Sioux': A gendered look at racial college sports nicknames." *Race, Ethnicity and Education, 9*(4), 325–340.

Williams, D. M. (2007a). "No past, no respect, and no power: An anarchist evaluation of Native Americans as sports nicknames, logos, and mascots." *Anarchist Studies, 15*(1), 31–54.

Williams, D. M. (2007b, December). "Where's the honor? Attitudes on the 'Fighting Sioux' nickname and logo." *Sociology of Sport Journal, 24*(4).

Index

Eastern Michigan University, 19–20,
134
Eaton High School (CO), 164, 171
education, 23
cultural literacy, 65–67
racially hostile environment, 27,
69–70, 79–86, 217, 223
Engelstad, Ralph, 123
Erwin High School (NC), 63
Eurich, Robert, 63
ethnic fraud, 97–102

Florida State University, 11, 148, 150,
152, 153, 155, 187

gendered colonialism, 43
genocide, 34–35, 37
George, Jeff, 183
Giago, Tim, 20, 175
Great Lakes Inter-Tribal Council, 15,
95
Guilford Native American Association,
111, 112

Harjo, Suzan Shown, 149
Hastert, Dennis, 179
Herman, Richard, 183
Honor the Chief, 42

In Whose Honor?, 11

Jefferson, Thomas, 34
Johnson, Glen, 153
Johnson, Timothy, 180

Kaufman, Stephen J. 180
Keelan, Matthew, 43
King, Larry, 20
Kupchella, Charles, 122

Lewerenz, Dan, 59, 60
Lick, Dale W., 153
Limbaugh, Rush, 167
Los Angeles School District, 148

Marquette University, 58, 124, 148, 150,
156, 164
McClaren, Peter, 4
Menomonie High School (WI), 72)
Miami University (Ohio), 7, 8, 64, 148,
155–156, 164
Minnesota Board of Education, 148
Minnesota State University, Mankato,
58
Morning Star Institute, 149, 163

Naperville High School (IL), 73
National Association for the
Advancement of Colored
People, 3
National Congress of American Indians,
3, 16, 148, 163–164
National Collegiate Athletic Association
(NCAA), 3, 7, 117, 120, 122,
125, 179, 181, 189
Minority Opportunities and Interests
Committee, 3, 58
National Education Association, 3
National Rainbow Coalition, 3
Native American Graves Protection and
Reparation Act (1990), 53
Native Americans
as victims of hate crimes, 86
as victims of violence, 86
invisibility, 10, 151
mental health, 27–28
suicide rate, 17
Native American mascots
ahistorical, 33, 51
authenticity, 16
change, 7, 20, 58, 64, 111–115, 117–
125, 148–149
costs associated with, 113
editorial policy in major dailies, 20
impacts of, 118
process of, 111–115, 117–125
resistance to, 36, 37
fan behavior, 61
gender, 41–45

About the Editor

C. Richard King, professor and chair of Comparative Ethnic Studies at Washington State University, has written extensively on the changing contours of race in post–Civil Rights America. His work has appeared in a variety of journals, including *American Indian Culture and Research Journal*, *Journal of Sport and Social Issues*, *Public Historian*, *Qualitative Inquiry*, and *Colorlines Magazine*. He is also the author/editor of several books, including *Team Spirits: The Native American Mascot Controversy* (a CHOICE 2001 Outstanding Academic Title), *Postcolonial America*, *Native American Athletes in Sport and Society*, and more recently *Animating Difference: Race, Gender, and Sexuality in Contemporary Films for Children*. Presently, he is at work on a monograph analyzing the production and consumption of media culture within white nationalist communities.